3-16-76

By Priscilla Sawyer Lord and Daniel J. Foley

The Folk Arts and Crafts of New England
Easter Garland

By Daniel J. Foley

Christmas the World Over
Christmas in the Good Old Days
The Christmas Tree
Little Saints of Christmas
Toys Through the Ages
Gardening by the Sea
The Flowering World of Chinese Wilson
Gardening for Beginners
Ground Covers for Easier Gardening
Garden Flowers in Color
Vegetable Gardening in Color
Annuals for Your Garden
Garden Bulbs in Color

Easter
The
World
Over

Illustrated with Photographs

PRISCILLA SAWYER LORD & DANIEL J. FOLEY

CHILTON BOOK COMPANY   PHILADELPHIA   NEW YORK   LONDON

For

MALCOLM STRANG SAWYER

Acknowledgments

A BOOK of this sort could hardly have been written without the aid of countless friends who have garnered for us bits of lore and forgotten traditions seldom seen in print. Alert librarians and dedicated staff members of various European consulates have shared their knowledge, and no query has seemed insignificant or petty to them. In many instances, current revivals of old customs and church observances dedicated to the retention of little-known traditions would have passed unnoticed in the press were it not for the sharp eyes of interested friends who share our hobby and sent us clippings.

Perhaps the most thoughtful assistance of all has come from those of our acquaintance who travel widely and never fail to bring back mementos, objets d'art, and simple trinkets and toys relating to Easter. Of all the items that came from overseas few are more fragile than eggs. Yet Mary Blackall, for one, managed to bring nearly two dozen from Spain without a single cracked egg. Nor was the effort of baking cakes and decorating eggs without its exciting moments. Uncounted hours of loving care went into their preparation, and a family of seven, father included, became deeply involved even to the youngest daughter, who found herself being photographed by a newspaper photographer. Furthermore, comparative strangers when queried not only shared their knowledge but in some instances offered recipes, samples of cookery and treasured eggs to be photographed.

Research involved not only the use of books, magazines, manuscripts and letters, but also endless numbers of scribbled notes and odd, sometimes cumbersome, objects which told a story and had to be studied at close range. Handling and storing these items often taxed the patience of families and friends alike, but silently they indulged the whims of overzealous writers anxious to document old customs and beliefs lest they be forgotten.

Perhaps the most heartwarming of all experiences is to have found so many kindred souls, anxious to share what they knew and to challenge what they doubted as the old tales were recalled. Preparing the manuscript and arranging for the photographs have involved many hands and considerable travel, but the burden has been lessened by a spirit of cooperation which has made even the drudgery pleasant. Had the authors found it necessary to gather personally all the materials used in the preparation of this book, they would have had to travel more than halfway around the world. Therefore, *Easter the World Over* belongs in part to all who have so generously helped us:

Abbot Public Library, Marblehead, Massachusetts
Mr. and Mrs. Moses Alpers
Mrs. Joseph G. Bettencourt
Miss Mary Blackall
Mrs. Vera Bockorec
Louise Alpers Bordaz
The Boston Athenaeum
Miss Margaret Brine
Mr. Julian Briz
Mr. and Mrs. John R. Burbidge
Mrs. John A. Burnham, Jr.
Mrs. Helen Buzby
Casa de Portugal of New York City
The Campbell Museum, Camden, New Jersey
Mrs. Minnie Chakonas
Dr. and Mrs. Timothy F. Clifford
Mr. Walton T. Crocker
Mr. Kevin Danaher
Mr. Rolando Diaz
Miss Mary Dowizey
Miss Nora Dowizey
Mrs. Robert D. Dykeman
Mr. Robert A. Edwards
Miss Margaret Foley
Carolyn M. Frost
Sara F. Gallagher
Mme. Jean Giroux, Paris, France
The Great Masterpiece, Inc., Lake Wales, Florida
Mrs. Richard E. Hale
Miss Inger Marie Hansen
Mrs. Herbert G. Howard
Mrs. Donald F. Hunt
Mrs. Francis E. Irwin

Mr. Hannes Jonsson, Consul General of Iceland, New York City
Hon. Juozas Kajeckas, Lithuanian Legation, Washington, D.C.
Mrs. Beatrice Knappik
Mme. Francis Laine, Marseille, France
Mme. Genevieve Legrand, Aix-en-Provence, France
Mr. David B. Little
Miss Beverley Lord
Joseph P. Lustenberger, Vice Consul General of Switzerland, New York City
Miss Katherine V. E. Lyford
Miss Eileen Lynch
Miss Marie Lynch
Mrs. Harvey L. Macaulay
Mr. Louis N. Mangifesti
Mrs. Donald K. Mason
Mr. Joacquin Noval Noredo
Norway Information Service, Washington, D.C.
Norway Memorial Library, Norway, Maine
Mrs. Bradley P. Noyes
Mrs. James A. O'Shea, Jr.
Mr. Sean O'Sullivan
Pan American Society of New England, Inc.
Mr. William C. Parker
Photographic Illustrations Corp.
Mr. Paul Picone
Dr. Frederick M. Piecewicz
Mr. Olli Pohjala, Vice Consul General of Finland, New York City

Mr. Robert H. Prew
Mrs. Mark Princi
Mrs. Gordon W. Roaf
Miss Betsy Ross, Bermuda
Salem Public Library, Salem, Massachusetts
Mrs. Frank H. Sawyer
Mrs. Robert Simpson, Jr.
Mrs. Foster Stearns

Mrs. Edwin A. Sturgis
Mrs. Francis Sullivan
Swedish Information Service, Washington, D.C.
Dr. Joseph Szovrffy
Mr. George Taloumis
Mrs. David P. Williams
Woburn, Public Library, Woburn, Massachusetts

PRISCILLA SAWYER LORD
Marblehead, Massachusetts

DANIEL J. FOLEY
Salem, Massachusetts

Contents

Easter
The
World
Over

The Meaning of Easter

IN tracing the name "Easter" to its roots in the languages of Europe, we learn that it refers to the season of the rising sun, or the dawn. This meaning for Easter long antedates the Christian era, and was adopted as appropriate to designate the Resurrection, the "Feast of the New Life." That illustrious monk and writer of the medieval Church, the Venerable Bede, is often quoted as referring to Easter as being derived from *Eostre,* the name of an Anglo-Saxon goddess, but present-day scholars claim that no such person was known in German mythology.

Also referred to as the "Great Night" and the "Great Day," "The Feast of Feasts," this "Solemnity of Solemnities" is spoken of in Hungary as the "Feast of Meat," indicating that the Lenten fast is over.

Most of the nations of Europe refer to Easter as *Pasch,* a Greek term derived from the Hebrew, meaning "Passover." Christ was crucified on Passover Day. This important feast in the Jewish calendar was observed in thanksgiving for the deliverance of the Israelites the night before they fled from Egypt. The firstborn of each Egyptian family was destroyed by the angel of God, but the children of the Israelites had been spared. Moses, proclaiming the command of God, ordered that each Hebrew family should slay a lamb without blemish and sprinkle its blood on the doorframe of each house. Following this sacrifice, the lamb was roasted and eaten with the traditional unleavened bread, and garnished with bitter herbs. As set down in the Jewish law, the ceremony was to take place annually on the eve of the Passover, and is still practiced by Orthodox Jews. Christ participated in this rite the night before His crucifixion. The sacrificial lamb of the Hebrews became the Christian symbol of Christ, the "Lamb of God, which taketh away the sin of the world" (John 1:29).

The sharing of a meal is the central feature of Passover, for eating together denotes kinship the world over. Our word "companion" means "one who shares bread with" another; likewise, the Gaelic word for "family" is "cuedich," meaning those who eat together. In his book *Passover, Its History and Tradi-*

I

tions, Theodor Gaster has written: "The original purpose of the paschal meal was to recement ties of kinship, infuse new life into the family, and renew the bonds of mutual protection at the beginning of each year." These rites were far more significant than a family reunion; they also involved man's relationship with God, thereby assuring divine protection.

What is eaten at the Passover meal is as important as the manner in which it is consumed. There are three cardinal features of the Passover meal: haste, because there was the danger in the past that the food might spoil; unleavened bread, which contained no fermentation and hence could not spoil; and bitter herbs, which were served as a cathartic to neutralize any impurities. The sacrificial lamb was chosen as part of the meal because the Egyptians worshiped the ram, and the Israelites wanted to show their disapproval of such idolatry. The blood from the sacrificial lamb was smeared on the side posts and the lintel of the door of each Jewish home as a reminder of the three patriarchs: Abraham, Isaac, and Jacob. It was applied with hyssop to symbolize the House of Israel—lowly but bound together by God's grace.

The Seder is the most important and familiar feature of Passover. This service is held in the home the first two nights of Passover and now takes the place of the sacrifice and paschal meal. All leavened food such as bread, flour, beer, and other items are removed from the house before the festival begins. The night before Seder, the master of the house carefully searches the premises with a lighted candle and sets aside any leavened food to be burned the next morning. Today, this ceremony is symbolic since the housewife has previously done a thorough job of "spring cleaning"—even substituting new dishes for old and polishing all the silver needed for the occasion. Yet she leaves a few crumbs so that her husband can "discover" them and sweep them up.

The traditional table is set with symbolic foods and the stirring story of the Exodus of the children of Israel is read from the *Haggadah* (the "Bible" of the Jewish people). Although Passover deprives Jewish homemakers of certain everyday foods, it is still possible to serve well-balanced and easily prepared meals. To simplify holiday cooking, many traditional Passover foods are now available in quick and convenient packaged form.

In front of the head of the house (who reads and recites from the *Haggadah* the story of the Passover), the following are placed, either on a Seder plate or on a group of small plates:

Three whole matzoth (unleavened bread)—covered or inserted into the matzoth dish. A piece (the afikomen) of the middle one is hidden for a child to find.

A *roasted lamb bone*—to the right—to commemorate the sacrifice made by the Israelites in Egypt before leaving for the Promised Land.

A *roasted egg*—to the left of the host—in mourning for the destroyed Temple.

Maror or *bitter herbs* (radish, horseradish, onions, scallions)—in the center —as a reminder of the bitterness of Israel's slavery in Egypt.

2

The ram's horn (shofar), used by the Jews in high religious observances. (*Courtesy, Israel Gov't Tourist Office*)

Charoseth (chopped almonds, grated apple, wine, sugar, and cinnamon)—to symbolize the mortar with which the Jews were forced to make bricks for the Pharaoh.

Karpas (celery, parsley, any greens)—which in Hebrew means "600,000", the number of Israelites that left Egypt.

Salt water—symbolizing the Red Sea, that parted miraculously to let the Israelites escape.

Elijah's cup—traditionally a precious item filled with wine—placed on the Seder table to await the beloved prophet.

The Seder is traditionally begun by dipping a hard-boiled egg in salt water. As an alternative, a tasteful appetizer is gefillte eggs, prepared with fish and bread crumbs.

In recent years, on Holy Thursday, the "Meal in the Upper Room" has become a special Holy Week service in some of the Protestant churches of the United States. Traditional Passover food, similar to that eaten in the Holy Land in the time of the Savior, is served. In the Hebrew tradition, the sharing of food has always been in itself a pledge of friendship and loyalty. The meal includes lamb, cheese, spinach, rice, olives, matzoth, grapes, figs, walnuts, and grape juice. The service is carried out in silence, with readings from the Gospels and the Psalms interspersed. A large seven-branch candelabra, typical of the kind used at Passover, is lighted when all have gathered at the table, and the room is illuminated entirely by candlelight. Selections from Psalm 113 from the Hebrew *Hallel* are read as the candles are lighted, followed by the Passover Thanksgiving Prayer, also taken from the *Hallel*, Psalm 118.

The variable dates of Easter are sometimes confusing, especially to those who deal in commerce. The possibilities of fixing the date for Easter so that it occurs at the same time annually have been discussed on many occasions, but the method of determining Easter has remained unchanged for more than 1600 years. The celebration of the Passover, governed by the moon, had been set according to custom for generations at the time of the birth of Christ. The early Christians, following this ancient practice, declared that Easter should be observed on the first Sunday following the full moon that occurs on or following the spring equinox, near or on March 21. The meeting of the astronomers of Alexandria under the direction of the archbishop of that great city resulted in the Council of Nicaea, which set the method of calculating the date of Easter in A.D. 325. Thus, Easter is spoken of as a movable feast which may occur as early as March 22 or as late as April 25. During the past fifty years, Easter has been observed four times as often in April as it has in March.

The Lenten season covers a forty-six-day period which begins on Ash Wednesday and ends on the eve of Easter. Since the six Sundays in Lent are not actually a part of Lent, the Lenten season itself comprises forty days. Sundays, commemorations of the first Easter, have always been excluded from the Lenten fast. The date of Ash Wednesday is determined by the date of Easter. Holy Week, the last week in Lent, begins with Palm Sunday.

The busy crowded streets of the Old City of Jerusalem echo to the steps of Christian, Jewish, and Moslem pilgrims. The city is sacred to three major religious faiths and houses such sites as the Church of the Holy Sepulcher, the Wailing wall, and the Mosque of Omar. (*Courtesy, Israel Tourist Office*)

Worshipers carrying palm leaves walk from Bethphage along the slopes of the Mount of Olives. Following the route of Jesus' triumphal entry into Jerusalem on the Sunday before his Crucifixion, the procession files past the Garden of Gethsemane and across the Kidron Valley into walled Jerusalem on Palm Sunday. The crenellated medieval walls of the Old City and the huge Dome of the Rock, a beautiful Moslem shrine, can be seen in the background. (*From United Press International*)

Lent may be said to have developed from two sources. Originally it was a period of fasting which preceded Easter in the early church. In the early days of the church this period of fasting was held on Saturday, the day before Easter, lasting until 3 A.M. Easter morning, when the Eucharist was celebrated. This ceremony symbolized the belief that Christ rose from the dead early in the morning. Later this fast was extended to six days and eventually was absorbed into the events of Holy Week. Actually, the observance of Holy Week is an older custom than that of the entire Lenten season.

The second source for this season of Lent was the baptism of candidates into the faith on the eve of Easter. Since the early church was an "underground movement," candidates were carefully screened, and there was a long period of preparation. The strictest part of this probationary period came, as would be expected, just before the time of baptism. A fasting period of forty days was required, the length of which was suggested by our Lord's fasting in the wilderness, Moses' fasting at Mt. Sinai, and Elijah's fasting on the way to the Mount of God—each lasting forty days. Eventually, this period of preparation for baptism evolved into a general period of preparation for Easter to be observed by all Christians.

The word *Lent* probably comes from the Anglo-Saxon *lencten,* meaning spring, and the German *Lenz,* meaning the time when the days lengthen.

The Lenten season, then, is a period of penitence in preparation for the highest festival of the church year, Easter. There seem to have arisen, however, two misunderstandings about the Lenten season. First, the penitential tone of the season has crept into the Sundays within the season, obscuring them as commemorations of the first Easter.

Second, the days of Lent themselves seem to have become dominated by meditation on the sufferings of Christ and sometimes even by morbid introspection. A study of the Passion of Christ is often extended over the entire Lenten season. The study of the Passion, however, should be the special subject of Holy Week. Edward T. Horn III states in his *The Christian Year*: "Sermons and meditations at midweek Lenten services are usually concerned with the events and characters of the Passion. Often the result is that, by the time Holy Week arrives, both people and clergy are weary of the details of the narrative which is proper to the week before Easter."

Certain days of Holy Week have been given special significance. The first is Palm Sunday, which takes its name from Jesus' triumphal entry into Jerusalem. In medieval days there was a ceremony of blessing the palms followed by a procession. This is still observed in the Roman Catholic Church, and some Protestant churches, too, recall that historic event with a procession of palms.

Thursday in Holy Week is the anniversary of the institution of the Lord's Supper, which was held the evening before the Crucifixion. The name "Maundy Thursday" is derived from the Latin *mandatum,* meaning "command," referring to the foot-washing ceremony at the Last Supper, when

Jesus spoke of the "new commandment" to love one another as He himself had loved (John 13:1-35).

Friday in Holy Week, of course, is the anniversary of the Crufixion. The term *Good* Friday probably came from "God's Friday" just as *good-bye* comes from "God be with ye."

The story of Easter is summed up in the words "hope" and "eternal life." Around this "Feast of Feasts," which commemorates the greatest of miracles, the Resurrection of Christ, have evolved a host of traditions and legends. In ritual, in hymns, in folk customs, it manifests itself in the humblest of every-day practices, from the foods we eat to the new clothes we put on. The outward manifestations of nature mirror in a variety of ways the spirit of hope that wells up in human hearts at Easter. Spring and Easter are synonymous. Symbols reveal themselves in the flowers of the field, the birds of the air, and the familiar animals.

The spirit of Christmas is best expressed in the joy of children who marvel at the birth of the Saviour in an image they understand, for He is like them— a child, yet the King of the World. Easter is somewhat more complex, for the very concept of the risen Christ requires the mental grasp of the growing child old enough to have attained the use of reason. But the message of Easter, when described in terms of the eternal symphony of spring, becomes a supreme lesson of faith for mankind.

Aside from the Christian concept of Easter and its Hebrew· roots, the pre-Christian or pagan myths and folklore that surround this feast of spring have clothed its observance in a worldwide blending of ancient traditions. Down through the ages, the fear and mystery surrounding death have been no less puzzling than the renewal of life and the rebirth of the spirit. "Except a corn of wheat fall into the ground and die, it abideth alone: but if it die, it bringeth forth much fruit." In these simple words Christ summed up the mysterious truth that life depends on death (John 12:24).

Myth and symbol go hand in hand as historical facts are related and blended with age-old beliefs and customs which attempt to explain eternal truth and historic fact as Christ did in giving the parables to His first followers. In a book which attempts to bring together history, myth, symbols, folklore and traditions, the aim must be to relate and yet to distinguish the various categories that provide the threads that make the marvelous tapestry of Easter in all its glory, radiance, and richness.

Popular in the eighteenth century were these soup tureens in the form of a rabbit. Made of soft-paste porcelain in Chelsea, England, between 1752 and 1756, these rabbits are life-sized, unlike smaller versions used for dessert dishes. The back of each rabbit is a removable cover, the ears serving as handles. At least seven of these tureens have survived. Two are included in the collection of the Campbell Museum. (*From the Campbell Museum Collection, Camden, N.J.*)

This brightly lithographed toy train, run by a spring-wound clockwise motor, made by The Girard Model Works, Girard, Pennsylvania, in the early 1930s. This concern was one of several attempting to compete with the importation of metal toys from Germany. (*From the collection of Richard Merrill*)

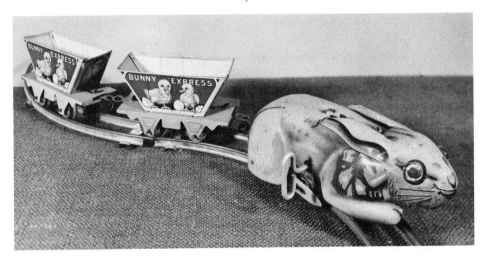

White Russian Easter charms made about 1900. Women and girls wore them on necklaces. The number of these charms owned by an individual was evidence of her popularity. Stones in charm at left are garnets. Larger jewel is made of gold. (*From the collection of Mrs. Robert D. Dykeman; photo: Richard Merrill*)

The Message of Easter

(According to Matthew 26:17–56 (*The Jerusalem Bible*))

Preparations for the Passover supper

Now on the first day of Unleavened Bread the disciples came to Jesus to say, 'Where do you want us to make the preparations for you to eat the Passover?' 'Go to so-and-so in the city,' he replied, 'and say to him, "The Master says: My time is near. It is at your house that I am keeping Passover with my disciples."' The disciples did what Jesus told them and prepared the Passover.

The treachery of Judas foretold

When evening came he was at table with the twelve disciples. And while they were eating he said, 'I tell you solemnly, one of you is about to betray me.' They were greatly distressed and started asking him in turn, 'Not I, Lord, surely?' He answered, 'Someone who has dipped his hand into the dish with me will betray me. The Son of Man is going to his fate, as the scriptures say he will, but alas for that man by whom the Son of Man is betrayed! Better for that man if he had never been born!' Judas, who was to betray him, asked in his turn, 'Not I, Rabbi, surely?' 'They are your own words,' answered Jesus.

The institution of the Eucharist

Now as they were eating, Jesus took some bread, and when he had said the blessing he broke it and gave it to the disciples. 'Take it and eat,' he said, 'this is my body.' Then he took a cup, and when he had returned thanks he gave it to them. 'Drink all of you from this,' he said, 'for this is my blood, the blood of the covenant, which is to be poured out for many for the forgiveness of sins. From now on, I tell you, I shall not drink wine until the day I drink the new wine with you in the kingdom of my Father.'

Peter's denial foretold

After psalms had been sung they left for the Mount of Olives. Then Jesus said to them, 'You will all lose faith in me this night, for the scripture says: I shall strike the shepherd and the sheep of the flock will be scattered, but after my resurrection I shall go before you to Galilee.' At this, Peter said, 'Though all lose faith in you, I will never lose faith.' Jesus answered him, 'I tell you solemnly, this very night, before the cock crows, you will have disowned me three times.' Peter said to him, 'Even if I have to die with you, I will never disown you.' And all the disciples said the same.

Gethsemane

Then Jesus came with them to a small estate called Gethsemane; and he said to his disciples, 'Stay here while I go over there to pray.' He took Peter and the two sons of Zebedee with him. And sadness came over him, and great distress. Then he said to them, 'My soul is sorrowful to the point of death. Wait here and keep awake with me.' And going on a little further he fell on his face and prayed. 'My Father,' he said, 'if it is possible, let this cup pass me by. Nevertheless, let it be as you, not I, would have it.' He came back to the disciples and found them sleeping, and he said to Peter, 'So you had not the strength to keep awake with me one hour? You should be awake, and praying not to be put to the test. The spirit is willing, but the flesh is weak.' Again, a second time, he went away and prayed: 'My Father,' he said, 'if this cup cannot pass by without my drinking it, your will be done!' And he came again back and found them sleeping, their eyes were so heavy. Leaving them there, he went away again and prayed for the third time, repeating the same words. Then he came back to the disciples and said to them, 'You can sleep on now and take your rest. Now the hour has come when the Son of Man is to be betrayed into the hands of sinners. Get up! Let us go! My betrayer is already close at hand.'

The arrest

He was still speaking when Judas, one of the Twelve, appeared, and with him a large number of men armed with swords and clubs, sent by the chief priests and elders of the people. Now the traitor had arranged a sign with them. 'The one I kiss,' he said, 'he is the man. Take him in charge.' So he went straight up to Jesus and said, 'Greetings, Rabbi,' and kissed him. Jesus said to him, 'My friend, do what you are here for.' Then they came forward, seized Jesus and took him in charge. At that, one of the followers of Jesus grasped his sword and drew it; he struck out at the high priest's servant, and cut off his ear. Jesus then said, 'Put your sword back, for all who draw the sword will die by the sword. Or do you think that I cannot appeal to my Father who would promptly send more than twelve legions of angels to my defense? But then, how would the scriptures be fulfilled that say this is the way it must be?' It was at this time that Jesus said to the crowds, 'Am I a brigand, that you had to set out to capture me with swords and clubs? I sat teaching in the Temple day after day and you never laid hands on me.' Now all this happened to fulfil the prophecies in scripture. Then all the disciples deserted him and ran away.

THE DEATH OF JESUS

According to Luke 22: 66–71 and Luke 23: 1–46

Jesus before the Sanhedrin

When day broke there was a meeting of the elders of the people, attended by the chief priests and scribes. He was brought before their council, and they said to him, 'If you are the Christ, tell us.' 'If I tell you,' he replied, 'you will not believe me, and if I question you, you will not answer. But from now on, the Son of Man will be seated at the right hand of the Power of God.' Then they all said, 'So you are the Son of God then?' He answered, 'It is you who say I am.' 'What need of witnesses have we now?' they said. 'We have heard it for ourselves from his own lips.' The whole assembly then rose, and they brought him before Pilate.

Jesus before Pilate

They began their accusation by saying, 'We found this man inciting our people to revolt, opposing payment of the tribute to Caesar, and claiming to be Christ, a king.' Pilate put to him this question, 'Are you the king of the Jews?' 'It is you who say it,' he replied. Pilate then said to the chief priests and the crowd, 'I find no case against this man.' But they persisted, 'He is inflaming the people with his teaching all over Judaea; it has come all the way from Galilee, where he started, down to here.' When Pilate heard this, he asked if the man were a Galilean; and finding that he came under Herod's jurisdiction he passed him over to Herod who was also in Jerusalem at that time.

Jesus before Herod

Herod was delighted to see Jesus; he had heard about him and had been wanting for a long time to set eyes on him; moreover, he was hoping to see some miracle worked by him. So he questioned him at some length; but without getting any reply. Meanwhile the chief priests and the scribes were there, violently pressing their accusations. Then Herod, together with his guards, turned him back to Pilate. And though Herod and Pilate had been enemies before, they were reconciled that same day.

Jesus before Pilate again

Pilate then summoned the chief priests and the leading men and the people. 'You brought this man before me,' he said, 'as a political agitator. Now I have gone into the matter myself in your presence and found no case against the man in respect of all the charges you bring against him. Nor has Herod either, since he has sent him back to us. As you can see, the man has done nothing that deserves death, so I shall have him flogged and then let him go.' But as one man they howled, 'Away with him! Give us Barabbas!' (This man had been thrown into prison for causing a riot in the city and for murder.)

Pilate was anxious to set Jesus free and addressed them again, but they shouted back, 'Crucify him! Crucify him!' And for the third time he spoke to them, 'Why? What harm has this man done? I have found no case against him that deserves death, so I shall have him punished and then let him go.' But they kept on shouting at the top of their voices, demanding that he should be crucified. And their shouts were growing louder.

Pilate then gave his verdict: their demand was to be granted. He released the man they asked for, who had been imprisoned for rioting and murder, and handed Jesus over to them to deal with as they pleased.

The way to Calvary

As they were leading him away they seized on a man, Simon from Cyrene, who was coming in from the country, and made him shoulder the cross and carry it behind Jesus. Large numbers of people followed him, and of women too, who mourned and lamented for him. But Jesus turned to them and said, 'Daughters of Jerusalem, do not weep for me; weep rather for yourselves and for your children. For the days will surely come when people will say, "Happy are those who are barren, the wombs that have never borne, the breasts that have never suckled!" Then they will begin to say to the mountains, "Fall on us!"; to the hills, "Cover us!" For if men use the green wood like this, what will happen when it is dry?' Now with him they were also leading out two other criminals to be executed.

The Crucifixion

When they reached the place called The Skull, they crucified him there and the two criminals also, one on the right, the other on the left. Jesus said, 'Father, forgive them; they do not know what they are doing.' Then they cast lots to share out his clothing.

The crucified Christ is mocked

The people stayed there watching him. As for the leaders, they jeered at him. 'He saved others,' they said, 'let him save himself if he is the Christ of God, the Chosen One.' The soldiers mocked him too, and when they approached to offer him vinegar they said, 'If you are the King of the Jews, save yourself.' Above him there was an inscription: 'This is the king of the Jews.'

The good thief

One of the criminals hanging there abused him. 'Are you not the Christ?' he said. 'Save yourself and us as well.' But the other spoke up and rebuked him. 'Have you no fear of God at all?' he said, 'Remember me when you come into your kingdom.' 'Indeed, I promise you,' he replied, 'today you will be with me in paradise.'

13

The death of Jesus

It was now about the sixth hour and, with the sun eclipsed, a darkness came over the whole land until the ninth hour. The veil of the Temple was torn right down the middle; and when Jesus had cried out in a loud voice, he said, 'Father, into your hands I commit my spirit.' With these words he breathed his last.

THE RESURRECTION
According to Luke 24: 1–31

The empty tomb. The angels' message

On the first day of the week, at the first sign of dawn, they went to the tomb with the spices they had prepared. They found that the stone had been rolled away from the tomb, but on entering discovered that the body of the Lord Jesus was not there. As they stood there not knowing what to think, two men in brilliant clothes suddenly appeared at their side. Terrified, the women lowered their eyes. But the two men said to them. 'Why look among the dead for someone who is alive? He is not here; he has risen. Remember what he told you when he was still in Galilee: that the Son of Man had to be handed over into the power of sinful men and be crucified, and rise again on the third day?' And they remembered his words.

The apostles refuse to believe the women

When the women returned from the tomb they told all this to the Eleven and to all the others. The women were Mary of Magdala, Joanna, and Mary the mother of James. The other women with them also told the apostles, but this story of theirs seemed pure nonsense, and they did not believe them.

Peter at the tomb

Peter, however, went running to the tomb. He bent down and saw the binding cloths but nothing else; he then went back home, amazed at what had happened.

The road to Emmaus

That very same day, two of them were on their way to a village called Emmaus, seven miles from Jerusalem, and they were talking together about all that had happened. Now as they talked this over, Jesus himself came up and walked by their side; but something prevented them from recognizing him. He said to them, 'What matters are you discussing as you walk along?' They stopped short, their faces downcast.

Then one of them, called Cleopas, answered him, 'You must be the only person staying in Jerusalem who does not know the things that have been happening there these last few days.' 'What things?' he asked. 'All about Jesus of Nazareth,' they answered, 'who proved he was a great prophet by the things he said and did in the sight of God and of the whole people; and how our chief priests and our leaders handed him over to be sentenced to death, and had him crucified. Our own hope had been that he would be the one to set Israel free. And this is not all: two whole days have gone by since it all happened; and some women from our group have astounded us: they went to the tomb in the early morning, and when they did not find the body, they came back to tell us they had seen a vision of angels who declared he was alive. Some of our friends went to the tomb and found everything exactly as the women had reported, but of him they saw nothing.'

Then he said to them, 'You foolish men! So slow to believe the full message of the prophets! Was it not ordained that the Christ should suffer and so enter into his glory?' Then, starting with Moses and going through all the prophets, he explained to them the passages throughout the scriptures that were about himself.

When they drew near to the village to which they were going, he made as if to go on; but they pressed him to stay with them. 'It is nearly evening,' they said, 'and the day is almost over.' So he went in to stay with them. Now while he was with them at table, he took the bread and said the blessing; then he broke it and handed it to them. And their eyes were opened and they recognized him; but he had vanished from their sight.

Asia Minor

The Holy Land

NEARLY two thousand years ago, in the Sermon on the Mount, Jesus said: "Consider the lilies of the field, how they grow; they toil not, neither do they spin: and yet I say unto you, that even Solomon in all his glory was not arrayed like one of these." This was a reference to the glorious wild flowers that burst forth in Jerusalem at Easter time when the barren hillsides are vivid with red, blue and white field anemones and a score or more of other spring flowers including narcissus, iris and choice alpines. Neither the flowers nor the atmosphere of this hallowed city has changed greatly in two thousand years. Bitterness and hate prevail among the various racial groups of the population and the resulting strife, then as now, creates a spirit of unrest.

The various episodes of Holy Week took place between two great hills which reach nearly 3000 feet above sea level—Mount Zion and Jerusalem to the east and the Mount of Olives to the west. The steep Valley of Kidron divides them. Bethany, on a ridge below the crest of the Mount of Olives, is the quiet village from which Jesus rode out on his donkey to enter Jerusalem on Palm Sunday. This was the community where Martha and Mary and their brother, Lazarus, lived. Visitors to the Holy Land at Easter and at other seasons of the year never fail to revel in the superb view eastward from Bethany, looking into the Jordan Valley, Jericho, and the Dead Sea. Jesus chose Bethany, coming to it, it is believed, from Jericho in the last week of his ministry to find quiet and comfort in the home of friends away from the excitement and confusion of Jerusalem in Passover season.

It has been surmised that he walked back and forth between the city and the village, a distance that can be covered in thirty-five to forty minutes. If so, he passed the Garden of Gethsemane at the foot of the Mount of Olives—

16

the place where he prayed on Maundy Thursday night. The spot remains a beautiful garden with flower beds and ancient olive trees, a thousand years old or more, that provide welcome shade. Nearby now are two landmark churches, one for the Roman Catholics, and the other the property of the Russian Orthodox congregation. Yet, in the adjoining fields little has changed; it is the same pastoral landscape where sheep still graze and patches of land are cultivated that Jesus knew.

The walls of honey-colored stone around the old city are not original, having been constructed by Suleiman the Magnificent in the sixteenth century, but they enclose the area known in the time of Christ. According to tradition, He entered Jerusalem through the Zusan Gate of Herod, which was replaced in the fifth century by what is called the Golden Gate in the east wall of the Temple. In Jewish belief it is through this gate that the Messiah will enter and for the Moslems it is held that the last judgment of Mohammed will occur here. The effect of the sun shining on these honey-colored walls has evoked the expression "Jerusalem the Golden."

Within the walls, at the southeast corner of the old town, is perhaps the most impressive of the holy places, the Temple area on Mount Moriah, which is now a Moslem shrine. Originally this was the site of the Temple from which Jesus drove the money changers, but nothing remains except a stretch of wall outside and below the present enclosure, a wall for centuries sacred to Jewry as the Wailing Wall. However, worshiping Jews were denied access to it in 1948, when the fighting in Palestine resulted in the separation of the Old City from the New. Both the Old City and the New City are now held by the Israelis. The Temple area, known now as Haram Esharit, is a vast open space paved with flagstones, in the center of which the Dome of the Rock rises, a restrained example of architecture, covered with porcelain tiles of blue and gold. At its southern end is the Mosque of Aqsa, once a Crusader church.

The spot in the city most revered by Christians is the Church of the Holy Sepulchre, away to the northeast, but within the medieval walls. To reach it, the pilgrim must walk over narrow, winding, cobbled streets, lined with open-front stalls, since no cars are permitted. Everybody who walks rubs shoulders with Arab peasants in head cloths and ankle-length dress, women from the surrounding villages in gay embroidery and white veils, priests from the Eastern and Western churches, as well as tourists.

Entering through an archway, and looking across a courtyard, one sees the squat square bell tower built by the Crusaders in the twelfth century. However, most of the rest of the exterior, including the dome, dates only from the eighteenth century, when much of the church was rebuilt to prevent its collapse. Beneath are rock tombs and cisterns protected by a vault which was also the work of the Crusaders. The first church built on this site was erected in the fourth century, when, according to tradition, Helena, mother of the Roman emperor Constantine, found relics of the Cross here. Some of the stonework of this early church remains under the roof of the present building.

17

Jerusalem, the City of Peace, shown here in a bird's-eye view. The Jaffa Gate is in the foreground, the Temple Mount in the center and the Mount of Olives can be clearly seen in the background. (*Courtesy, Israel Govt. Tourist Office*)

The Damascus Gate, which leads into the old walled city of Jerusalem, is one of the busiest of the many city entrances. On the Jerusalem skyline are the twin domes of the Church of the Holy Sepulchre. (*Courtesy, Israel Govt. Tourist Office*)

The meandering alleys and streets of the Old City of Jerusalem are in sharp contrast with the broad avenues of the New City. Monks, nuns, priests, Moslem kadis, and Jewish rabbis add color to the interest-crammed scene. (*Courtesy, Israel Govt. Tourist Office*)

The Garden of Gethsemane on the slope of the Mount of Olives is revered as the site where Jesus rested after the Last Supper. A number of churches and shrines are contained in the garden area, which is just outside the eastern walls of Jerusalem. (*Courtesy, Israel Gov.'t Tourist Office*)

The Church of the Holy Sepulchre is one of the most sacred Christian sites in the Holy Land. Situated on Golgotha, where ancient tradition says the skull of Adam is buried, it also marks the site of the Crucifixion, burial and Resurrection of Jesus. (*Courtesy, Israel Govt. Tourist Office*)

The Room of the Last Supper is a sacred site to the many Christians who visit Jerusalem each year. Located on Mount Zion, just outside the walled section of the city, it is traditionally the place where Jesus supped with his disciples. (*Courtesy, Israel Govt. Tourist Office*)

Pope Paul VI prays in the Room of the Last Supper, the Cénacle. It was here that Jesus instituted the Holy Eucharist, elevated the apostles to the priesthood and where, at a later date, the apostles received the Holy Spirit on Pentecost. (*Courtesy, Israel Govt. Tourist Office*)

Many seeing the Church of the Holy Sepulchre for the first time are disappointed. Its façade is partly hidden by a network of steel girders erected after the earthquake of 1927 to prevent the building from falling down. It is a maze of chapels and passageways on various levels, where ancient denominations jealously and fiercely guard their traditional rights. Since the days of Saladin in the twelfth century, a Moslem family has policed the sacred precincts to prevent strife between the rival Christian persuasions.

Tradition has it that within the church are the sites of both Calvary, where Jesus was crucified, and the tomb where Joseph of Arimathaea subsequently laid His body. A hole in the floor of the chapel at an upper level is said to mark the place where the Cross stood, and a large rectangular structure under the dome is reputed to have been the tomb.

Nevertheless, to recapture the spirit of the first Easter morning, one must visit the Garden Tomb, just outside the Damascus Gate of the Old City. At the close of the nineteenth century, a hollow cave was excavated, believed to have served as a tomb at the time of Jesus. The entrance was closed by a huge circular stone, like a millstone, rolled before it. St. Luke, it will be recalled, described the sepulcher of Joseph of Arimathaea as "hewn in stone, wherein never man before was laid."

As one traveler expressed it: "Here at dawn, within a low wall amid flowers and trees, where nature is unspoiled by any human construction or incongruous intrusion, the Easter hymns ring true. Here one can hear the angel saying: 'He is not here: for he is risen, as He said. Come, see the place where the Lord lay.' And here one can picture the joyful scene as the sorrowing Mary Magdalene recognized that prophecy was true and that Jesus had indeed risen from the dead. This is the Jerusalem that assuredly will remain a holy place for the rest of human history."

Down through the ages, many plants have been associated with the Holy Land and the Holy Family. Then, too, legends and traditions have literally sprung from the earth in various parts of the world, due in part to the similarity or relationship or resemblance of some local plant to one found in the Holy Land. Moreover, when looked upon as symbols of memorable events or as simple reminders of faith, they serve to convey the message intended. One of the common briers with showy red blossoms (*Rubus coronaricus*) is believed to have derived its color from the Savior's blood.

Was the crown of thorns, that was plaited by the soldiers and placed on Christ's head in mockery, actually a wreath of rose canes, as implied by some of the great Renaissance painters? No other flower that grows in gardens or in the wild is richer in lore than the rose. This emblem of love, beauty, and youth can be traced back five thousand years or more, and its associations with the Holy Family are numerous. It is often referred to as the flower of the martyrs. The name "rose" has been used for many plants that are not true roses or related to the rose family. The term Rose of Sharon has been applied to a wild tulip and a handsome flowering shrub which blooms in summer (*Hibiscus syriacus*). Other plants referred to as roses are the oleander, the crocus, and the narcissus. In many parts of Europe, the wild rose is referred to in folklore as the plant used in Christ's Passion. The flowers were originally white, but changed color, having been dyed with the blood of the Savior as the crown rested on His brow. There are several kinds of wild roses native to Palestine, and Bible scholars have written voluminously about the word "rose" as used in the Bible.

In Germany, France, and Great Britain, tradition has it that the white hawthorn (*Crataegus oxyacantha*), familiar shrub of English hedgerows and gardens, was the plant used. Other plants mentioned are the box thorn (*Lycium europaeum*), the wild hyssop (*Capavris spinosa*), and the bramble (*Rubus fruticosus*). The common barberry (*Berberis vulgaris*) is pointed out in Italy as the source of the crown.

Of all the plants mentioned as the source of the torturing crown, none is better known than the hawthorn. So abundant are its white blossoms in spring that its long, spiny thorns are hardly noticeable, but they are capable of inflicting a painful wound and their sharpness is soon apparent when branches are carelessly handled. An age-old tale recalls that on the way to Calvary a bird fluttered down to the head of the weary Christ and pulled out a thorn that was piercing His brow. The sacred blood colored the breast feathers of the little creature, who has worn the mark since that day, and we know him as robin redbreast.

In England, the hawthorn often blooms during mild periods in winter, and the famous Glastonbury Thorn has frequently put forth flowers at Christmas. According to tradition, this holy thorn was brought to England in the first century by Joseph of Arimathaea, when he settled there and taught Christianity to the Britons. He had been banished from the Holy Land after the Resurrection. On reaching Wearyall Hill, near Glastonbury, he struck his walking staff into the earth to indicate the location of his new home. Left thus in the soil, the staff stirred to fresh life, put forth leaves, and flourished for centuries as a revered tree. It was finally destroyed by the Puritans as a Romish superstition, but scions were perpetuated and one planted from the original tree on the grounds of the National Cathedral in Washington, D.C., has bloomed on five occasions since 1918.

The fabled hawthorn is truly rich in Scriptural tradition. A little-known story reveals that, while Christ was resting in a grove during His most perilous hours, the magpies covered Him with hawthorn boughs, which the swallows, "fowls of God," removed as soon as His enemies had passed. From this episode the plant gained holiness. A tale concerning Charlemagne related that he knelt before the crown of thorns in the church of Saint Chapelle in Paris, which was believed to have been made of hawthorn. He was overcome when the wood, dry for centuries, burst into bloom and the air was filled with a wondrous fragrance.

The crown of thorns (*Euphorbia splendens*), a familiar house plant in cold climates noted for its bright vermilion flowers, is probably the plant most frequently associated in the popular mind with Christ. Its woody stems are heavily set with the sharpest of spines of various sizes, making it exceedingly difficult to handle. Yet this woody vine-like shrub, native to Madagascar, was unknown in Bible times.

An acacia, known to the Israelites as the shittah tree, is referred to in the Near East as the source of the crown of thorns. It was chosen, sacred tree that it was, because the leaves between the thorns resembled those of ivy, with which kings and princes and great heroes were crowned. No form of mockery could have been more subtle, for the wood of the acacia was considered sacred by the Hebrews. They had brought the acacia out of Egypt and used the wood to build both their Tabernacle and the Ark of the Covenant.

In parts of the Orient a plant called butcher's-broom, or prickly-rush (*Ruscus aculeatus*), is believed to be the plant used in the mock coronation. This plant, grown commercially on the West Coast of the United States and known as ruscus, is dried, dyed red and used in Christmas decorations.

Visitors to the West Indies are shown the cashew (*Anacardium occidentale*), and told that it was used to make Christ's painful crown.

One old legend not commonly heard concerns the willow. Its branches were used to make the ignoble wreath since this plant originally had thorns. However, the tree wept and drooped at having caused the Savior so much pain, and the sharp thorns changed themselves into soft, sad-colored leaves that they might never cause any more suffering.

The Christ thorn (*Paliurus spina-Cristi*), a plant with thin pliable twigs and fiercely sharp spines found abundantly in Palestine, has received its common name from its supposed use. This plant is believed to be the source of the "wreath of thorny twigs" that was placed on Christ's head as he stood in a scarlet cloak.

One noted scholar maintains that the plant actually used was the spiny burnet (*Poterium spinosum*), a tangled shrub with curious reddish flowers and delicately cut leaves which disappear in the heat of summer. Commonly used as fuel for limekilns and ovens, it is gathered and cut with pruning hooks. It burns with a noisy crackling spitting sound, and is the plant referred to in Ecclesiastes 7:6, "For as the crackling of thorns under a pot, so is the laughter of the fool . . ."

The true lily of the field (*Anemone coronaria*), or windflower, a superb wild flower of Palestine widely cultivated in greenhouses and gardens today, appears in many colors, including white, purple, pink, and red. It is traditionally associated with the Passion of Christ. It is claimed that those with red flowers owe their color to the drops of blood which fell on the flowers as Christ hung on the Cross.

At the time of the Crusades, Umberto, Bishop of Pisa, suggested that ships returning from the Holy Land should bring back good soil, instead of sand, for ballast. The sacred earth so obtained was spread on the ground of Campo Santo and Pisa, and the marvelous windflower appeared there, where it is now naturalized.

Another favorite flower, the lily of the valley, is said to have sprung from

24

the tears of Mary, the mother of Jesus, as she wept at the foot of the Cross, yet this flower is unknown in the Holy Land. But it is beautiful in form, pure white, as precious as any jewel, and in the language of myth and legend serves as a kind of parable. Flowering plants have been a never-ending source of joy to poets, painters, and peasants down through the ages: They speak the language of the heart.

A wild verbena known as American blue vervain (*Verbena hastata*), which resembles a species found in Brittany, is known as the "herb of the Cross," for it is said to have been found at the foot of the Cross.

Selma Lagerlöf, noted Swedish writer of stories and legends, has produced a memorable story entitled "St. Veronica's Handkerchief." This is recounted in the chapter about Russia.

A curious plant found in Jericho, Syria, and the Mediterranean area which botanists refer to as the Palestine tumbleweed is popularly known as the resurrection plant (*Anastatica hierochuntica*). To the Jewish people it is the Rose of Jericho. In the Old World it is known as Rosa-Mariae, the Rose of the Virgin, or Mary's hand. Yet it in no way resembles a rose. The Moslems call it Kaf Marjam, and to all it has been a cherished plant for centuries. According to legend, it sprang up wherever the Holy Family rested on the flight into Egypt. It is said to have blossomed at the Savior's birth, closed at the Crucifixion, and opened again at Easter; thus the name resurrection flower. When withered, the plant rolls up like a ball, but it resumes its natural form whenever it is placed in water or exposed to dampness. It is sometimes offered in novelty shops as a curiosity, and from time to time has been featured by street peddlers and hawkers of strange merchandise. In Psalm 83:13 we find this passage: "O my God, make them like a wheel; as the stubble before the wind"—a reference to the resurrection plant.

The crown imperial, or fritillary, is a curious plant with bulb-like roots, sometimes grown in gardens, and native to Iran. The bell-like flowers, which are usually red or yellow, were originally white. According to an old German legend, this flower failed to bow in the Garden of Gethsemane during the Agony of the Savior, and since that time it has hung its head, blushing red with shame, and with tears of repentance in its eyes. The tears are drops of standing sweet dew in the white centers of the blossoms.

The showy reddish fruit of the pomegranate is a symbol of the Resurrection often found in Christian art, including painting, sculpture, and embroidery. This plant is linked with Proserpine, who was the daughter of Ceres, goddess of the earth, and who was kidnaped by Pluto. She finally returned to her mother, but because she had eaten six pomegranate seeds, she had to remain with Pluto for six months each year in his underground kingdom. This old Roman legend was transferred to Christian tradition to signify that the Lord had power to burst forth from the tomb and live again.

On the night of the Crucifixion, we read in John 19:39, 40, Nicodemus came "and brought a mixture of myrrh and aloes, about an hundred pound weight. Then took they the body of Jesus, and wound it in linen clothes with

A nun of the Franciscan convent on the Mount of Beatitudes looks out over the Sea of Galilee from the archway of the church, which is on the summit. (*Courtesy, Israel Govt. Tourist Office*)

The YMCA camp on the shore of the Sea of Galilee is used as a retreat for Israel's Protestant citizens and for visitors from abroad. The camp is set in a grove of pine and cypress. (*Courtesy, Israel Govt. Tourist Office*)

Traditionally the location where Jesus preached the Sermon on the Mount. The church on the summit belongs to the Italian Franciscan nuns. The mount overlooks the Sea of Galilee. (*Courtesy, Israel Govt. Tourist Office*)

Galilean shepherd.
(*Courtesy, Israel Govt. Tourist Office*)

Donkeys are still a common sight on the streets of Nazareth. These hardy animals are as useful to the current residents of the city as they were to its inhabitants some 2000 years ago. (*Courtesy, Israel Govt. Tourist Office*)

The saddle-shaped hills known as the Horns of Hattin mark the place where Saladin defeated the Crusaders in 1187. (*Courtesy, Israel Govt. Tourist Office*)

the spices, as the manner of the Jews is to bury." Myrrh is derived from a thorny bush in the form of a gum resin which comes from the branches. It is an astringent and cleansing agent used by the ancient Hebrews and other races in embalming. Since it was not found in Palestine, it had to be imported from Arabia or Africa in Bible times. Aloe is a plant with stiff succulent leaves, not unlike the century plant in appearance, with spikes of showy red flowers. Like the century plant which grows in our American deserts, it grows in hot, dry places, but was not native to Palestine and was also imported from Africa. In Jesus' time this drug was used in embalming and was considered costly.

A legend beloved by children relating to Jesus concerns the larkspur. It relates to the Garden of Gethsemane, where Jesus loved to walk. There the grass was greener, the sky bluer, and the sun brighter than anywhere else; there colorful flowers bloomed and little animals lived. For a while Jesus did not come to the garden. All His little friends missed Him, and particularly a small rabbit, who waited day and night for the return of the Master. Early on the third day Christ came—and as He walked into the sunshine He gave the rabbit a loving smile. Later, when Jesus' friends came to the garden to pray, they found a path of beautiful flowers—the larkspurs. To this day one may see in the center of each blossom an image of the little rabbit who waited three days to greet the risen Lord.

Thomas, beloved apostle of Jesus, was grief-stricken by the crucifixion of his Master and as much as he wanted to believe in a resurrection, his mind could not grasp such a miracle. Three days after the Master's death, Thomas was walking a familiar path to Galilee when he noticed a lovely flower growing by the wayside. Only weeks before, the plant had been withered and brown— dead to all appearances. *It has been reborn*, thought Thomas. *Could this be an example of resurrection as our Lord explained it to us?* His heart bursting with new hope, Thomas hurried to the place where the apostles were gathering. And there he found his Lord, risen from the dead as He had promised. Thomas never forgot the lesson he learned from the iris. Even today this lovely flower is a symbol to Christian hearts everywhere of new hope and new life.

The British author Mary Drewery, who has traveled often to the Holy Land, has written a tale for all ages, called *Hamid and the Palm Sunday Donkey*. She paints a graphic word picture of Old Jerusalem and the Garden of Gethsemane as a backdrop for a young Arab boy, Hamid. Through many adventures and mishaps with his donkey, Hamid has his eyes opened to the importance of this extraordinary land, rich in Biblical history.

The United States

WHEN the Dutch settled in New Amsterdam, they brought the Easter egg customs to the New World along with Santa Claus, the Maypole, ice skating, golf, and bowling. A rough-and-tumble sport enjoyed in rural areas by Dutch farm boys at Shrovetide was called "pulling the goose." A live goose was thoroughly greased and suspended between two poles, whereupon the contestants, one after the other, rode toward it on horseback and tried to catch and hold it. However, Governor Peter Stuyvesant disapproved of the game as being too "pagan" and forbade it. Even in the New Netherlands, the Puritan spirit made itself felt at an early date.

Charles Burr Todd in *The Story of the City of New York* has given us this record: "Paas, which we observe on Easter Monday, may be traced back to the early Saxons, from whom the Dutch are sprung. Paas means 'egg cracking,' and a favorite game on that day is called 'playing for eggs.' The sweetheart holds an egg in her hand and challenges thee to break it by striking it with thy egg, the broken one belonging to that which remaineth whole. On that day, too, the shops are gay with boiled eggs, tied with red and blue ribbons, or colored by mixing potent pigments in the water which hath boiled them. On Paas Day no true son of St. Nicholas tasteth other food than eggs."

During the Revolution, a British lieutenant, Thomas Anburey, kept a journal of his experiences as a soldier and prisoner while in the colonies. Apparently he moved about considerably during his stay and being interested in sports, recorded what he saw. In 1781, he was a captive near Frederick, Maryland, and described the Easter holiday: "The young people have a custom, in this province, of boiling eggs in logwood, which dyes the shell crimson and though this color will not rub off, you may, with a pin, scratch on them any figure or device you think proper. This is practiced by the young men and maidens, who present them to each other as tokens. As these eggs are boiled a considerable time to take the dye, the shell acquires great strength and the children divert themselves by striking the eggs against each other, and that which breaks becomes the property of him whose egg remains whole."

29

Pre-Lenten celebrations took root in the United States long before the penitential season or Easter itself was widely observed on the national level. Yet, to those of Puritan background and the populace at large, such bacchanal revels were to be heartily frowned upon for several generations. The celebration of Carnival and Mardi Gras were Old World customs enjoyed and understood only by those of French, Italian, and Spanish heritage. The American melting pot had not yet begun to boil, but like so many other transplanted customs, these revels soon became regional events of prime interest throughout the country.

The name "Mardi Gras" applies literally to one day only, the Tuesday before Ash Wednesday, but in New Orleans, the term Mardi Gras is used to refer to a six-day period which begins with the parade of Comus on the preceding Thursday evening and ends with the parade and ball in tribute to Comus on Shrove Tuesday, Mardi Gras night. Although Mardi Gras evolved from the original Carnival, the two are not synonymous in New Orleans. Each year Carnival is launched there on Twelfth Night with an elaborate ball. This marks the beginning of a long season of feasts, plays, masquerades, dances, and elaborate entertainment. In the early days, street travesties were popular. The exact date of the first Carnival observance has never been established. Tradition has it that Jean Baptiste de Bienville, the founder of New Orleans, launched a celebration in 1718.

Local chroniclers claim that Mardi Gras began in 1827, the result of a revel by a group of young Creoles recently returned from private schools in Paris. Infected with the gay spirit of Paris, they donned weird costumes and danced merrily through the streets of the Old French Quarter. Prior to that time, the Carnival season was observed with fancy dress balls and masquerades

The elaborate Mardi Gras floats, fifteen to twenty in each parade, are worked on secretly for a whole year by the various organizations sponsoring them and are not seen by the public until they appear in one of the parades. Papier-mâché fantasies of brilliant colors, employing ingenious mechanical devices, are built on wheeled flat cars about twenty feet long and eight feet wide. (*Courtesy, The New Orleans Tourist and Convention Commission*)

Mardi Gras in New Orleans is often referred
to as "the greatest show on earth." Although
Carnival season begins officially on Twelfth
Night, Mardi Gras is celebrated the two weeks
preceding Ash Wednesday. Its origin dates back
to the early French settlers, but the street celebrations in their present form began in the mid-
nineteenth century. (*Courtesy, The New Orleans
Tourist and Convention Commission*)

Rex, the king of Carnival, made his first appearance in 1872. His parade takes place on Mardi Gras morning. He is toasted by thousands as he and his entourage move through the streets of New Orleans. Each year an outstanding civic leader is chosen to be king of Mardi Gras. (*Courtesy, The New Orleans Tourist and Convention Commission*)

At night the Mardi Gras parades are lit by flambeaux or oil torches carried by boys dressed in white robes who strut along the traditional parade routes. On Tuesday evening, the final parade of Mumus is held, after which the crowds return home and the music stops. (*Courtesy, The New Orleans Tourist and Convention Commission*)

held in private homes or auditoriums to which invitations were issued on the basis of social standing. The history of Mardi Gras for the past hundred years makes exciting reading and few have told it better than Hartnett Kane in his *Queen New Orleans: City by the River,* and in other books from his pen.

In 1857, an organization known as the Mistick Krewe of Comus was formed to manage the event. Fifteen years later, Rex, the acknowledged ruler of Mardi Gras, began his reign. In the years that have followed, other groups or societies have been organized. Each year Mardi Gras grows bigger and bigger, with more and more excitement, until it would seem that local residents know only two seasons of the year—Carnival and after the Carnival. As Mr. Kane has written, "He who tastes of Mississippi water, he'll be back. . . . He who tastes of Mardi Gras, he will also return. It's the maddest, fastest, giddiest, most absurd, most magnificent thing in New Orleans."

In Biloxi, Mississippi, there is a Mardi Gras celebration that claims to be older than that held in New Orleans, since the city was founded in 1699. Mobile, Alabama, began its observance in 1830. All three cities vie with one another for publicity and all that goes with it to make visitors welcome in Carnival time.

Like the Christmas tree, the Easter rabbit is one of several notable contributions to American folklore made by the Pennsylvania Dutch. All across this broad land, it is the Easter rabbit or bunny who is supposed to bring the Easter eggs and other confections as well as the wide variety of gifts that attend the celebration of the greatest of spring holidays.

This fascinating custom introduced by the German settlers who began to arrive here in the 1700s was "childhood's greatest pleasure in the Pennsylvania Dutch country, next to the visit of the Christ-Kindel on Christmas Eve." Anticipation ran high as the children prepared a nest for the "Oschter Haws," as they called the Easter rabbit. They knew that if they had been good, he would come on Easter Eve and lay a whole nestful of colored eggs. Nests were built indoors in some secluded corner, in a sheltered place in the garden or even in the barn. The Easter rabbit was a shy creature, hence the need for a secluded spot. The boys used their caps and the girls their bonnets, or if father's old hat could be borrowed, it might serve as the nest. Sometimes nests were made with fancy paper. The notions about elaborate baskets came much later when the tradition spread over the entire country.

For several religious sects, it was not considered truthful to tell the story of the Easter rabbit as the giver of eggs, so these families placed the gaily decorated gifts at the children's plates at the table or on the broad windowsills of the farmhouses.

Although this pleasant way of observing Easter was dear to the hearts of the German settlers wherever they made their homes, in Pennsylvania, Virginia, the Carolinas, Tennessee, New York State, or Canada, it was more than a century before their English, Quaker, and Scotch-Irish neighbors adopted the custom. Children have a way of communicating ideas and enthusiasms which often make a deeper imprint than the sternest admonition from the pulpit. In the years following the Civil War, the Easter rabbit had become sufficiently popular to merit more than casual comment in the press each year as Easter approached. The various ways in which plain white or brown eggs could be decorated with colorful designs which made them look like alluring jewels reflected the enduring quality of folk art, so integral a part of Pennsylvania Dutch culture. These sturdy people, with their intense love of the soil, had a way of expressing their faith, their folklore, and their love of life in simple art forms which captured the imaginations of their neighbors.

Baking a special kind of Easter cake in the shape of a rabbit, which had a raisin for an eye and a colored egg protruding beneath its tail, was a popular practice in parts of the Dutch country. Local bakers made them in quantity, using the same dough they prepared for bread, but sometimes these cakes were homemade.

A curious form of egg decoration formerly seen in Pennsylvania Dutch homes was the Easter egg bird. These were decorated shells in which four holes were made—one for the head, two for the wings, and one for the tail—plus an opening for attaching the bird to a thread so that it could be hung. These were popular a century ago and lasted indefinitely if handled with care.

As early as 1789, Easter eggs were ornately decorated with scratch carving by the Pennsylvania Dutch. A sharp knife or pointed tool was used to scratch the dyed surface of the egg. Considerable effort was put into making the designs, and these eggs were often inscribed as presentation pieces. Naturally, they were cherished as keepsakes, and some have been kept for a hundred years or more. Typical Pennsylvania Dutch folk art designs including tulips, distelfinks, hearts, butterflies, and elephants were used. This craft had been practiced in Germany and Switzerland for generations. Scratch-carved eggs were obviously popular in Switzerland in the 1880s, for there are interesting accounts of such eggs brought to Pennsylvania at that time.

Binsa-graws was a name for a type of meadow rush familiar to those who decorated eggs with the pith of that rush found in low ground. The woolly pith was forced out of the rush with a match and wound around the egg surface with a paste made of flour and water. Then pieces of brightly colored calico cut in a variety of shapes were added for further embellishment.

Onion skins boiled in water were used to color the eggs. For yellow effects, alder catkins and hickory bark did the job. Madder root produced light red, and coffee and walnut shells made brown tones. Wrapping eggs tightly in calico made it possible to transfer patterns easily.

In nineteenth-century Pennsylvania, men and children used to challenge each other to egg-eating contests, as their forebears along the Rhine had done for generations. "Picking eggs" on Easter Sunday and Monday was the name given by children to testing the strength of the shells by striking the ends together. The broken egg was the prize for the fellow whose egg broke it. The custom is of ancient origin and is enjoyed as well in far-off Syria, Iran, and Iraq, and in various parts of Europe.

Another sport introduced from Europe is rolling hard-boiled eggs against each other or downhill. The child who retains the last uncracked egg is the winner. This pleasant pastime has been observed on the lawn of the White House in Washington for more than 150 years, since the Presidency of James Madison, and many fascinating stories about this custom have been written. In 1922, Robert Shackleton in his *Book of Washington* recorded his impressions of this colorful event:

1905463

"The children gather by thousands, boys and girls, and all young. No adults are admitted, except such as are in definite charge of a child. What may be termed the childless fathers of Washington (not the fatherless children) form a long unbroken line, along the stone base of the enclosing iron fence, standing tiptoe and eager to watch the gay scene within. I took my chance with the general public, and was curtly refused admission by a particularly stern policeman whom I noticed turning back one adult after another. I briefly said a half dozen words to the effect that I was a stranger in the city, who had not brought a child. Apparently he did not hear me. He looked sternly over my shoulder at the Washington Monument, and in a growling undertone responded to 'go back a little and adopt a child.' So within five minutes I was within the grounds—and it was astonishing how soon that adopted boy was lost!

"The sweeping grounds were thronged. Every moment more were arriving. They came in singles and twos and threes and they came in a succession of little throngs as street car after street car unloaded; they came, very many, in motor cars. And in the closed cars the little children, gathered half a dozen or so in a car, looked like crowded nests of brightly plumaged birds, for it was a gathering that included every class. The rich and the well-to-do were there; the poor were there, proud of their colored eggs.

"There was no formal procedure. Each child carried its eggs, all fancifully decorated, and most of them sat quietly on the grass on knolls where their eggs rolled easily.

"There was, oddly, a general appearance as if there were only children, for the elders were practically lost, practically unnoticeable, among the gayly colored throng of little ones. Quite amazingly colorful were the children and their accessories: their parasols, their many-colored toy balloons, held by strings, the bright baskets, the eggs themselves, the hair ribbons, the jackets and hats and skirts, in reds and blues and lavenders, in mustards and pinks—there were children like lilies, all in white, children in pale linen, children like yellow daffodils, seated on the pale green grass.

"Some were moving about in gentle happiness. A great fountain was gloriously playing and all the lilacs were in delicate flower. Intermittently came the music of the Marine Band; and always was the softly chirring sound of children's voices.

"It makes the most picturesque scene in America, with its noble background of the White House: it was like some unusually beautiful fete day for children in France, with the beauty of grass and shrubs and trees and costumes accented by the noble jet d'eau."

35

Crowds gather at the White House on Easter Monday for the annual Easter Egg Roll, a capital tradition of long standing. (*Photo: United Press International*)

Among the first arrivals for the annual Easter Egg Roll are this brother and sister pair. Each year thousands of children, equipped with their baskets of gaily colored eggs, flock to the south lawn of the White House. (*Photo: United Press International*)

The game proved to be so rough on the grass that, for a time, the location of the festival was changed from the White House to the Capitol terraces. This annual fete has changed but little over the years. In fact, it would hardly be Easter Monday in Washington without it. Small children continue to get lost in the great crowd, parents become bewildered, but each year the Marine Band, attired in colorful uniforms, plays on. In the days before the Civil War, this custom was preceded by Sunday-school picnics and Easter parades.

Another game consisted in throwing colored eggs into the air, like balls. The game ended when the last egg was broken.

Following World War II, an annual Easter Egg Rolling Contest, inaugurated by Arnold Constable and the Department of Parks, has been held in New York's Central Park. Children from five to twelve, using wood spoons, roll wooden eggs across a prescribed area of the lawn. Prizes include popular toys and cash awards.

Eggs laid on Good Friday and eaten on that day or on Easter Sunday insured good fortune and were used in folk medicine by the Pennsylvania Dutch to cure many ailments. No sensible farmer would sell eggs laid on this day, for it meant parting with good fortune. These and many other interesting folk beliefs are included in *Eastertide in Pennsylvania,* by Alfred L. Shoemaker, published by the Pennsylvania Folklife Society at Kutztown, Pennsylvania.

The Easter egg tree, in many ways the counterpart of the Christmas tree, has become a fairly recent tradition in America because of the widespread popularity of Katherine Milhous's delightful children's book, *The Egg Tree.* This custom of decorating evergreens or leafless trees with colored eggs, a novelty among the Pennsylvania Dutch, had its origin in the years following the Civil War. The older practice of suspending or impaling eggs in their natural colors on bushes and small trees outdoors was a custom of earlier date. Of German origin, this fashion was vividly portrayed in the color lithographs circulated in this country before the turn of the century. It was also practiced in other northern European countries.

Making such a tree required considerable skill to obtain perfect shells for painting. Eggs to be used for the great Easter feast were not broken, but carefully punctured with a needle at both ends, and the contents blown into a bowl. Then the shells were ready to be painted or dyed, or otherwise decorated, and placed on the tree. An article which appeared in *Lothrop's Annual,* 1895, tells the story:

"The Easter-tree is a delightful feature of the Easter season in Germany. It is not so universal as the Christmas-tree; for in Germany there is no household so poor but the Christmas-tree finds a place in it, even though its branches may spread scarcely wider than the flowers of a good-sized bouquet. The Easter-tree is more common in northwestern Germany than elsewhere, and the tree-frolic is something all young people ought to know about.

"For an Easter party, at which the frolic is to take place, a large tree, set upon a good-sized table, stands in the center of the room. The larger the room the better. The tree is hung with *Oster Eier* (Easter eggs) of every color and

37

size. During the year the children gather many varieties of birds' eggs and save them for decorating the Easter-tree. Hens, geese and turkeys' eggs are also colored by boiling them in solution of dye-stuffs—a strong one to make the deep colors, a weak one for the more delicate shades.

"Loops of bright-colored ribbons, always of contrasting shades, are pasted upon the eggs to hang them by, tip downwards. Tinsel ornaments and pendants; curious sugar people, cake animals, especially lambs and rabbits; Easter hens and chickens; and dainty chocolate and sugar confections of every conceivable variety are fastened to the boughs, while underneath, upon the table or pedestal, sitting in special state the wonderful Easter rabbit, or sometimes the Easter lamb, presides over the gifts and favors concealed in the *Oster Hase's* nest."

In Germany it was often the practice to gild eggshells, fill them with candy and suspend them on ribbons. Decorated trees were often used in spring festival parades during the Easter season. Among the natives of the Virgin Islands, the fashion of placing decorated eggshells on the spiny stems of yucca plants was a practice of long standing. Decorated eggs, sometimes gilded, sometimes decorated like a globe to represent the world or elaborately ornamented with decalcomanias, used to be popular for decorating Christmas trees in various parts of Germany. Occasionally these are seen in America.

Several authors of children's books have contributed to the universal place of love that the rabbit holds in the affections of the peoples of the world. The noted English writer, Beatrix Potter, with her inimitable *Tale of Peter Rabbit,* published nearly a half century ago, awakened people to the bunnies and inspired many writers. In America this rabbit lore has been greatly increased by Joel Chandler Harris with his *Bre'r Rabbit Tales,* Thornton W. Burgess by his *Adventures of Peter Cottontail,* and Robert Lawson, whose devotion to rabbits shines forth from his *Rabbit Hill,* in which the rabbits wistfully hope that the new occupants of the house will welcome spring as "growing-folks."

In an article in *Friar,* a religious magazine, Ade Bethune, noted authority on religious art, posed the question " 'Has the Easter bunny become a menace to the Paschal season?' Sticklers for realism are apt to disapprove of him. 'As if it weren't bad enough,' they figure, 'to disgrace the holy season with a silly rabbit, how in heaven's name do you reconcile the creature with the Easter egg?'

"Some parents will let their children have the eggs, but put their foot down against the bunny. And, yet, it's hard to avoid him. Come spring, and lo, from every store and poster over the land he stares at you. Every child in vernal finery who is not seen carrying a potted hyacinth to grandmother is at least clutching a lavender stuffed toy twice his own size and ornamented with large overhanging ears.

" 'Christmas already has been all but ruined by the Santa Claus cult, and now Easter in turn is being subverted,' so our friends of realism are apt to complain. But, as far as I am concerned, they are missing the proverbial boat.

"The rabbit's burrow, like the tomb wherein Christ lay, is a dark hole in the earth. From this 'tomb' he too arises, and with bounding agility skims over hill and dale, a figure of our bodies as they will rise on the Last Day in the likeness of our Risen Lord.

"If you be risen with Christ, seek the things that are above, and as you do so, incidentally, see in the rabbit, not so many pounds of meat and fur, but also the springing joy of the spirit alert to God's ways."

Long ago, it was believed that Easter Day was best begun by rising early enough to see the sun dance as it rose in the sky. If the viewers were in the right spot and carried a piece of smoked glass to look through, they might see the symbol of the risen Savior—the image of the Lamb of God with the banner marked with a red cross. It was sometimes referred to as "the lamb playing." Instead of walking in the fields, there were those among the country folk in the British Isles who placed a pan of water in an east window that they might see the reflection of the sun as it danced. This old myth was the subject of considerable discussion in the seventeenth and eighteenth centuries, and even earlier. Some scorned it; others pondered the idea philosophically, and still other writers recorded it for what they believed it to be—mere superstition.

Yet, men have seen strange and wonderful sights in the sky at various hours of the day, century after century, down through the ages. Who can challenge the flights of imagination to which some men are subject or the visions which they claim? Surely there are many forms of imagery that have meaning for those who experience them.

In France, there is an old belief that the rays of sunlight penetrating the dawn clouds on Easter morning are angels dancing for joy at the Resurrection. It used to be said in Scotland that the sun whirled around like a mill wheel and gave three leaps. An old Irish custom was a dance of joy to greet the sun on this day. The women of the village baked a cake for a prize, and the men performed the dance. The best dancer was awarded the cake, and from this bit of jollity came the expression "He takes the cake." Dancing to honor the sun after the vernal equinox is associated with the lore of many countries.

Among the many curious folk beliefs relating to Easter morning is an ancient practice once observed on the Island of Malta. The men of the community made their way to the village church and transported a statue of Christ to a nearby promontory, running uphill as fast as they could while ceremoniously carrying aloft the revered figure. This rapid movement signified the Resurrection.

It was on an Easter morning, March 27, 1513, that Ponce de León first sighted the land which he named Florida, from the Spanish *Pasqua Florida*. The words originally meant "Palm Sunday," but were later applied to the entire Easter week. Centuries later, on Easter Day, 1772, a Dutchman named Roggeveen expressed his feeling of joy and hope when he discovered an island in the Southeast Pacific which he named Easter Island. Often referred to as "the loneliest little island in the world," it was called by the natives "Eye which sees heaven" and "Frontier of heaven."

Down through the ages, palm leaves have been distributed each year on

Palm Sunday in Christian churches throughout the world. In some countries both the palm and the olive are used; in others, where palm is not available, willow and boxwood yew take its place. Palm leaves are also used at the Passover services in Jewish temples. Most of the palm used on Palm Sunday in the United States is harvested in Florida. Thousands of acres of cattle land in Florida are leased by a single person for the rights to cutting the buds of the cabbage palm for use in Palm Sunday and Holy Week services. The cabbage palmetto, as it is commonly referred to, grows in profusion in both salt marshes and fresh-water swamps, as well as on hummock land. This palm, which is native to the United States, is the state tree of both Florida and South Carolina. At the top of the tree, deep within the crown of fronds, is the heart of the palm, the terminal bud by which the tree's growth is continued. The bud is protected by a fibrous casing or "bootjack." It is from this point that the great leaves yield the creamy golden spray of new growth which varies from four to six feet in length. This new growth is the kind desired for Palm Sunday.

The bud is sliced from the center of the crown with a palm hook or hatchet, and care is taken not to cut so deeply as to cause injury to the tree. The saw palmetto, *Serenoa repens,* enemy of the cattle rancher, is lower in habit and yields a smaller bud. Approximately three months before Easter, hundreds of workers begin collecting these palm buds from remote swamplands, which include the 36,000-acre Seminole Indian Reservation. Buds are carefully sorted and, after drying, are wrapped in burlap bags. The cured palms are transferred to huge warehouses for final shipment in refrigerated trucks and railroad cars to churches in various parts of the country.

The folklore and the traditions of every country in the world are, to a large extent, the accumulated customs and manners blended with signs and symbols that serve as reminders of religious practices and historic associations. In those countries that are rich in folk culture, one nationality is dominant; such a homogeneous atmosphere is conducive to the creation and development of a distinctive folklore. When national groups have colonized new areas of the world, they have, in most instances, perpetuated their beloved customs and traditions, which live on, slightly changed and in new guise, but ever cherished as links with the past. Such is the Easter sunrise service, which has become popular all over America in recent years.

"Millions of Americans will greet Easter this year with sunrise services of worship—the first of these at the summit of Cadillac Mountain on Mt. Desert Island, Maine, where the sun first touches the United States, and then in hundreds of similar services as the dawn moves westward across the land.

"There will be sunrise services in nineteen of our National Parks, including Grand Canyon and Death Valley, and on our Navy ships at sea. At Aspen, Colorado, worshipers will travel by ski lift for services atop 11,300-foot Ajax Mountain. Perhaps 100,000 people will gather at midnight Easter Eve in the mountains near Lawton, Oklahoma, to witness a six-hour pageant depicting episodes from the life of Christ and concluding at dawn with the Resurrection story. Other thousands will assemble in the vast outdoor amphitheater at the

Easter Day, 6:46 A.M. Mountain Time, in the Amphitheater, Mount Rushmore National Memorial. (*Courtesy,
National Park Service*)

Park of the Red Rocks at Denver, and a reverent multitude will fill the Hollywood Bowl." Thus, Joseph R. Siroo, of George Washington University, recently described the widespread scope of Easter sunrise services in various parts of the United States.

A group of Spaniards exploring North America, from Key West to Southern California, are believed to have held the first sunrise service on Easter Sunday in the year 1609. The Moravians who settled at Winston-Salem, North Carolina, in 1773 established a beautiful custom which continues to this day. With great dignity and true religious fervor, they gather in front of the old Home Moravian Church several hours before daybreak, to give the traditional salutation that opens the service, *The Lord is Risen!* Continuing with other hymns of joy that express their simple faith, they walk quietly in long lines at daybreak to God's Acre, the Moravian cemetery. There they reaffirm their faith. Great throngs of visitors gather each year to witness this ceremony, which reflects the cherished beliefs of a sect that has preserved its folk customs in all their simplicity and beauty.

A similar service takes place in Bethlehem, Pennsylvania, where the Moravian Trombone Choir, organized in 1754, adds greatly to the annual Easter sunrise service. The choir moves through the center of the city playing chorales at the principal intersections of downtown streets between midnight and dawn, and then proceeds to the church, where part of the service is conducted. In accordance with old custom, the remainder of the observance is held in the churchyard. A second service is given later in the morning, and a third at night. An account of the beginning of this impressive ceremony, written by J. Max Hark for the Lancaster *Intelligencer,* April 24, 1886, gives us a word picture couched in the elegant phrases of the Victorian era:

"Very early on Sunday morning, long before the first penciling of dawn gives outline to the darkness, there mingle strangely with the sleepers' dreams the sounds of far-off soft and sweetest melody. Wafted from a distance through the fresh and fragrant morning air, like angels' whispers from on high they seem, as gently falling on the semi-conscious ear. Near and more near they approach. Slowly the dreamer awakes, and in rapture dwells on the mellow strains. It is the music of the trombone choir that thus early goes forth to usher in the gladsome Easter morn, and with its sweet old chorals gently arouses the slumbering villager, and bids him prepare for the worship of the day. The effect of this ancient custom on the mind surpasses all powers of description. It must be experienced, and then will never be forgotten. The profound stillness of the rural night, unbroken by the clatter of machinery, the roll of wheels, and restless tramp of feet, so absolute and perfect; the clearness and purity of the air at this the most delicious period of the budding spring; the weird and touching sounds of the trombone, so peculiarly adapted to the music of the old chorals; together with the frame of mind induced by the services that have absorbed the attention of the entire previous week, and tended to make the whole soul more exalted and impressionable—all these help to make this part of the Moravian Easter ceremonies striking and beautiful beyond expression."

The Oklahoma *Oberammergau* is an Easter sunrise service based on the traditional Passion play, and staged at Holy City in the Wichita Mountains, not far from Lawton. Begun on a modest scale in 1926 by the pastor of the First Congregational Church, it has developed into a great presentation which attracts thousands of interested spectators every year. They begin to gather in the 640-acre tract at sunset on Easter Eve, finding desirable vantage points in the hills overlooking the mammoth natural stage. The setting for the pageant includes replicas of Biblical landmarks such as the inn, the manger, the walls and gates to the city of Jerusalem. The Judgment Hall, the Upper Room, Calvary, the appropriate settings for the triumphal entry on Palm Sunday, the meeting with Pilate, the Lord's Supper, and the Crucifixion are a part of the permanent background. Each year, the six-hour pageant is an unforgettable experience despite the uncertainties of the weather. Those who attend bring with them all the equipment needed to keep comfortable in the cold spring air.

In 1921, the Garden of the Gods at Colorado Springs first became the setting for an annual Easter sunrise service. Music predominates at this assembly, and frequently the 300-voice *a cappella* choir of Colorado Springs High School participates. Attendance has increased greatly over the years.

One of the most elaborate sunrise services in America is staged at the Hollywood Bowl in Hollywood, California. It was started forty years ago, and

The annual Easter sunrise worship service held in Hollywood Bowl, California. (*Photo from H. Armstrong Roberts*)

each year the overflow crowd increases by thousands. They begin to gather at midnight on Easter Eve in the subdued light of the amphitheater. Thousands of calla lilies are massed in front of the band shell. A "living cross" of 250 teen-agers, a choir of 100 adults, an organist, and a symphony orchestra take their places on the stage shortly after dawn. Girl trumpeters, strategically placed, open the program of music, prayers, and sermon. Special features vary from year to year.

A most unusual Easter service, sponsored by 500 Aztec Indians, is held near San Diego. Mounted on horses, they gather in Alvarado Canyon to greet the sunrise with song, assisted by a trumpeter.

At dawn on Easter, an impressive program, inaugurated in 1935, is broadcast annually from Grand Canyon National Park. Amid the splendor of the myriad tints of pink and gold, a radio announcer for a national network describes the service, composed of hymns, prayers, Scripture reading, and a brief sermon.

Mountain ranges and craters, historic sites, public parks, college campuses, ancient landmarks, village squares, and city plazas have become centers for these observances in recent years. No community church is so small that it has not organized a group of enthusiastic participants to hold an Easter sunrise service. Thus, another age-old folk tradition has become a part of our American heritage.

Reaching out into the Atlantic Ocean, the State of Maine becomes the official greeter of Easter dawn as worshipers gather to watch the sunrise from Cadillac Mountain, the easternmost pinnacle of the United States. The entire State of Maine is the sunrise country of America. The last ceremony on the mainland of America is held at Yosemite National Park, because of the time required for the sun to rise above the 5000-foot Half Moon Dome so that it can shine on Mirror Lake. At dawn in Tampa, Florida, thirty-three white pigeons are released, signifying the years of Christ's life on earth. Lincoln's birthplace in Hodgenville, Kentucky, serves as the setting for a service while in Utah the most spectacular service is held on the steps of the capitol at Salt Lake City. At Rindge, New Hampshire, the widely known Cathedral of the Pines forms one of the most impressive backdrops in all New England to salute the sun on Easter morning. And as sunrise comes to the Pacific, the Hawaiians in Honolulu gather for their salutation in the Punchbowl National Memorial Cemetery.

These sunrise services, typical of the Easter-morning gatherings all across America, had their origin in the Middle Ages when joyful voices, the shooting of cannons, and the ringing of bells all helped to announce to the world that Christ was risen, as He truly said.

For centuries the eternal spirit of hope, symbolized in the most ancient of all images, the rising of the sun, has left its imprint on many a heart. At Easter, the symbolism becomes all the more meaningful as we commemorate the Resurrection of Our Savior and its significances, and this eternal truth repeats itself in every sunrise. On a summer morning in 1893, Katharine Lee Bates, a New England schoolteacher, had a profound experience as she viewed the

An Easter parade in the early
1900s in New York City was
a sedate and stately affair.
Ladies and gentlemen attired
in the latest fashions prom-
enaded on the sidewalks or
rode in horse-drawn carriages
in front of St. Patrick's Cathedral. (*Photo: United Press International*)

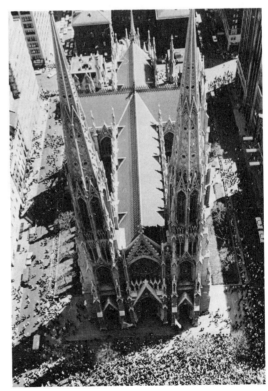

Sixty years later a milling throng of
more than a million persons jam a
police-barricaded ten-block area on
Fifth Avenue for the Easter Sunday
"parade." Millions more watch the
spectacle on television and read
about it the next day in the newspapers. (*Photo: United Press International*)

sunrise from Pikes Peak, Colorado. There, standing as close to heaven as any mortal could, she contemplated what she had seen in the world of her day. America—the melting pot of the nations, welding together men and women of all races and creeds, their ideals, customs, traditions, and beliefs—symbolized a growing spirit of brotherhood such as no nation had ever achieved.

On that very day she wrote the hymn "America the Beautiful," which has become known and loved the wide world over—a hymn that is a humble prayer, echoing the commandment given at the Last Supper—to love one another:

> *O beautiful for spacious skies,*
> *For amber waves of grain,*
> *For purple mountain majesties*
> *Above the fruited plain!*
> *America! America!*
> *God shed His grace on thee,*
> *And crown thy good with brotherhood*
> *From sea to shining sea.*

Practically all of the Easter traditions we cherish in America have come to us from the Old World. The Easter bunny, the sunrise service, the Easter lily (described under "Bermuda"), and the wealth of folk customs that have been blended with our way of life are adaptations often colored with a distinct American flair. They are ours by inheritance, to cherish and to keep alive. However, the great humanitarian movement that launched the annual Easter Seal drive for aid to crippled children is truly American. Yet, the idea of using seals to raise money for charitable purposes came from Elmer Holboll, a Danish postal clerk, in 1903. He it was who originated the Christmas seals for the control of tuberculosis.

On Memorial Day, 1907, in Elyria, Ohio, a streetcar accident occurred, involving a group of young people returning from a holiday excursion. Many died of injuries that could not be properly treated in the town hospital. Others were maimed for life. The effects of this tragic accident might have been confined to one remote community, but the event was destined to have world-wide significance. Fourteen years later, the National Society for Crippled Children and Adults was founded. This organization of volunteers is dedicated to a program of enlightening the public on what can be done for the crippled, and of mobilizing public and private resources to develop needed services.

One of the boys who died in the tragic accident in Ohio was eighteen-year-old Homer Allen. The boy's father, Edgar F. Allen, keenly aware of the inadequacy of local hospital facilities, spearheaded a drive for a new general hospital. A crippled boy who was brought to the hospital made Mr. Allen aware of a new and different need—that of crippled children for special medical care and treatment. He saw what proper care had achieved in restoring the boy from a hopeless condition to one of optimism and expectation for a normal life. Then he began to visualize what it would mean to countless others to have similar

46

care. Through his contact with the boy, who affectionately dubbed him "Daddy," Edgar Allen was led into the activity which was to be a lifelong career of service.

Once his interest was aroused, the first logical steps for "Daddy" Allen were to conduct a survey to find out how many crippled children there were in his home county and to organize community support to build the Gates Memorial Hospital for Crippled Children. He then embarked on an even more ambitious program of arranging for crippled children elsewhere in Ohio to be brought to the hospital, where care and treatment were provided without cost. To accomplish this great humanitarian task, he enlisted the interest and support of Rotarians. In turn, it was the Rotarians who spearheaded the founding in Ohio in 1919 of the first state crippled children's society, an organization of volunteers dedicated to a program which provided privately supported services, while it sought extension of and increased support for public services for the crippled.

The program of the Ohio society flourished. By 1921, "Daddy" Allen saw sufficient evidence of similar interest on the part of Rotarians in Michigan, New York, and Illinois to convince him that the time had come for national action. He sought official endorsement of expansion of the "Ohio Plan" through Rotary International. Although Paul P. Harris, founder of Rotary, was particularly receptive to the idea and did much to promote it, formal action did not come about. However, the interest shown by the Rotarians in the problem greatly aided the spread of the crippled children's movement throughout the nation.

Meanwhile, in 1921, a dedicated group of volunteers, headed by "Daddy" Allen, launched the National Society for Crippled Children, with headquarters in Elyria, Ohio. The first president was "Daddy" Allen, who served until 1937.

In the early years, he stimulated much of the interest among Rotarians single-handedly. Later he was aided by a small staff. Once the national society was launched, the movement spread quickly. Michigan and New York societies were organized in 1922. Kentucky, Pennsylvania, Tennessee, West Virginia, and Illinois followed in 1923. By the end of 1929, there were twenty-three state societies for crippled children.

The society was a pioneer in its field. It stood alone at that time as the only national voluntary agency speaking and acting on behalf of the crippled. Federal-state crippled children's programs were not enacted for almost a decade. The Federal Vocational Rehabilitation Act of 1920 provided for a very limited program and was not to be expanded for more than twenty years. State tax-supported programs were very few. Prior to the founding of the society, there had been no concerted attack on the problem of rehabilitating the crippled citizens of America, by either voluntary or public agencies.

The Crippled Child, a magazine, was established in 1923. A Bureau of Information and a library began operation in 1924. One of the greatest tasks of the national society in the early years was to encourage and aid in the drafting of special state legislation to meet the medical, educational, and vocational needs of the crippled. In 1935, provisions were made in the Social Security Act, due largely to the efforts of the society.

In 1922, the name of the society was changed to International Society for Crippled Children in order to encourage the development of similar voluntary organizations in other countries. Eight years later it became advisable to separate the national and the international organizations.

It was in 1934 that the Easter Seal was adopted as a fund-raising device. The conventionalized Easter lily, adopted in 1952 as the symbol of the organization, is now widely known, and the societies for crippled children and adults are called informally "The Easter Seal Societies."

In 1945, the headquarters of the national society was moved to Chicago. In succeeding years, the national organization was extended to include state and local member societies in all of the forty-eight states, the District of Columbia, and the then territories of Alaska and Hawaii, as well as Puerto Rico. A national staff of professional consultants in care and treatment, organization, public education, and fund raising was developed.

The Easter Seal Research Foundation was established in 1953, thus creating a means for implementing a third major objective of the society, added to those of care and treatment and education that had been pursued since 1921. By 1958, the national headquarters built and occupied its own building in the West Side Medical Center in Chicago.

Services, which started literally with care for one crippled child, in 1957 reached more than 160,000 crippled children and adults. These direct services are provided by more than 1600 state and local affiliates which operate some 1400 rehabilitation and treatment centers, clinics, camps, sheltered workshops, home employment, physical, occupational and speech therapy programs, and other related services. The professional personnel staffing these programs, together with administrative personnel, now total more than 2000.

In 1933, Paul H. King, who followed Mr. Allen as president of the society, originated the idea of selling Easter seals. As he expressed it, "Thoughts of Easter and the crippled child harmonize wonderfully. Easter means Resurrection and New Life; and the rehabilitation of crippled children means . . . new life and activity, complete or partial, physically, mentally, and spiritually."

The first seal was designed by J. H. Donahey, the famous cartoonist of the Cleveland *Plain Dealer*. Copies of the 1934 seal have become exceedingly scarce, and prices quoted to collectors by dealers are on the increase. The next two seals were also based on appealing cartoons drawn by Mr. Donahey. After the 1935 Easter seal sale, nobody doubted any longer that the Easter seal for crippled children was here to stay. From 22,000,000 in 1934, distribution of Easter seals has risen to more than a billion. More than $3,000,000 worth of seals is sold annually, and distribution is constantly on the upgrade.

Daffodil Cake

1 cup cake flour	½ tsp. vanilla extract
1½ cups sugar	½ tsp. almond extract
1⅓ cups egg whites	4 well-beaten egg yolks
¼ tsp. salt	2 tbsp. cake flour
1¼ tsp. cream of tartar	1 tsp. lemon extract

Sift 1 cup flour with ½ cup sugar 3 times. Beat egg whites until frothy; add salt and cream of tartar; beat until stiff but still glossy. Add 1 cup sugar a little at a time (sprinkle over egg whites); fold in thoroughly. Add vanilla and almond extracts. Sift flour mixture over top, a little at a time; fold in lightly with a down-over-up motion. Divide batter into two parts. Into one half fold egg yokes, 2 tbsp. flour, and lemon extract. Spoon batter alternately into 10-inch ungreased angel cake pan. Bake in moderate oven (325° F.) for one hour. Invert pan to cool.

This ceramic plate with raised decoration was made in an American pottery. (*Photo: Photographic Illustrators Corp.*)

Ice Cream Easter Bunnies

Use firm vanilla or Hawaiian pineapple orange ice cream. Use a large scoop for the body, a smaller scoop for the head. Place the two scoops one on top of the other and decorate with gumdrop sticks for ears, cinnamon drops for eyes, marshmallows for mouth and tail. Hold in freezer until serving time, then line up on pastel-tinted coconut.

Roast Lamb, Extraordinaire

1 leg of lamb, 5 to 6 lbs.	1 large onion, sliced
Soft butter	2 large carrots, sliced
Salt and pepper	2 cups hot strong coffee
Paprika	1 tbsp. sugar

1 tbsp. cream

It is optional whether to remove the parchment covering on the leg of lamb. Rub the leg of lamb with the soft butter and season by sprinkling with salt, pepper, and paprika. Make a bed of the onion and carrot slices on the

49

Tin molds for Easter cakes and confections of European origin. (*From the collection of Priscilla Sawyer Lord; photo: Richard Merrill*)

Lead molds for Easter ices were popular at the turn of the century. (*From the collection of Mrs. John R. Burbidge; photo: Richard Merrill*)

A collection of Easter Sunday cookies based on old recipes. Some bear the sun motif because it was believed that the sun danced on that festive day. (*From Mrs. John R. Burbidge; photo: Richard Merrill*)

rack on the bottom of the roasting pan. Then lay the roast on top of the vegetables. Roast uncovered in a preheated oven at 325° F., allowing 20 minutes to a pound. Mix the two cups of hot strong coffee with sugar and cream; pour over the leg of lamb ½ hour before the lamb is done. Baste frequently. Remove the lamb to a hot platter and place in turned-off oven to keep warm. Remove onions and carrots from pan; then remove excess fat. Make a gravy by placing the pan on top of the stove over a medium flame. While the liquid is simmering, scrape all the brown drippings clinging to the pan into the gravy, and stir. Serve in a warm bowl as an accompaniment to the roast. Serves 6.

Tansy Pancakes

Beat 2 eggs, add ¼ pint of cream, 2 tablespoons of flour, 1 ounce fine, granulated sugar. Beat together very well, then add a teaspoonful of tansy juice with a dash of nutmeg. Beat again and fry as pancakes in a pan greased with butter. Serve hot, garnished with sections of orange and dredged with fine white sugar.

Europe

Austria

To celebrate Gschnasfest, in Vienna, three great fancy dress balls are held—each ball with its own particular name and theme, and all who attend wear appropriate costumes. Prior to 1654, the festival was Carnival only, but it became necessary in that year to issue a municipal edict threatening arrest and heavy fines for "lascivious behavior and the carrying of firearms" at Carnival time. This prohibition had to be issued annually during the seventeenth and eighteenth centuries until Carnival itself was banished. Since indoor amusements were permitted, the fancy dress ball came into fashion with people dancing throughout the night to the strains of Johann Strauss's waltzes.

The strangest of all the Shrove Tuesday celebrations is the Dance of the Phantoms, performed every third year in the Tyrolean town of Imst. There will be one in 1973. Usually this celebration takes place in February, symbolizing the ever recurring battle between winter and spring, with spring victorious. This "battle" dates back to primitive times when people believed that winter demons who created the short dark days of winter could be frightened away by the wearing of hideous masks. Highlighting the festival is a special group of men, wearing grotesque masks, who mingle with the dancers and revelers, shaking their heads and performing antics. The more lurid and diabolic the mask, the more prized it becomes. Some, however, are exceptionally beautiful, decked with flowers and mirrors which reflect them; others are elaborately plumed headdresses. Naturally, the maskers are noisy as they shout, jangle bells and sing boisterously so that the winter demons may be driven out completely. During Lent, the Passion Play is presented at both Fulpmes and at Thiersee.

Lent is announced by the solemn ringing of church bells at the stroke of midnight on Shrove Tuesday. Again the following morning on Ash Wednesday, the bells call the faithful to the ceremony of the ashes.

On Maundy Thursday, in olden days in Austria, the Emperor, attended by the Archdukes of the Blood Royal, first washed the feet of twelve old men and then feasted them at a splendid dinner of many courses. Today it is the clergy who perform this washing ceremony. Green eggs alone are used and eaten on Maundy Thursday.

Mid-Lent Sunday, known as Laetare Sunday, is the day for announcing the engagements of young couples.

In Austrian cities, pretzels are distributed to the poor on various days during Lent. Throughout the country, children carry pretzels suspended from "palm" bushes on Palm Sunday. Austrian farmers, accompanied by their families, walk through their fields, pastures and farm buildings on the afternoon of Palm Sunday, praying and singing ancient hymns. They place a sprig of the blessed palms from the morning church service in each pasture lot and in each building. Thus they avert the punishment of tragedies inflicted by weather or disease.

Good Friday is a favorite day for devout pilgrimages to some distant shrine or church. At one of these "processions," in the Austrian Tyrol, people often walk for ten hours each way. Another custom of the day is concerned with eating a loaf of bread which bears the imprint of the Cross.

Francis X. Weiser reminds us that the Ascension Play was performed in churches in the Austrian Tyrol until the present century. Sometimes it happened that one of the angel figures which met the statue of Christ in midair had its candle blown out by a draft; in such cases the angel would quickly fly back to "heaven" to have it lighted again. With brightly burning light the figure slowly returned, to the great glee and enjoyment of all the children.

In the Alpine provinces of Austria, Easter fires are lighted on the mountaintops after sunset on Holy Saturday. Children carrying lighted torches follow bands of musicians who play hymns while they march through the valleys.

It is a widespread legend that on Easter Day all running water is especially blessed because the Risen Lord sanctified all life-giving elements and bestowed upon them special powers for the one great day of His Resurrection. In Austria, bridegroom and bride sprinkle each other with such water (saved from that drawn on Easter) before going to church on their wedding day.

Young Austrians go pace-egging, singing:

> *We sing, we sing the Easter song:*
> *God keep you healthy, sane and strong.*
> *Sickness and storms and all other harm*
> *Be far from folks and beast and farm.*
> *Now give us eggs, green, blue and red;*
> *If not, your chicks will all drop dead.*

In pace-egging, hard-boiled eggs are rolled against each other on the lawn or down a hill; the egg that remains uncracked at the end is called the "victory

A mechanical toy rabbit, made in Austria about 1890. A country tune from the concealed music box adds to the delight of this unusual toy. (*From the Richard E. Hale collection; photo: Wm. W. Anderson*)

egg." Little nests containing eggs, pastry, and candy are hidden in spots out of doors and the children are told that the Easter Hare has prepared the nests.

In Austria, Easter bread is make with milk, eggs, and raisins, and baked in oblong loaves of twisted or braided strands. Another kind of Austrian bread is the Easter loaf, a large, flat, round loaf marked with the cross or an image of a lamb.

Easter Monday is a traditional day of "switching" or Gsundschlagen, stroke-of-health day. Cut brush is used to whack one's friends gently on the shoulder or the back to wish them good luck and good health.

TRADITIONAL RECIPE
Guglhupf

Guglhupf, coffee cake baked in a Turk's head pan (a tube mold with a swirled design), dates back to the Austrian and Polish kitchens of the Middle Ages. Then, it was leavened with barm, the yeast formed on beer during fermentation. By the time it reached France, during the reign of Marie Antoinette, yeast replaced barm and its flavor became more delicate. Marie Antoinettte loved *guglhupf* and, some historians say, made it famous:

2 packages active dry yeast	Grated rind of 1 lemon
¼ cup warm water	4 eggs
¾ cup warm milk	¼ cup blanched almonds
4 cups all-purpose flour	½ cup each of diced citron, white
1 cup butter or margarine	raisins and currants
1 cup granulated sugar	Confectioners' sugar
½ teaspoon salt	

Dissolve yeast in warm water. Add milk and 1½ cups flour; beat until smooth. Cover and let rise in a warm place 1 hour. In an electric mixer cream butter and beat in granulated suger; add salt and grated lemon rind. Add eggs one at a time, beating well after each addition. Add yeast and remaining flour. Beat 10 minutes. Butter a 10″ tube pan and decorate bottom and sides with blanched almond halves. Pour in half the dough; sprinkle citron, raisins, and currants over the top. Cover with remaining dough; this should half-fill the pan. Cover and let rise in a warm place until dough just reaches top of pan (about 1½ hours). Cake will be coarse and dry if allowed to rise too long. Bake in moderate oven (350° F.) 45 to 55 minutes. Cool in pan 5 minutes, then carefully remove to cake rack. Serve sprinkled with confectioners' sugar.

Belgium

THE Carnival of Gilles at Binche, which takes place each year on the three days prior to Ash Wednesday, is based on traditional pageantry that reaches back more than four centuries. It is the chief ambition of every male in Binche to play the role of a *gille,* or clown, at least once during his lifetime. The costly and elaborate costume worn by a *gille* consists of a brightly colored blouse, filled out with straw, and bell-bottomed trousers, trimmed with numerous rows of the famous handmade Binche lace. The collars of the blouses are deep gold, lace-trimmed and decorated with tinkling bells. A broad sash ornamented with signs of the zodiac lends an additional flourish. To complete his outfit, the clown wears heavy wooden shoes, which he uses to stamp out the dance rhythms that make him a truly joyful *gille*. Each performer carries on his left arm a basket of oranges from which he tosses the fruit to every acquaintance within reach.

This spectacular carnival is believed to have originated in 1549, when the provinces of the Low Countries, which make up present-day Belgium as well as The Netherlands and Luxembourg, were part of the empire over which Charles V ruled. Charles had sent his son, who later became Philip II, ruler of Spain, to visit the provinces. Marie of Hungary, Charles's sister and regent of the Low Countries at the time of her nephew's visit, gave a great entertainment in honor of his visit since it coincided with the news of the recent Spanish conquests in Peru. At Marie's great party, the *gilles* wore enormously tall, plumed headdresses and colorful Inca costumes as they performed a ballet of foot stamping to strange rhythms. The ballet was a tribute to the conquistadores, who, under Pizarro's leadership, had subdued the Peruvians.

On Vastenavond (Shrove Tuesday) housewives are busy preparing the traditional pancakes (*koekebakken*) and waffles (*wafelen*). In some parts of Belgium, as in other countries, the boys and girls go about begging for food, singing an appropriate ditty. They are given nuts, apples, and strips of bacon. When they have gathered enough, they hold a picnic at which they broil their bacon on long willow sticks as their parents did in their youth.

Walloon farmers believe that eating cabbage on Shrove Tuesday will prevent flies and caterpillars from destroying the cabbage crop in their gardens during the coming year.

A celebration peculiar to Belgium in some parts of the Ardennes, observed on the first Sunday in Lent, is known as Erste Zondag Van Dere Vesten (Sunday of the Great Fires), so-called because of the bonfires which are ignited on hilltops. Children go from house to house begging for wood to keep the fires going. Those who refuse fuel are pursued the following day by the children, who attempt to smudge their faces with the ashes remaining from the bonfires. The young people dance and sing around the bonfires until only smoldering embers remain. Then they jump over the ashes, thus assuring themselves of good luck in marriage, freedom from colic, and good crops both for their family's future and for their own. According to Belgian folklore, anyone who can glimpse seven Lenten fires in an evening is assured of protection against witches. Parents tell their children that at Easter they will receive as many eggs as they can count fires seen on the first Sunday in Lent. An old peasant belief held that neglect to kindle "the great fire" meant that God would kindle it Himself—that is, He would set fire to one's house.

Witte Dondeday, Holy Thursday, is the day when the church bells become silent until Holy Saturday. Belgians and other European folk once held the notion that at this time the bells flew to Rome "to visit the Pope and dine with him," as well as "to make their own Easter and their own confessions" and "to look for the eggs which they will drop on their return for the boys' and girls' Easter egg hunt." The silencing of the bells was considered a time for extra caution against the powers of darkness, since it was thought that the sound of church bells acted as a repellent to evil spirits and to bad weather as well. When, on Easter Saturday, the bells returned, bringing Easter eggs, and rang out the joyous good tidings of the season, it was the custom, on hearing them, to bend down and embrace one's chair, or bench, if in church. Those who were out of doors fell and embraced the earth.

Tradition and religion play a vital role in most Belgian celebrations and fetes. Loyalty, dignity, and piety are obvious manifestations in the observance of Easter whether displayed in the Procession of the Holy Blood at Bruges or the Stations of the Cross at Furnes, where the sculptures depicting Christ's Passion are placed throughout the streets of the town. The "March of the Penitents" which follows is the essence of solemnity.

Twelve old men from "God's House," the term used for the alms house in Belgium, are chosen on Holy Thursday to play the roles of the twelve apostles in the ceremony of foot washing. The clergy bathe the feet of the old men and bestow bread and alms upon them.

On Good Friday, Goede Vridag, the churches are draped in black and a funereal air is prevalent across the land.

After the Easter Glory Service on Holy Saturday, Zaterdag voor Pasen, when the "returned" bells have rung, parents tell their children that the bells "sow colored eggs in the gardens." The children, in turn, scramble out of doors to hunt for the bells' eggs behind shrubs, stone walls, in the grass or in the crotches of trees. The candy and pastry shops, their windows and showcases filled with beautiful bell confections and eggs of colored sugar, chocolate, and marzipan, also testify that the bells have returned. Many of the candies are decorated with artificial flowers and pretty ribbons. On Sunday the children hold another egg hunt for those overlooked on Saturday. Having exhausted all the hiding places on their parents' grounds, they hurry to see what has been left near the homes of their grandparents and other relatives.

On Easter Monday, the adults indulge in a prank referred to as "shoe-stealing." Men hide their wives' shoes, which are redeemed for a small forfeit the following day. Women usually retaliate by stealing the men's caps, which are easier to come by than shoes or firmly laced boots.

Czechoslovakia

n Czechoslovakia, early in March, the village folk make a dummy of Old Woman Winter, using a sack stuffed with straw. Children go from door to door carrying little trees hung with colored bows, singing as they go:

St. George, the saint of spring,
Will soon be here to unlock the earth with his keys.
Our trees will soon grow,
Like the ones we are holding.

Then they parade to the river, swinging Old Woman Winter from side to side, the townspeople following. As the dummy is tossed into the river and floats away, the people shout:

Death is floating down the river,
And spring will soon be here.

On Green Thursday (Holy Thursday) the Czechoslovakians eat "Judases" and greens—a soup of green herbs followed by a green salad. Housewives busy themselves with the preparation of the Easter foods that will be consumed on the holy weekend. They say:

Soon will come Green Thursday
When we shall bake the Lamb;
We shall eat Judases farina
And three spoonfuls of honey.

"Judases" are served with honey at breakfast in Czechoslovakia. These are breakfast cakes of twisted dough, made to look like rope, suggesting the fate of Judas the Betrayer, who "went and hanged himself" in remorse after he had identified Jesus to His enemies. Honey is considered a preventive against disaster.

On Good Friday, Czechoslovakian cooks prepare their Easter bread (coffee cake) which must not be cut or eaten until the priest says, "Christ is Risen." The bread is always marked with a deep cross.

TRADITIONAL AND REGIONAL RECIPES

Mazanec (A rich Czechoslovakian yeast bread)

1 lb. all-purpose flour	1 tsp. vanilla
1¼ sticks unsalted butter	1 cake yeast
Pinch of salt	4 egg yolks
¼ lb. sugar (powdered)	1 cup milk
Grated lemon rind	¼ lb. raisins
¼ lb. almonds	

Sift flour and cut the butter into it. Place in a large bowl. Add salt, powdered sugar, lemon rind, vanilla. Let yeast rise in a little cream to which sugar has been added. Add to the flour mixture. Beat egg yolks slightly in the milk and add to the rest. Work the dough first in the bowl, then transfer to a board covered lightly with flour. The dough should be fairly heavy but must be kneaded thoroughly. Then add the raisins and slivered blanched almonds, place the dough back into the bowl, cover with a clean napkin and let rise in a warm place for ¾ of an hour. When the dough begins to rise, form into a round loaf and place on a buttered cookie sheet and allow to rise for another ¾ of an hour. Before placing in the oven, take a sharp knife and cut a cross on top of the loaf. Beat an egg and spread it all over the top. Let dry and then repeat, this time covering the whole loaf with slivered almonds. (They will stick to the egg and not fall off.) Bake 1 hour.

Note: The proportions of the ingredients and the taste of this Easter bread are very much like those of the Russian *Kulich*.

Bábovka is a round Czechoslovakian coffee bread served with hot coffee on Easter morning. It is generally baked in one of the round fluted cake forms with a hole in the middle. The word *bábovka* covers a wide variety of cakes ranging from yeast-risen "coffee-cake" breads to the pound-cake variety. Some of the recipes are very similar to those for the *Mazanec* and for the first of the two lamb-cake recipes which follow. There are at least thirteen recipes for *Bábovka*. This one is called:

Bábovka si šlehanon smetanon (with whipped cream)

⅓ lb. confectioners' sugar	Juice from ½ lemon
6 egg yolks	6 egg whites beaten stiff
1 tsp. vanilla	1 heaped cup sifted all-purpose flour
Lemon rind	1¾ cups whipped cream (sweeten
1 bitter almond	to taste)
	Chocolate frosting

Beat the sugar, egg yolks, vanilla, lemon rind and grated almond for 25 minutes by hand. Add lemon juice, a drop at a time. Then add alternately the stiffly beaten egg whites and the sifted flour. In the meantime, prepare the form, butter or flour it, and pour the dough in it. The *bábovka* should be baked in a moderately hot oven for ½ to ¾ hour. Allow to cool and take out gently. The next day, cut off the top (about ½ inch) of the *bábovka*. (By "top" here is meant the portion which is on top when baking, but is actually the bottom of the finished cake.) Cut the slice carefully, because it will be used later and should remain whole. Now make a big hollow in the cake without letting the sides collapse. Fill the cake with sweetened whipped cream and cover the top and reverse on a plate. (The top is now at the bottom.) Cover the cake quickly with chocolate frosting and place in refrigerator before serving.

Beránek (Velikonočhi beránek—Easter Lamb Cake)

½ lb. confectioners' sugar	Juice and rind of ½ lemon
2 whole eggs	1 bitter almond
5 egg yolks	5 egg whites beaten stiff
1 tsp. vanilla	½ lb. all-purpose flour (roughly
	2 heaped cups)

The sugar, eggs (2) and yolks (5), vanilla, and lemon rind are beaten together by hand for 30 minutes (or an equivalent time with mixer). Then add the grated bitter almond and the lemon juice. Very slowly fold in, alternately, the stiffly beaten egg whites and the flour (sifted).

The utensil shaped like a lamb is buttered and sprinkled with bread crumbs. The cake mixture is then slowly poured into it and baked in a medium hot oven (375° F. for an hour). The cake is allowed to cool before frosting.

Frosting

Beat 1 egg white with ¼ lb. confectioners' sugar and 1 tsp. lemon juice until the mixture thickens. Spread over the lamb cake. Add 2 raisins for eyes, and a sliver of candied cherry for the mouth. When the frosting dries, tie a red ribbon around the lamb's neck.

Lamb Cake Variation (Not Frosted)

1 stick unsalted butter	1 tsp. vanilla
¼ lb. sugar	1 cake yeast
4 egg yolks	1 lb. sifted all-purpose flour
Salt	1½ cups milk (about)
Lemon rind	1-2 oz. blanched almonds (slivered)
1-2 oz. raisins	

Cream the butter and add sugar, egg yolks, salt, lemon rind, and vanilla. Beat for 20 minutes. Then add the prepared yeast, sifted flour, and lukewarm milk (enough to prepare a medium heavy dough). Add the slivered blanched almonds and raisins and knead the dough thoroughly. Allow to rise. Prepare the lamb form as in the previous recipe, fill it with the prepared dough, and allow it to rise farther in the form. Preheat the oven in the meantime, then close the form before baking. Bake at 375° F. for an hour. (With some forms, the lamb cake should be turned over once to have it baked equally on both sides.) Cool the baked lamb cake and remove carefully from form. Immediately sprinkle it with confectioners' sugar, add raisins for eyes, tie a red ribbon around its neck, and place on a lace doily.

On Easter Monday (Pomlăzka, the Day of Whipping) in Czechoslovakia, a highly popular youth festival is celebrated. Boys braid willow branches into whips, which they festoon with flowers and colored ribbon streamers. The boys then roam about, caroling for eggs and whipping the village girls "so they won't be lazy or have fleas." This is a pre-Christian purification rite and supposedly brings good luck.

Denmark

SHROVETIDE, the Sunday, Monday, and Tuesday before Ash Wednesday, is the time of the year when everyone indulges in eating as many Shrovetide buns as he can. As in Norway, the children make "Lenten birches," decorated birch switches which they use to waken their parents and any other adults who are found sleeping early in the morning. Inflicting resounding smacks with their switches on the bedclothes, they cry: "Give buns, give buns, give buns!" From somewhere the awakened adults produce the coveted buns.

A long time ago the children, wearing strange costumes and more-than-strange masks, used to join together in a custom known as "beating the cat out of the barrel." A lightweight wooden cask with a cat inside was suspended by a wire or rope. All struck at the barrel with sticks, and whoever broke the barrel enough to release the poor frightened cat earned the title of "cat king." Today a cat has no part in this old custom; instead an empty wooden barrel, with one or more painted cats on it and sometimes paper flowers as well, is suspended, and young people riding horses with decorated bridles take turns in striking the barrel. The one who completely smashes the barrel becomes Shrovetide "cat king."

In many Danish seaport towns, a *Fastelvan* (Shrovetide) boat is used as the feature of Shrovetide activities to collect money for sick and needy seamen. A large boat, manned by twelve seamen, is placed on a truck drawn by several horses and paraded through the streets. Horn players seated beside the driver furnish the musical flourishes. Members of the Seamen's Guild, led by a marshal carrying the Danish national flag, head the parade. As he marches along, the marshal announces the approach of the ship, and the onlookers shout, "The ship is coming! The ship is coming!" When the musicians play, the men stop and dance.

In both the towns and the villages, the older children dress up in costumes with weird masks and make the neighborhood rounds as they sing for buns and rattle their collection boxes vigorously:

> *Buns up, buns down,*
> *Buns for me to chew!*
> *If no buns you give*
> *I'll rattle till you do!*

Once again they jingle the boxes in which they collect coins for a *Fastelvan* feast.

There are all kinds of games for the children; one which they thoroughly enjoy is trying to take a bite of a bun which has been suspended from a chandelier by a string. The bun is set in motion and whoever can get a bite, without using his hands to steady the bun, wins it.

Early on Easter morning, the boys and girls get up early to hunt in the garden for the "hare's nest." The hares leave not only dyed hen's eggs, but also chocolate and sugar ones decorated with delicious pink and yellow "frosting" roses. After the Easter morning services, the children engage in egg-rolling contests. The owner of the egg that rolls the farthest wins the contest.

England

TRADITION has been an integral part of the English way of life for so many centuries that the folklore simply described as the knowledge of the common people—their customs and beliefs—has retained a high degree of vitality. The legends associated with feast days and holidays and the customs attendant on them continue to evoke a sense of delight and pleasure for vast numbers of people. In the present era of science, sophistication, and mechanization, young and old find the reenactment of many ancient practices a refreshing respite from the hustle and bustle of everyday life.

Tradition dies hard as has been proved down through the centuries. Yet every era has had its scoffers and prophets of doom who declared that the best loved of customs would die out, given time. But folklore continues to flourish in England in research, writing, and practice. Periodic revivals of old-time customs never fail to capture the attention of the press. Furthermore, the vast body of literature dating back more than two centuries and still being published is evidence enough of the esteem in which old customs are held. Modern scholars have evolved the science of ethnology so that English museums as well as those in various other parts of the world display with pride artifacts which tell the story of the various races, their characteristics, customs, and beliefs.

Spring comes early to the Scilly Islands, thirty miles off the coast of the Cornish mainland. Four little islands—St. Mary's Tresco, St. Martin's, St. Agnes' and Bryhr—are noted for their mild frost-free climate, ideal for the culture of flowers and vegetables which provide the economy. Three flower shows are held on the islands annually. The first comes on the second Saturday of January followed by a show on the first Friday and Saturday in March and the third at Easter. Bulbs and other spring flowers are featured for those who attend. Meanwhile the English flower markets display quantities of these welcome blossoms for sale to lift the spirits of the flower-loving English.

Shrovetide, in both church and folk tradition, is the English name for the last four days before the beginning of Lent: Egg Saturday, Quinquagesima Sunday, Collop Monday, and Shrove Tuesday. In bygone days on Egg Saturday, the first day of Shrovetide, the children went Lent-crocking, demanding gifts of eggs or meat, and hurling broken crockery at the doors of those who refused them.

On Collop Monday, now forgotten, eggs and collops appeared on the table for the last time before Lent. The term "collop" referred to pieces of meat, such as ham, bacon, or any other meat that was cured by being salted or hung to dry, in contrast with the term "steaks" for slices of fresh meat. It was a day when potluck meant infinite variety, a little of this and a little of that. But one fact was certain—there would be no more meat served until Lent was over. In Cornwall, during the evening, known as Knickanan Night, garden gates, tools and whatever was lying loose around the premises were in danger of disappearing.

Shrove Tuesday is the Tuesday before Ash Wednesday. The bell that once called the churchgoers to confession—that is, to be shriven, or to have one's sins forgiven—became known as the Pancake Bell, and Shrove Tuesday came to be called Pancake Day. In England, this same day was sometimes called "Guttit," "Goodish," or "Goodies" Day because of the many good things that were served. *Poor Robin's Almanack* for 1684 gives a vivid description of the ringing of the Pancake Bell, which was a signal for cooks to rush to the frying pan, and for apprentices and clerks to cease work and join in the day's festivities:

> *But hark, I hear the pancake bell,*
> *And fritters make a gallant smell;*
> *The cooks are baking, frying, boyling,*
> *Stewing, mincing, cutting, broyling,*
> *Carving, gormandising, roasting,*
> *Carbonading, cracking, slashing, toasting.*

One puritan polemicist described pancakes as "sweet bait which ignorant people devour very greedily."

There are two celebrated pancake ceremonies in England. At Westminster School a pancake is annually scrambled for in the ceremony known as the Pancake "Greeze." At eleven o'clock on Shrove Tuesday, the cook, preceded by the verger with the silver-topped mace, enters the Great Schoolroom, carrying a frying pan from which he tosses a pancake over the high bar separating the old Upper and Lower Schools. The assembled boys scramble for it as it falls to the ground, and he who secures it, or the largest part of it, receives a guinea from the dean. The cook is also rewarded for his essential part in the affair. At one time, all the boys in the school took part in the scramble, but now each form chooses one of its members to represent it.

Throughout England, children sing this song on Pancake Day:

> *Dibbity, dibbity, dibbity, doe,*
> *Give me a pancake and I'll go;*
> *Dibbity, dibbity, dibbity, ditter,*
> *Please to give me a bit of a fritter.*

The other Pancake Day ceremony concerns a race. In England, in bygone days, it was the custom for the housewives to drop whatever they were doing and hurry to the church at the tolling of the bell on each Shrove Tuesday. In 1445, a wife in Olney, England, started baking her pancakes rather late on Shrove Tuesday. The pancakes she was making were flat cakes made in a frying pan, and would be eaten to sustain her, for she would have a long wait to be shriven on that day. The pancakes were not quite finished when the church bell rang, but she hurried off to her shriving, carrying her griddle and pancakes with her. Thus an annual sporting event was born.

In Liberal, Kansas, this five-hundred-year-old event of pancake racing, which consisted of racing over a 415-yard course from the "town pump" to the church, became a challenge. In 1950, urged on by the local Junior Chamber of Commerce, the housewives of Liberal, Kansas, U.S.A., challenged the house-

In 1950, housewives of Liberal, Kansas, challenged the housewives of Olney, England, to a pancake race. The British housewives accepted and the International Pancake Day Race has since become an annual event, fostering international understanding, as symbolized by this float in the Liberal Pancake Day Parade. (*Photo: Southwest Daily Times*)

These present-day housewives of Liberal carry on an old English tradition as they race, skillets in hand, against their English counterparts in the International Pancake Day Race. Courses of identical length are set up in each country and times of winners are compared by transatlantic telephone. (*Photo: Southwest Daily Times*)

These cooks are kept busy on International Pancake Day in Liberal. Started by the Liberal Junior Chamber of Commerce, the festival now runs for several days. (*Photo: Southwest Daily Times*)

wives of Olney, Bucks, England, to a pancake race. The British housewives, through the Reverend R. C. Collins, vicar of Olney, accepted the challenge. For the running of what has become the international Pancake Day Race, over courses of identical distance, times of the winners in both Olney and Liberal are compared by transatlantic telephone.

Pancake Day in Liberal has reached staggering proportions, and several days of festivities are now scheduled. This is the pancake rhyme from Liberal:

> *Shrove Tuesday's the day (it happens each year)*
> * Pancakes are flipping—far and near*
> *Promoting world friendship,*
> * Good cheer and good will . . .*
> *Come help us celebrate,*
> * Eat to your fill . . .*
> *And when the day's over*
> * You'll remember it long,*
> *You, filled with pancakes,*
> * Your heart with a song.*

Such primitive customs or sports as dog-tossing, cockfighting, thrashing the hen and others have long been forgotten. Games of various kinds were popular also. Egg shackling, as observed in the Sedgemoor villages of Stoke St. Gregory and Shepton Beauchamp, is a curious custom indeed. On Shrove Tuesday children carry eggs to school with their names written on them; the eggs are placed in a sieve and shaken until all but one are cracked. The owner of the uncracked egg gets a cash prize, bequeathed in an old legacy, but the cracked eggs are not wasted; rather, they may be sent to a local hospital or carried home to make pancakes.

"Remember, man, that thou are dust, and to dust thou shalt return" is the central theme of the solemn services on Ash Wednesday. These words were repeated as the priest made the sign of the cross on the forehead of each member of the congregation who approached the altar for the distribution of ashes. The ashes were obtained by burning palm leaves saved from the previous Palm Sunday. This symbol of penance and sorrow for one's sins marked the beginning of the forty days during which Christ fasted in the wilderness. Although the Church of England no longer follows this ritual, it is still observed in the Roman Catholic Church. For nearly a thousand years the first day of Lent has been known as Ash Wednesday. Prior to that time it was called the "Beginning of the Fast."

The practice of fasting during Lent is no longer widely observed. Abstaining meant giving up the use of all flesh-meat and all its by-products such as milk, cheese, butter, and eggs, and formerly only those in delicate health were released from this rigid practice.

In London, members of the Worshipful Company of Stationers attend a service in the crypt of St. Paul's Cathedral, following which they are served cakes and ale at Stationers' Hall. The custom originated under the will of

Alderman John Norton, a prominent member of the Company of Stationers and one of the Royal Printers, who in 1612 left £150 in his will for this purpose.

In his book *Endless Cavalcade,* Alexander Howard relates the following: "Until the reign of George I a queer ritual was observed on Ash Wednesday. An officer of the Royal Household, appointed to act as the King's Cock Crower, had to crow the hours of the night within the palace precincts as the watchman used to cry the hours in the City streets. It is believed that the custom was intended to serve as a reminder of the crowing of the cock which is supposed to have brought St. Peter to repentance.

"A story says that George II, when Prince of Wales, was having supper in his apartments when the door opened and H. M. Cock Crower burst in and crowed in a shrill voice that it was ten o'clock. The Prince, who had scanty knowledge of English and even less of the customs of the country, jumped to the conclusion that he was being mocked. That ended the ritual."

On Ash Wednesday, children in villages in Hampshire and Sussex used to pick a "black-budded twig of ash" to put in their pockets. A child who forgot could expect to have his feet trodden on by every child who possessed a twig, unless he was lucky enough to escape until midday. Even then, punishment might be meted out on the way home. It is believed that the demand for an ash twig may be a transference from Royal Oak Day (29th of May) in the nineteenth century, when Wiltshire children carried a sprig of oak before midday, exchanging it for a sprig of ash in the afternoon.

In the Yorkshire area, the Friday following Ash Wednesday was known as Kissing Friday. On this day boys could kiss girls without expecting any resistance. The practice was tried even in the schoolroom and one teacher to whom it was unfamiliar soon learned that order was best kept by accepting it. Apparently this custom was carried out on other days as well. Another old custom was practiced on Nippy Lug Day, when boys pinched one another's ears.

The fourth Sunday in Lent is called "Mothering Sunday" in many European countries. On mid-Lent Sunday in England, the parishioners in outlying hamlets, who normally worshiped in chapels-of-ease (as the small churches of the great houses were called), went to the mother church of the parish, bringing their offerings. How early the idea of honoring one's own mother on that particular day began is not certain.

On Mothering Sunday, above all, it was customary that every child dine with his mother. This pleasant custom dates from the sixteenth century. In those days young girls who had hired out as servants for the first time at the New Year hiring fairs were given a holiday in mid-Lent so that they could visit their families. To prove their cooking skill, they brought home a gift of "mothering" or "simnel" cake. And because the Lenten fast in those times was rigorous, they used a rich mixture so that the cake would keep until Easter.

As well as evidence of her newly acquired cooking skill, the girl sometimes brought home for family approval her newly acquired sweetheart. And

66

if she happened to be a dairy maid or laundry maid, the sweetheart bought or had made for her the mothering cake. There is an old verse which goes:

And I'll to thee a simnel bring
'Gainst thou goest a-mothering;
So that when she blesses thee
Half the blessing thou'st give me.

In "Richard Symonds Diary" (1644) may be found the quotation: "Every Mid-Lent Sunday is a great day, when all the children and grandchildren meet at the head and chief of the family and have a feast."

John Brandt writes that "it was customary in the eighteenth and early nineteenth centuries, for servants or others working away from home to be given a holiday then, so that they might visit their mothers and present them with a cake of their own or their mistress's making, and little nosegays of violets and other wild flowers gathered in the hedgerows as they walked along the country lanes. Whole families attended church together and there was a dinner of roast lamb or veal, at which mother was treated as queen of the feast she had prepared herself, and everything was done to make her happy." This custom never reached the shores of the Americas, where the idea of Mother's Day, the second Sunday of May, was conceived much later. Mother is feted—the token is only a carnation—and there are always gifts.

The cakes made for mothers were called simnels. The name "simnel" is derived from *simila,* a fine wheaten flour. There are two legends connected with this name. One relates that the father of Lambert Simnel (one of the two known pretenders to the throne in Henry VII's reign), a baker, concocted a certain cake and named it for his notorious son. The other account states that a man named Simon quarreled with Nell, his wife, as to whether the mixture (cake) should be baked or boiled. They compromised by doing both, and since then the cake has been known by a combination of the two names.

The simnel cake is described thus: "The crust was made of flour, water and saffron, to envelop a filling of mixed plums, lemon peel and many good things. The edges were pinked, the top duly criss-crossed, the whole boiled in a cloth, then glazed with egg and finally baked." The cakes were sold at a guinea apiece and were so large and so hard that it is small wonder that one mother new to the region used hers for a footstool!

A curious ceremony known as Church Clipping or Clypping takes place in Sussex on Mothering Sunday. It is believed to have had its origin in the pagan festival of Lupercalia, in which Pan of Lycia, who guarded the flocks against wolves, was honored. A sacred dance was performed around an altar on which goats and young dogs were sacrificed to Pan. The Luperci, or priests who performed the sacrifice, followed it by roaming through the streets, belaboring the women of the village with thongs of goatskin. Today Clipping symbolizes the love of a parish for its mother church, as with All Saints, Hastings, Sussex, where the ancient ceremony was revived in 1952. Clipping means clasping or embracing. The parishioners embrace their church by clasp-

The Queen and the clergy carry nosegays of flowers as protection against fever and the plague as they distribute the Maundy Money. (*Courtesy, British Travel Assn. and Holiday Assn.*)

Shrovetide football at Ashbourne in Devonshire. (*Courtesy, British Travel Assn. and Holiday Assn.*)

At Hocktide the tutti men climb a ladder to kiss the girls who reside on the second floor. (*Courtesy, British Travel Assn.*)

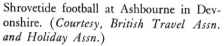
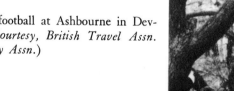

At St. Michael's Church, Bristol, buns are given to several hundred boys on Easter Tuesday. (*Courtesy, British Travel Assn. and Holiday Assn.*)

Beating the Bounds at the Tower of London. Thirty-one boundary stones are beaten with willow wands. (*Courtesy, British Travel and Holiday Assn.*)

The Biddenden Dole is still dispensed during the Eastern season in accordance with the terms of an ancient will. (*Courtesy, British Travel Assn.*)

Shoeing a "colt" is an ancient Hocktide custom. (*Courtesy, British Travel Assn.*)

Pancake Day at Westminister School. (*Courtesy, British Travel Assn.*)

ing hands, forming a circle, and walking round the building in a clockwise direction with due ceremony.

Following the Reformation, palms were no longer distributed to the faithful in the Church of England on Palm Sunday, but the spirit of the day was not forgotten. Instead of palm, which had to be imported from Spain, branches of willow catkins were used together with sprigs of boxwood and hazel. Formerly, men and boys went "a-palming" early in the week and brought home sprouting boughs to deck their houses. The age-old belief, held elsewhere in Europe, that these branches brought good fortune and protected the house from evil was shared in England.

Palm Sunday was sometimes called "Spanish Sunday." As Christina Hole reminds us, "This rather unexpected title comes from the children's habit of making a sweetish drink from broken pieces of Spanish licorice shaken up in a bottle of water. No ordinary water from a tap may be used on this occasion. It has to be drawn from some particularly holy or wishing well in the neighborhood, and a special pilgrimage must be made to fetch it. At one period, not so long ago, such wells were visited by crowds of children from all the nearby parishes and even in these sophisticated days, little groups can often be seen, solemnly walking three times round the well, filling and shaking their bottles, and happily drinking the resulting concoction." This custom undoubtedly had its roots in ancient well worship.

Fig Sunday and Carling Sunday were other names for this day. Figs were eaten on this day or fig pudding was served at the noonday meal, and children were presented with small clusters of dried figs commemorating the parable of the barren fig tree. Carlings are gray peas soaked in water and then fried in butter. Also known as parched peas, they are served in northern England either on Palm Sunday or on "Carling" Sunday, the fifth Sunday of Lent. From Berkshire comes this jingle:

> Beef and bacon's out of season,
> I want a pan to parch my peas on.

A popular pastime with the young folk in bygone days involved fortunetelling games on this day. Whoever managed to get the last pea in the dish was thought to be the first to marry. Care Sunday was another English folk name for Palm Sunday; like the name Passion Sunday it signified the care or sorrow expressed in view of the approach of Holy Week.

Alexander Howard has also recorded the *paxcake* tradition. "Lady Scudamore is recorded to have charged the revenues of Boysham Court in 1570 with an annual sum of money to defray the cost of a meal of cake and ale to be served in the parishes of Hentland, Sellack and King's Chapel, near Ross-on-Wye, Herefordshire, on Palm Sunday.

"The object of this kind gesture was to promote the spirit of peace and good fellowship through a communal meal, and the reason she chose Palm Sunday for the purpose was to ensure peace amongst the parishioners before their Easter Communion.

"Originally a huge cake was made and presented by the church-wardens to the vicar who cut the first slice and had the remainder carried to each person to be eaten in church. Passing round glasses of beer, part of the original custom, has long been discontinued, and nowadays small individual cakes called Pax Cakes are handed to the parishioners on leaving the church after service.

"These cakes bear the imprint of the Paschal Lamb, and in handing them to his parishioners the vicar utters the time-honoured greeting: 'God and Good neighborhood.' "

On Thursday of Holy Week, known as Maundy Thursday or Royal Maunday, it was customary for the English king and queen to wash the feet of as many poor subjects as they were years old, commemorating Christ's similar service to his apostles. Queen Elizabeth I, when thirty-nine years old, performed this ceremony for the last time in her life. In 1530, Cardinal Wolsey performed a similar act for fifty-nine poor men. To each he gave "twelve pense in money, three ells of good canvas to make them shirts, a pair of new shoes, a cast of red herring, and three white herrings; and one of them two shillings." Until 1689 during the reign of James II, the king went each year to Westminster Abbey to perform the ancient rite. The water was mixed with sweet herbs, and after the ceremony was completed, small gifts were bestowed on each of the men. Since that time the ceremony has been replaced by the giving of Maundy Money, which is distributed on behalf of the king by the Archbishop of Canterbury. Those who participate carry nosegays of flowers and herbs to recall the days when the Yeoman of the Laundry performed a preliminary ablution of the feet of beggars with ceremonial herbs, prior to the ceremony carried out by the sovereign.

Kings George V, Edward VIII, and George VI all made personal appearances at Westminster for the ceremony, and one of the first public engagements of Elizabeth II, after her accession, was to attend the Maundy Service.

Formerly, food and clothing were also given to those among the poor who attended. When Elizabeth I "made her Maunds" in 1572, she gave to each person enough broadcloth for a gown, a pair of sleeves, half a side of salmon, ling (a kind of fish, common in Europe), six red herrings, bread and claret. Queen Victoria in 1838 gave woolen and linen clothing, shoes and stockings to the men, and 35 shillings to the women in lieu of clothes.

The Maundy Money now used for the ceremony is presented in small white purses containing specially minted silver penny, twopenny, threepenny and fourpenny pieces to the value of a penny for each year of the sovereign's age; these tiny coins have not altered in size since the time of Charles II.

In 1952, when Westminster Abbey was being prepared for the coronation, the distribution was made at St. Paul's Cathedral. In 1955 the custom was observed by the queen at Southwark Cathedral to mark the jubilee of the Southwark diocese. In 1957 it was held for the first time at St. Albans Abbey, where thirty-one men and the same number of women, equal to the number of years of the queen's age, were selected from the diocese of St. Albans as the recipients.

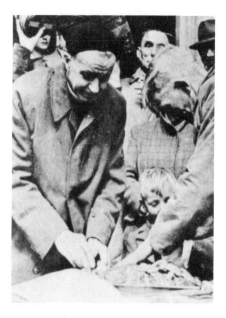

The International Pancake Day Race at Olney, Buckinghamshire, on Shrove Tuesday. See U.S. section for American counterpart. (*Courtesy, British Travel Assn. and Holiday Assn.*)

Cutting the Hare Pie. (*Courtesy, British Travel Assn.*)

"Pace-egging" is more than simple child's play. (*Courtesy, British Travel and Holiday Assn.*)

Hot cross buns have notable keeping qualities as shown in the buns hanging from the ceiling in a village pub. (*Courtesy, British Travel Assn. and Holiday Assn.*)

Good Friday is a day of mourning in many Christian churches in all lands. It was observed as the strictest fast day in the eary church. Many superstitions surround this day, one being that water dipped before sunrise without a spoken word has healing power and will stay pure all year.

Bread baked on Good Friday, if hardened in the oven, could be kept all year, and its presence protected the house from fire. Sailors took loaves of it on their voyages to prevent shipwreck. Three Good Friday loaves thrust into a heap of corn were often used to protect it from the ravages of rats, mice, and weevils. The commonest use of such bread or buns was as a cure for diarrhea, dysentery, and a hundred other complaints. The bread was finely grated, mixed with milk or water, and given to the patient as a medicine.

In England, Good Friday and hot cross buns are synonymous. An old notion was held that if you did not eat a bun on this day, your house would be burned, but everybody ate buns so there was no danger of fire. A favorite cry of London, one shouted by the bun sellers and the children as well was this little ditty:

> One a penny, two a penny,
>   Hot-cross buns;
> If you have no daughters,
>   Give them to your sons;
> But if you have none of these merry little elves,
> Then you may keep them all to yourselves!

The cross on the hot cross buns is believed by many to be a purely Christian emblem. It is, however, far older than the advent of Christainity. The cross was a pagan symbol long before it had any Holy Week significance. The first crosses appeared on cakes associated with the worship of Diana. The little

The ancient game of marbles is played on Good Friday in many an English village. (*Courtesy, British Travel Assn. and Holiday Assn.*)

Egg shackling in the village of Stoke St. Gregory. (*Courtesy, British Travel Assn. and Holiday Assn.*)

wheaten cakes that are known to have been made at primitive spring festivals were similarly marked. Two small loaves, each with a cross on it, were discovered under the ruins of Herculaneum, the city that was encased by volcanic ash in A.D. 79.

An English tale states that at an inn in London called the "Widow's Son," a bun is ceremonially laid in a basket containing many others by a sailor who receives free beer as his reward. In the early nineteenth century, the licensee of this inn was a widow. If her sailor son happened to be at sea on Good Friday, she laid aside, every year, a hot cross bun against the day of his return. One year he did not return, then, or ever again. The widow would not give up hope, and continued her practice of keeping a bun for him, hanging it up in the bar parlor until the next Good Friday came around, when she put it with the accumulation of buns. After her death, later tenants followed the same custom, and now a clause in the lease enforces the custom. During World War II, the collection of buns was housed in a skittle alley under the bar to insure its safety during air raids. Many of the older buns are still in a state of perfect preservation, but some of those made with inferior flour during the two wars are already crumbling away.

For centuries the ancient game of marbles has been played on Good Friday in England. It may well be a vestige of the practice of dice throwing linked with the Roman soldiers at the foot of the Cross. Roman children enjoyed the game long before the time of Christ. In Surrey and Sussex Good Friday used to be known as Marbles Day, and the entire Lenten season was the time of year when young and old enjoyed the game. Every year on Good Friday at Tinsley Green, near Crawley, Sussex, a game is held and the champions carry off a silver cup, while the runners-up receive a firkin of ale. Marble players have shot their "tolley" here since Elizabethan days, when a local girl was said to have persuaded her suitors to fight for her hand at a game of marbles. The annual contest used to be held each year at the Old Greyhound Inn.

Forty-nine marbles are placed on a sand-covered concrete ring six feet across. Teams of six compete in a contest. Each competitor shoots a tolley— a ¾-inch marble—and tries to knock as many marbles as he can from the ring. If he knocks any out and his tolley remains in the ring, he shoots again. If his shot is unsuccessful and his tolley is in the ring, it must stay there until his turn comes round once more. The player must grip his tolley between the forefinger and thumb and shoot by moving only the thumb. If he moves his hand he is penalized for *fudging*. Experts from all parts of England gather to take part in the marble championships. Local hopes rest on the Tinsley Green Tigers, who compete with teams of equally colorful names: Cherry Pickers, Bulldogs, Copthorne Spitfires, Artful Alberts, Telcon Terribles. To give an international flavor an American team called the Grosvenor Gobs frequently enters the contest.

A strange custom that produced a special name for Good Friday—Long Rope Day—was commonplace at Brighton in Sussex until a century or more ago. In this fishing community whole families walked down to the beach and there did some skipping with ropes taken from the boats. Finally it became fun for children only and gradually was forgotten. However, at Alciston and South Heighton outside Newhaven, as well as in a village near Cambridge, skipping with ropes long enough to stretch across the road has not died out entirely.

Many old Easter customs took the form of charitable distributions in accordance wtih ancient bequests. On Good Friday at the Church of St. Bartholomew-the-Great in Smithfield, poor widows of the parish are given a silver sixpence and a hot cross bun over the tomb of the charity's founder. The founder remains unknown because all the records were lost in the Great Fire of London in 1666. There is a similar Good Friday charity in the Sussex village of Hartfield, where over the grave of Nicholas Smith the old-age pensioners are given a silver bounty. Smith was a fairly wealthy man but in earlier days had traveled all over the country dressed as a tramp in search of kindness and charity. These virtues he had found at Hartfield and left this bounty to the aged in gratitude for the successful end of his search.

The day on which Christ was buried was regarded as a good time for sowing seed. Some people believed that any seed put in the ground on this day would thrive, and in England the belief has been attached especially to parsley, for "if you want to have parsley all the year round it must be sown on Good Friday."

"Cramp rings" were hallowed by the king on this day, to be worn by those suffering from cramps. "A number of rings were placed in a silver basin on the floor of the chapel, near a cushion, on which rested a crucifix. A piece of carpet was spread in front of the cushion, and the king knelt down, crept along on his hands and knees, in token of his humility, to the crucifix. Here with his almoner kneeling beside him, he made his prayer, blessed the rings, and retired."

It was considered most unlucky on the Isle of Man to poke the fire with an iron poker on Good Friday. A stick made of the mountain ash was used instead, and all the fire irons were hidden away—presumably because of an association between Christ and fire.

Rural folklore relating to Good Friday is rich in dos and don'ts. It was a good day to shift bees; to plant potatoes, peas, and beans; to prune roses; to eat salt fish for dinner; to go into the open to jump rope or spin a top. It was *not* the day to drive nails, shoe a horse, plow with a horse, go to sea, catch fish, or wash clothes.

In the South End of Liverpool early on Good Friday morning, children of all ages used to gather on the streets in groups; each group carried an effigy which they called "Judas," who had been carefully dressed in a suit of old clothes complete with a comic mask for a face. As the sun rose, Judas was hoisted on a pole and one of the children proceeded to knock on bedroom windows while the rest of them called out, "Judas is a penny short of his breakfast." They kept up the noise until they had collected a fair share of pennies, calling at as many houses in their neighborhood as they could. Then they made a pile of wood, straw, shavings, and anything else that would burn, which they had been collecting for weeks, and started a small bonfire to burn Judas, who, according to an old belief, had to be destroyed by eleven A.M. But since more fires were lighted in the middle of the street "amid scores of children whooping for joy and throwing wood and straw on them," the police had to take over and put out the fires. Judas was usually carried off by a policeman much to the distress of the children, who, in true rowdy fashion, followed him down the street calling him "Judas." For a few days following, every policeman in the area was pursued by similar catcalls. This raucous performance went on year after year on this day.

It was considered lucky in earlier centuries to put out all fires on Easter Eve and light them afresh with flint and steel as a special protection against lightning as well as an inducement to good luck:

> On Easter Eve the fire all is quenched in every place.
> And fresh againe from out the flint is fetched with solemn grace;
> The priest doth halo this against great daungers many one,
> A brande whereof doth every man with greedie minde take home,
> That, when the fearfull storme appeares or tempest black arise,
> By lighting this he is safe may be from stroke of hurtful skies.

Many people rose before dawn on Easter morning to see the sun dance in honor of the Resurrection. This verse was printed in the *British Apollo* in 1709:

> Phoebus, the old wives say
> That on Easter Day,
> To the musick o' the spheres you do caper.
> If the fact, sir, be true
> Pray let's the cause know,
> When you have any room on your paper.

(The god Phoebus replies:)

> "The old wives get merry
> With spiced ale and sherry
> On Easter, which makes them romance;
> And whilst in a rout
> Their brains whirl about,
> They fancy I caper and dance."

Sir John Suckling wrote in "The Bride":

> But oh, she dances such a way,
> No sun upon an Easter Day
> Is half so fine a sight.

"That the sun really did dance was solemnly discussed and argued, and combated by grave old scholars, who took the trouble to demonstrate that, while the king of day might shine more brightly on Easter morning, he did not, and could not, dance." This comment was made by Helen P. Patten in *This Year's Festivals*, written nearly seventy years ago.

Wearing new clothes for Easter meant that the wearer could expect to have something new to enjoy all year. Another notion had it that new Easter clothes insured good fortune in love affairs during the coming year—a thought that suggests the importance of the new Easter bonnet:

> *Last Eyster I put on my blew*
> *Frock cuoat, the vust time, vier new;*
> *Wi' yaller buttons aal o' brass,*
> *That glitter'd i' the zun lik glass;*
> *Bekaise 'twor Eyster Zunday.*

Easter Day weather lore offered these thoughts which were widely quoted:

If the wind on Easter Sunday is east, "it is best to draw *Easter water* and bathe in it to prevent ill effects from east wind, throughout the remaining months of the year."

Much importance was attached to rain's falling on Easter Day:

> "A good deal of rain on Easter Day
> Gives a good crop of grass, but little good hay."

If the sun shines on Easter morning it will shine until Whitsunday.

Sussex weather lore: "If the sun shines on Easter Day, it will shine, if ever so little, every day during the year; while if it be a rainy Easter, there will be rain every day in the year, if only a few drops fall."

The dry spots on the grass where there is no dew are called "fairy rings." If you run around a fairy ring on Easter morning, the fairies will rise and follow you and bring you good fortune for the rest of the year.

Egg lore in England is not only deeply rooted in tradition but also in the ways in which it is interpreted. Groups of jolly boys (more often groups of girls), dressed in weird costumes, went from door to door asking for eggs while reciting a ditty. Games with such names as "shackling," "dumping," "jarping," "booling," and "conkers," whatever their origin, referred to knocking one egg against another to determine who held the strongest shell. Usually the victor collected all the eggs he succeeded in breaking. Rolling eggs on a grassy slope until they broke, sometimes referred to as egg races, was and remains a favorite pastime in some villages. This custom, shared with many countries, undoubtedly dates back to the spring festivals of pagan times, and later was adapted to symbolize the rolling away of the stone from Christ's tomb. Prior to the Reformation, eggs were blessed in the churches during Eastertide. Old records indicate that the royal household used quantities of colored eggs. The process of coloring in the days before vegetable dyes came into common use involved onion skins, flowers and leaves of several plants, chips of logwood (a tropical tree), cochineal and other materials. Decorating depended largely on individual skill, in which wax was used for tracing or coating and a sharp knife for scratching. Bright colors had strong appeal, especially red. Black eggs held a strange fascination for children in some areas because in Tunstall one granny claimed that "the egg had been laid by a black hen which only laid eggs at Eastertide and they were always black;" whereupon her granddaughter added: "She blacks them with blackett."

The Easter egg hunt held on Easter morning has been traditional with children for generations. Each child carries a basket into the garden and looks for the hidden treasure knowing that the prize for the day goes to the one who finds the greatest number of eggs. Youngsters are familiar with the tradition of other countries in which the Easter bunny is credited with being the purveyor of the eggs. Both the rabbit and the hare have been familiar creatures in the English countryside for so long a time that their antics, their legends, and their folklore are common knowledge.

Another Easter game is called "Egg Picking." A player challenges another player by calling:

> *Who's got an egg?*
> *Who's got an egg?*
> *Who's got a Guinea egg?*
> *Who wants to pick an egg?*
> *One pick,*
> *One pick,*
> *Who's got an egg?*

The first player holds his egg firmly in his hand with only the small end of the egg showing. The other player uses one of his own eggs to try to crack the first player's egg without breaking his own. If he succeeds he wins an extra egg from the first player. If his own egg cracks he has to pay with one of his eggs.

Egg-rolling games, usually reserved for Easter Monday, were sometimes held in parks at specially designated sites where young folks congregated for the occasion. There were plenty of eggs gay with color for the excited contestants. Before the turn of the present century, chocolate and sugar eggs became popular as well as cardboard egg-shaped boxes filled with toothsome sweets. These were much more appealing and the demand for colorful hens' and ducks' eggs gradually waned except for use in games.

Pace-egging on Easter Monday in Cheshire and Yorkshire was an amusing bit of good-natured nonsense based on a sixteenth-century play relating to a battle involving St. George and a motley crew of characters with storybook names. These included Bold Hector, the Black Prince of Paradise, the Fool, the King of Egypt, the Doctor, Tosspot, and Bold Shasher, impersonated by boys wearing brightly colored tunics, fantastic hats weirdly decorated, and wooden swords. When the antics of the battle were over, Tosspot passed the basket, once meant for eggs, for whatever coins the spectators might offer. The cast did its level best with a traditional rhyme which ends:

> *Just look at St. George,*   *A star on his breast*
> *So brisk and so bold*   *Like silver doth shine;*
> *While on his right hand*   *I hope you'll remember*
> *A sword he doth hold.*   *It's Pace-Egging time.*

This old custom has revealed itself as having many variations in costume, characters represented, and the kind of rhymes sung, but all are directed at getting goodies to eat and a few pence to spend. In Westmoreland the ditty clearly stated what was wanted.

Now we're jolly pace-eggers all in one round.
We've come a pace-egging, we hope you'll prove kind:
We hope you'll prove kind with your eggs and strong beer,
For we'll come no more near you until the next year.
Fol de diddle ol, fol de dee, fol de diddle ol dum day.

In the northwest of England, the plea had a different pitch as children sallied forth to the houses of relatives and neighbors, their faces daubed with soot and lipstick, singing:

Please will you give me an Easter egg,
Or a flitch of bacon,
Or a little trundle cheese
Of your own making.

In the villages of Far and Near Sawrey near Ambleside, the verse had six parts. The leading singer was Old Betsy Brownbags, accompanied by Jolly Jack Tar, Old Paddy from Cork, and Lord Nelson as well as the familiar Old Tosspot with a pig's tail sewn to the seat of his trousers. The concluding verse went like this:

Now ladies and gentlemen who sit by the fire,
Put your hands in your pockets, that's all we desire.
Put your hands in your pockets and pull out your purse,
And give us a trifle, you won't feel much worse.
Fol de diddle ol, fol de dee, fol de diddle ol dum day.

For 800 years the poor people of Biddenden, Kent, have received bread and cheese on Easter Monday. The founders of this charity were Siamese-twin sisters, joined at the hips and shoulders, who bequeathed twenty acres of land for this purpose. To this day revenue from their property, called Bread and Cheese land, annually provides each needy inhabitant with two to four pounds of bread and one pound of cheese. A token is also available to visitors in the form of a cresecent or small cake on which are imprinted the date of the custom's inception and a portrait of the sisters. The cake is too hard to eat but makes an interesting souvenir. These are called the "Biddenden Cakes." A signpost carved in the form of the two sisters stands in the village as a remembrance of them.

In northern England or Scotland the custom of "lifting" or "heaving" used to be commonplace. A "chair" was made with the hands and the person to be "lifted" was tossed into the air three times and kissed afterward. The men "lifted" the women on Easter Monday, and the women returned the compliment on Easter Tuesday. A variation of this custom gave husbands the privilege of beating their wives on Easter Monday and wives dealt out the punishment on Tuesday.

It was also customary for men to remove the buckles from women's shoes to be redeemed only by offering a gift. The women retaliated in a similar manner. An old account from Warwickshire, written in 1849, tells a vivid story: "Many a time I have passed along the streets inhabited by the lower orders of people, and seen parties of jolly matrons assembled round tables on which stood a foaming tankard of ale. There they sat in all the pride of absolute sovereignty, and woe to the luckless man that dared to invade their prerogatives! As soon as he was seen he was pursued, as soon as he was pursued he was taken, and as soon as he was taken he was 'heaved' and kissed, and compelled to pay sixpense for leave and leisure to depart."

Another account describes the plight of a clergyman "who happened to be passing through Lancashire on Easter Tuesday and was staying an hour or two at an inn. He was astonished by three or four lusty women, who rushed into his room, saying they had come to 'lift him.' The clergyman stood aghast at such an intrusion, and asked them to interpret their unknown tongue. 'Why, your reverence,' they explained, 'we've come to lift ye 'cause it's Easter Tuesday. All us women was hove yesterday, and us heaves the men to-day—and in course it's our rights and duties to heave 'em.' But, after a little parley, the divine persuaded his visitors to relinquish their 'rights and duties' for half a crown." In the thirteenth century it was customary to seize all ecclesiastics during the period between Easter and Pentecost (because apostles were seized by Jews) and make them purchase their freedom with money.

Nowadays young people in Bristol stuff their mouths with sugary buns in observance of a custom which originated in the days when the poor had only black bread to eat. A charity provided that once a year on Easter Tuesday they have a meal of white bread. Today the sugar buns are a substitute for the bread.

On Easter Monday there are great goings-on at Hallaton in Leicestershire when the annual Hare-Pie Scramble and Bottle Kicking takes place. It seems that several centuries ago a woman in Hallaton was saved from being gored by a bull when a hare scuttled across the field through which she was passing. In gratitude she bequeathed to the rector a piece of land on condition that he and his successors would distribute hare-pie to all the parishioners once a year. More specifically the food was to consist of two hare-pies, twenty-four penny loaves and a quantity of ale which were to be scrambled for on the day after Easter on the rising ground, long known as Hare-Pie Bank, about a quarter of a mile from Hallaton. Since hare is out of season, mutton, veal or beef is now used in the pies which are prepared at the village bakehouse. The villagers gather at the Fox Inn and parade to the site with much ceremony and the music of a brass band. The wild scramble that follows is filled with animal spirits and indicates that this old folkway has not lost its vitality.

The same is true of the Bottle Kicking custom, which involves the men of Hallaton and those of the neighboring village of Medbourne. Not only are the pies carried in the parade to Hare-Pie Bank, but also the "bottles"—three small iron-bound barrels, bedecked with ribbons. Two are filled with ale and the third is empty. One of the filled bottles is strategically placed at the top of the bank after which both teams of men try to kick it over their own boundary, since the stream divides the villages. The winners get the ale. Then a battle ensues to capture the empty bottle and the rough-and-tumble struggle that follows compares favorably with a football game or a rugby match. To the victors goes the remaining barrel of ale with the leader getting the first drink. For a century or more, attempts have been made at intervals to divert the money expended to some charitable use, but on one occasion the village wags declared: "No pie, no parson, and a job for the glazier," and they meant it.

Until thirty or more years ago Ashton-under-Lyne sported an annual event on Easter Monday in which a dummy of a medieval knight dressed in black armor and a velvet cloak of the same color was paraded through the streets at the head of a procession followed by a group of men and boys, symbolizing the knight's retainers. The parade ended in an open field where the dummy was removed from the horse, pelted with stones and finally shot. The claim is made that the episode typified the practice by which Sir Ralph Assheton went "guld-riding" five centuries ago on his annual inspection of the land he owned. He had a passion for keeping down weeds, so the story goes, and the punishments he meted out to those tenants who neglected their fields were merciless. In consequence he was murdered by one of those punished. This annual event was supposed to signify the end of a form of tyranny, but it may have been linked with a much older practice relating to the destruction of dying winter or the elimination of hunger.

Stoolball, sometimes called the ancestor of cricket, similar in some ways to baseball, was once played during the Easter holidays. In Sussex women and girls still enjoy it. *Poor Robin's Almanac for 1740* carried these lines:

> *Much time is wasted now away,*
> *At pigeon-holes and nine-pin play,*
> *Whilst nob-nail Dick and simp'ring Frances*
> *Trip it away in country dances;*
> *At stool-ball and at barley-break,*
> *Wherewith they harmless pastime make.*

TRADITIONAL AND REGIONAL RECIPES

Shrovetide Pancakes

2 cups all-purpose flour	2 eggs
Pinch of salt	Milk to make batter thin

Mix together flour, salt, well-beaten eggs and just enough milk to make the batter thin. Have greased griddle very hot. Put 4 tbsp. of batter into a teacup and pour onto the griddle. Bake until golden brown on one side, then turn over and bake on the other.

Car-Cake

A small cake made with eggs and cooked on a griddle, and eaten on Shrove Tuesday in parts of Scotland and northern England. Sometimes served to children as a highly flavored pancake. A blood car-cake is a cake mixed with hog's blood and eaten on Easter Sunday.

Doughnuts

Doughnuts are not usually considered traditional English fare, but at Baldock, Hertfordshire, Shrove Tuesday used to be called Doughnut Day, since it was the practice on that day to make doughnuts rather than the more traditional pancakes. The doughnuts were fried in hog's fat, heated in small brass vessels. On the Isle of Wight, cottagers take the cakes out of the fat and drain them on clean straw.

1 cup milk	⅓ cup butter and lard mixed
¼ cake compressed yeast dissolved in ¼ cup lukewarm water	1 cup light brown sugar
	½ grated nutmeg or 1 tsp. cinnamon
	⅛ tsp. each of mace and cloves
2 cups sifted all-purpose flour	2 eggs
1 tsp. salt	Raspberry jam or currants

Scald the milk and cool to lukewarm. Dissolve the yeast in the lukewarm water. Add the yeast mixture to the milk, together with salt and enough flour to make a stiff batter. Set to rise overnight in a greased, covered bowl.

In the morning, work in the remaining flour, the melted shortening, sugar, well-beaten eggs and nutmeg. If the dough is too soft to handle, add a little more flour. Set the dough to rise again.

When dough is light, roll it out to ¾ inch thick on a floured pastry board. Cut out with small round cutter and work with fingers into small balls. Make a hole in the side of each ball, insert a little jam or a few currants in the center, close up the hole and seal with a little beaten egg. Place the balls of dough on the floured board and let them rise for 1 hour. Then turn them and let them rise once more.

Fry the doughnuts in deep hot vegetable shortening (370° F.) until brown, turning them when the first crack appears. Drain on absorbent paper.

When cool, drop 2 or 3 doughnuts at a time in a paper bag which is partly filled with granulated sugar. Shake bag until doughnuts are coated.

Fat for frying doughnuts must be kept at uniform temperature. Using a fat thermometer is the most accurate way of maintaining even heat, but another fairly sure method of testing temperature is to drop into the fat an inch cube of bread. If it turns golden brown in 60 seconds, the fat is approximately 370° F.

Fig pies were served on Carling Sunday in some parts of England.

Fig Pie

Short-Crust Shell

1¼ cups sifted all-purpose flour	⅛ teaspoon sugar
½ teaspoon salt	⅓ cup shortening
	About 3 tbsp. cold water

Sift together the flour, salt, and sugar. Add ½ of the shortening and work it in with pastry blender until the mixture looks like coarse meal. Add the remaining shortening and cut in until particles are the size of a small bean. Sprinkle the mixture with water, a tablespoon at a time, and work together lightly with a fork, until a soft dough is formed.

Roll out the dough ⅛ inch thick, prick with fork and loosely fit into the inside of a pie tin. Let the dough sag for 5 minutes, and then pat it firmly into pan with a small piece of dough. Trim the edge ½ inch larger than the pan, then turn it back and flute with the fingers. Bake 15 minutes in very hot oven (450° F.)

Fig Filling

2 cups cooked figs	½ tsp. mixed spices
¼ cup currants	1 tbsp. grated orange rind
¾ cup sugar	1 tbsp. molasses
	2 egg whites

Cut the figs into small pieces. Add the currants, sugar, molasses, spices, and rind. Beat egg whites until stiff but not dry, and fold into the first mixture blending well.

Pour into the baked shell. Bake in moderately hot oven (375° F.) 30 minutes. When cold, top with mixture of 1 cup heavy cream whipped, 2 tablespoons confectioners' sugar and ½ teaspoon vanilla flavoring.

Use of Tansy

The bitter juice of the tansy herb was used extensively in flavoring traditional Easter foods, especially the tansy cakes and puddings which were awarded to winners of the Easter games.

> *Soone at Easter cometh Alleluya,*
> *With butter, cheese and a tansay*

was written by a seventeenth-century poet, in reference to the custom of making tansy cakes at Easter. Since the cakes included such ingredients as butter, eggs, sugar, sack or ale, cream and fruit peels, the bitterness of tansy must have been largely disguised. British literature is rich in references such as "playing ball for a tansy cake," and "a game of stoolball for a tansy."

Hot Cross Buns

1 cup milk, scalded	3 cups flour
½ cup sugar	½ tsp. cinnamon
3 tbsp. melted butter	½ cup currants
½ tsp. salt	1 tsp. grated lemon peel
1 yeast cake	1 pinch ground cloves
¼ cup warm water	Confectioners' sugar and
1 egg, well beaten	milk

Combine milk, sugar, butter, salt. When lukewarm, add yeast cake dissolved in water. Then add egg and mix well. Sift flour and cinnamon together, and stir into yeast mixture. Add currants, lemon peel, and cloves, and mix thoroughly. Cover and let rise in warm place until double in size. Shape dough into round buns and place on well-buttered baking sheet. Let rise again. Brush top of each bun with egg. Make a cross on each bun with a sharp knife. Bake in hot oven (400° F.) for 20 minutes. Remove from oven and brush over lightly with a cross made of confectioners' sugar moistened with milk.

Finland

The Finnish name for Easter differs from that used in other countries. It comes from the verb *päästä* (to get free) and means the day on which people "get free from" the fast and begin again "to eat meat and fresh delicacies." Thus, this *Pääsiänen* was a great event in pre-Reformation times. From the religious point of view it undoubtedly signifies the day Christ *pääsi* (was freed from) the tomb, and it connotes the escape of the Jews from slavery in Egypt. As with the Hebrew Paschal Feast, the Finnish Easter observance is of eight days' duration.

In East Finland, Palm Sunday is known as Willowswitch Sunday (Virposunnuntai) while on the Karelian isthmus, the eve of Palm Sunday is called "Willowswitch Saturday" even to this day. The children used to rise early on Saturday and go from house to house with fresh-cut willow switches (*virpoja*), decked with multicolored cloth streamers. When they met the "woman of the house" the children would spank her lightly with their switches, reciting: *"Virpoi, varpoi, vitsat käyvät, tulevaks vueks tuoreeks, terveeks."* ("Switching, switching, switches go, wishing freshness and health for the year.") In addition to this bit of verse, good wishes were expressed. Similarly, the mistress of the family used a switch on her cows and sheep, wishing them health and well-being. Then the switches were stuck in the barn ceiling, to be used again when the cows and sheep were pastured in the open for the first time.

In some provinces, on Palm Sunday, the children had their fun switching eligible girls, all the while wishing them a happy marriage, riches, love, and position as mistress of a big house. A reward for the "switching service" was expected, and this was given on Easter Sunday, when the youngsters returned to collect goodies which were doled out generously.

In West Finland, children gathered branches of willow or birch from the snowdrifts, brought them home and put them in vases. It was believed that the forest trees would bud in as many weeks as it required days for the birch branches to sprout. In the Greek Orthodox Catholic Church, willow branches were blessed and distributed to the congregation, who used them to sprinkle "lucky water" on the cattle. According to old church traditions, the weather on Palm Sunday determined the prosperity of the crops. A clear and beautiful day on Palm Sunday signified a good year for barley.

Each day of Holy Week had its special connotation. In Savo province, they were: Stocking Sunday, Beam Monday, Splinter Tuesday, Bell Wednesday, *Kiira* Thursday (*kiira* means "evil spirit"), Long Friday, and Yarn Saturday. The names are still used and specific tasks are carried out on these days. Kindling splinters whittled on Splinter Tuesday are highly valued; the bell is tied around the cow's neck on Bell Wednesday. In the days when Finland was a Catholic country, all bells were silenced so that a quiet week was observed. From this practice comes the word *Tymintäviikko,* from the old Swedish *Dymbilvika,* meaning Dumb Week. Any activity involving noise, such as working with steel equipment, was prohibited during Holy Week. Likewise, laughing and whistling were considered outrageous.

On *Kiira* Thursday the *kiira* was banished from the farmyard. From an old record in Hankasalmi, we learn an old birch-bark tar basket, fastened to a stick, was ignited. One man pulled the flaming tar basket about the farmyard, twice clockwise and once counterclockwise. Another followed, striking at the birch basket with alder switches, saying, *"Kits kiira metsään!"* ("Away, evil spirits, to the woods!"). Usually the burning tar container was set on a sled to which was added a load of trash, such as old shoes, birch-bark curls and pieces of lumber, as well as implements like cowlstaffs, pot-hooks, mattocks, sickles, and scythes, the handles of which had to drag on the ground. As the sled was dragged about, chants were recited.

With the passage of time, this practice of exorcising took on a more dramatic form. For example, in the parish of Juva, the ceremony was performed by a man who ran around the yard with a fire poker and tar trough, as if chasing something. Another asked, "What are you chasing?" The reply was, "I'm chasing the *kiira* into the woods." The usual incantations followed.

In northern Savo province, it was customary, in driving away these evil spirits, to run around the house and barn with a cowbell around one's neck. The custom quickly became a children's game, with the run being performed in the house or out in a field. In Kuopio, in east central Finland, the bell was hung on an ash poker which was also adorned with trash; the performer circled the farm with an axe in one hand and the poker in the other. With the ax butt he struck at the corners of the buildings and recited: "Away, *kiira,*

85

to the woods." When the mistress of the house carried out this performance, she tied all kinds of domestic iron implements to her belt—shears, fire tongs, pokers, sickles, knives, and pliers—and added a flickering pitch torch.

The older generations banished the *kiira* so that snakes and other reptiles would not enter the yard in summertime. This banishment rite was important in preventing the forces of evil from entering the house. Since exorcising equipment also included cowbells, hay, and the farmwife's dress, we may surmise that the driving out of the *kiira* also was effective in getting the cows home on time during the summer, as well as insuring their general welfare. The practice undoubtedly stems from an ancient church purification rite. The "reeking birch-bark tar burner corresponds to the old church incense-burner."

"Tail Thursday," another reference to Holy Thursday, was so-called because it was customary on this day to trim the cow's tail and to prepare hair soup (not from the cow's hair, but from barley). Finnish folk hoped for good weather on Holy Thursday, for they believed that the following forty days would follow suit: "If Thursday night is cold, then the whole spring is cold."

"Long Friday" (Good Friday) climaxed the long fast. No one went visiting on that day; all sat quietly at home, fasting and reading the Bible; one did not neglect to go to church, however. If anyone laughed "so as to show his teeth" it was considered a sin. No fires were lighted and little was eaten except dried fish, sour bread, leftover stew and other cold foods; these were allowed only after sundown. Milk and cream were especially forbidden, even to babies and children. However, following the Reformation "fresh meat stew could be eaten even if the last sheep had to be slaughtered, so as to break the 'bad man's fast day.'" In West Finland, people whipped their children on Good Friday; this practice was also common to Germany and Sweden as a symbol of Christ's suffering.

Because the Finns believed that evil spirits ruled the day, Good Friday was an auspicious time for procuring powerful magical equipment. This equipment was to give a wide range of protection, from guarding cattle to fishing and healing the sick. It was believed that all sorts of evil spirits were about on the eve of Good Friday and Yarn Saturday: witches, trolls (*rullit*), and "pinch-noses." It was also customary to listen for omens of Easter on Saturday evening. This was best done by climbing the roof of a thrice-moved building or by standing at the crossing of three roads. Listeners could clearly hear the sound of Easter omens: "the striking of an ax, the clatter of boards, the pounding of a smith's hammer," which foretold news of death. It was believed that secret beings were building a coffin: whittling boards, piling them, and pounding nails in the smithy. The late-rising full moon added to the eerie effect of the night, for its pale glow and the resulting dark shadows made even familiar scenes unreal.

Trolls still play a notable part in the Easter eve activities in Finland; accounts of their doings still appear almost every year during Lent in West Finnish newspapers. These trolls are usually "short-witted, decayed old women of backward districts, whose attempts are based on unreasonable jealousy toward more fortunate neighbors. With dark deeds they try to do damage to the neighbors' livestock 'fortune' and at the same time improve their own poorly prospering cattle and sheep." They engage in such activities as milking cows dry and cutting pieces of fur and skin from farm animals, which is supposed to make animals sick, cows dry and sheep lose their wool. It was believed that by robbing the neighbors' animals of their "luck" and "prosperity," the trolls increased their own, because the "luck" would change places. Sometimes "the wool was mixed in with the wool on the troll's sheep, or else hidden in the sheep shelter. The pieces of hide cut out from the cows were nailed to the bottom of the churn, which caused increase in the amount of butter."

Some of the trolls did not care for livestock, but carried out their tricks out of pure jealousy. They damaged their neighbors' property maliciously. It was believed that if they took wool or hair from animals to a dwarf tree or to the cemetery, the affected animals would "wither away." Many supernatural attributes have also been given the trolls. Like witches, they fly through the air on all manner of implements on Good Friday Eve and on Easter Eve, procuring their supernatural powers from the "Evil One." It was believed that the troll would depart unseen from a brake, a thrice-moved building or from a chimney and could cover great distance in flight. It was also held that trolls went to supernatural gatherings where they consumed "snakes, lizards, frogs, rats, mildew, sticks burned at both ends, and other frightful objects." These were disguised as "rare delicacies," but if one forgot and blessed oneself, the food "changed immediately to its terrible natural appearance." After this feast, the troll had to fly back home to her parish church in time for the Easter service. In church, invisible to most parishioners, the trolls sat with pails over their heads and their backs to the altar so they wouldn't hear the sermon.

Many precautions were taken to keep witches away from homes and barns. A cross drawn on the door, metal implements placed in front of it, or the remains of an owl or hawk nailed above the door were all considered effective. Also, the lighting of fires was a general practice to frighten away evil spirits.

Many tales are still told by the old folks about attempts to capture witches. In southwest Finland, a troll was captured in a barn and "promised its deliverer a red skirt in return for freedom; when let free, the troll wounded the person; the blood-soaked skirt was the promised reward for the benefactor." Another tale concerns the hired hand "who anointed himself with witch-salve and then said the magic words wrong, getting himself a very bumpy and adventurous magic flight." The Finnish trolls are of western origin; the word *rulli* comes from the medieval Swedish *trull*, now *troll*.

On Easter Saturday evening Easter fires are burned on the plains of Osterbotten. These fires correspond to fires burned elsewhere in Finland on Midsummer's Eve and Ascension Day. Many Osterbotnians remember these fires from their childhood days. "During the dark night of this spring celebration," wrote Samuli Paulaharju, "when old trolls were active in the barns or flew about the parish with the demons, there flared up along the plains those scores of Easter fires. They flared and flickered over the night snowdrifts like terrible witch-fires, hesitated a bit, then flamed anew and sent out fiery sparks and embers into the dark heights. In every direction, one could see this dying out and rebirth, the sky flushed behind the forests as if the sky itself threatened to burst into flame. On all sides old tar-barrels flamed, kegs laced with tar stood about on the ends of posts, junipers sizzled, and, most of all, sheafs of straw gathered from the drying-house added to the multitude of fires. The young wild *Härmä* (from *Härmä* parish) flushed, jumped, and cavorted about the pyre, hurled firebrands into the air, sang and yelled and dragged more straw from the masters' drying-houses, although many quick-tempered old farmers stood, ax in hand, guarding their stores of straw."

It is interesting to note that the area of Finland in which these fires were built is the same area where witch persecution was the strongest. Of all the witches sentenced to death in the 1600s, more than half were from Osterbotten. Earlier customs indicate that the Easter fires of Osterbotten had a purpose other than the frightening away of witches and trolls. Originally, these fires were burned to insure good crops and prosperous herds. Nowadays, Easter fires are burned chiefly for the entertainment of the children, "but many of the younger children about the bonfire still believe they hear the dreadful whirring of the trolls' flight, and the wavering of their shadows on the snowdrifts seems like some evil spirit trying to escape from the lighted area."

The Finns also hold to the belief, prevalent among most European Christians, that the sun dances when it rises on Easter morning. In Helsinki, it was customary for children and servants to gather on the rocks of Alppila to watch this phenomenon. In other parts of Finland, people hike great distances early on Easter morning to observe the sun. It is considered the mark of a good year to see the sun "jumping." Better still, if the sun rises on a clear horizon, the year will be a good and bounteous one. If the sun frolics, a good year for grain and barley is predicted; but, if the sun rises behind clouds, the summer flowers will be killed by frost. A cloudy morning foretells a poor year for crops. A rainy Easter means a poor summer.

At Easter, the Finns find that their food supply is low. It is said of a pale person that "he has cheeks like an Easter saint." Another saying goes, "On All Saints' Day for all, on Christmas for most, but on Easter for the 'head-house,'" (meaning only the rich had food in the spring). The leavings from the fall slaughtering provide the food for Easter; it is "cow's head for Easter," or "pig's head for Easter," and, in many places, old folks remember a cow's head being served. A special Easter dish is "mämmi," a "thick paste-like dessert made from rye-meal and malt. It is cooked first from malt flour and baked in a birch-bark basket. Although blackish in color, it is unusually sweet, and is eaten at Easter in memory of unleavened bread-dough." Other delicacies include eggs, milk, blood sausage, pies, lamb, cheeses, and veal (if the cows have calved).

In southwest Finland, the children set up a kind of teeter-totter in the "branch-cutting garden" on Easter morning. Even today in some rural areas of Finland, Easter swings are made. It is the day for the home-spun dance, commemorating the wool spun and woven during the long days of winter.

France

$\mathcal{J}$N Aix-en-Provence there is a proverb that goes, "Christmas comes but once a year, but Easter is with us always." Of all the holidays and festivals celebrated there, Easter has a very special place in the hearts of the countryfolk. The inhabitants of Provence have a passion for legends and the folklore linked with them. They observe their countless fetes with great gusto, for many saints have trodden their dusty roads. This ancient crossroads of the Mediterranean which has inherited folkways from Italy, Greece, Spain, and other countries has blended the essence of these cultures with the same romantic spirit that inspired the troubadours to compose their songs of courtly love centuries ago. Long before Christ appeared, the Provençaux worshiped at the shrine of Venus in Arles. Friday was the day sacred to the goddess of fertility.

Yet, according to legend, in the early years of the Christian era, they gave shelter to the passengers of a small boat, without oars, set adrift from Palestine by those who wished to banish the followers of Christ. In this fragile bark were Lazarus, who had been raised from the dead; his sister Martha; Mary Magdalene; and the two Marys—Mary Jacobé and Mary Salomé—accompanied by their colored servant, Sara. Trophime, the friend of St. Paul, and Maximin, who became the first Bishop of Provence, were also passengers. They landed in Provence and came ashore to bring a message of salvation to the heathen Gauls. The natives can account for what happened to all the passengers, for there are holy places and shrines, as well as churches, named in their honor.

History reveals that many of the saints lived in Provence over a period of several hundred years, but the story is all one to the Provençaux. Since their beliefs and traditions are very real to them and all of this goes back to the "night of time," they see little point in drawing sharp lines of distinction or checking on historical accuracy. W. H. Johnson, in his *Folk Tales of Provence,* describes one section of this countryside as a "cradle of saints," and such it is.

Lazarus found a haven in Marseille, where he preached and performed so many miracles that he converted the residents to Christianity, became the first bishop of this second city of France and eventually its patron saint. It is said that he resided in catacomb-like quarters beneath the present Church of Saint Victor in Marseille. His feast day is observed annually on December 17. Surprisingly enough, there was another Lazarus who served as Bishop of Aix in the fifth century, and the two were no doubt confused as legends grew with the passage of time. Blended and broadened in their interpretation and scope, like so many of the ancient stories that have come down to us, some of the achievements and memorials of the Roman conqueror Marius were attributed to the man whom Christ raised from the dead.

Martha made her way to Tarascon and later established the first convent in Provence. She will be forever remembered in that ancient town and the surrounding countryside for her good works and her holiness. She had been hostess to the Savior and was personally inspired by His preaching and teaching to spread the Gospel among the heathen. People of Tarascon came to believe that she had miraculous power. Once the village was troubled by a horrible dragon who was causing great destruction, even to the point of devouring human beings. Martha's aid was invoked to subdue this monster. Sprinkling him with holy water to quiet him, she used her sash to bind him so that he could be destroyed by the men of the village. On St. Martha's feast day a replica of the dragon, known as the Tarasque, used to be paraded through the town with much merriment and frolicking. This observance, held on July 29, was established by good King Rene in the middle of the fifteenth century for the veneration of the saints and the delight of everyone.

Although the charming Provençal legend about Saint Martha seems to date back to her actual lifetime, she received no public recognition until late in the thirteenth century. Biographers of the saints tell us that another Martha, a Persian nun who was martyred near Hazza in 347 and whose relics were preserved at Tarascon, was identified with the Martha of Jesus' time. Still another Martha was closely associated with Provence before the Christian era. She was the Syrian prophetess Martha, confidante of Marius the great Roman general, uncle of Julius Caesar. This famous woman foretold the conquest of the German horde against whom Marius was fighting. Archaeologists believe that she is one of the persons portrayed in a stone sculpture cut in limestone, known as the Trimaie. It is of fairly recent origin and stands above a chapel at the foot of the ancient mountain town of Les Baux. She has been absorbed by the Christian tradition and her achievements have been modified and adapted to the saintly Martha of the New Testament.

It was this Martha who constantly reproached her sister Mary Magdalene for her evil ways and finally led her to Christ. The patroness of discretion and housekeeping, Martha is often depicted with a skimmer or ladle in her hand, or a large bunch of keys fastened at her waist. When represented in paintings, she is usually dressed in the plain garb of a housewife and stands out in marked contrast to her sister Mary Magdalene, who is portrayed in bright colors or in elaborate gowns. When they are shown together, Martha represents the contemplative life; Mary Magdalene, the worldly. In Provence, Martha is the household saint who keeps the light of faith shining with the same radiance that is reflected in the gleaming copper pots on the hearth.

Her sister Mary Magdalene visited Marseille and Aix and then repaired to a forest grotto which is now known as Saint Baume, where she spent her last thirty years praying and fasting in a gloomy cave. The site of her home was a mecca for the religious for many years after her death. Later a monastery was built there. This was destroyed by the Saracens in the eighth century. Nearly 500 years elapsed before interest in the holy place was revived. Then it received the attention of popes and princes and the peasants as well.

Mary Magdalene was as widely known throughout the region for her worldly deeds as for her conversion and repentance. She became the patron of all Provence. They believed she could give protection against lightning as well as comfort and advice to young lovers. Newly married couples visited her grotto to pray that their brood of children would be numerous and to ask the saint's help in rearing them.

The name Mary Magdalene as commonly used in Provence has composite significance. She is a blend of Mary of Magdala and Mary of Bethany. Mary from Magdala, a Galilean village, was one of the women who followed Christ on His journeys. She was present at Calvary and brought spices to His tomb, and it was she who first informed the apostles that the tomb was empty. In the Gospel of John we learn that she finally recognized her risen Lord in the garden at Gethsemane after mistaking Him for a gardener. Mary of Bethany, the sister of Martha and Lazarus, sat at the feet of Jesus while Martha prepared a meal for Him.

Any discussion of this name involves considerable Biblical scholarship, which was beyond the realm of the simple peasants of Provence. Tradition has it that Mary Magdalene was buried at Ephesus and that the Emperor Leo VI, in the year 899, moved her relics to a monastery in Constantinople. However, it was not until the tenth century that special devotion was paid her.

About 1050 the monks of Vezelay claimed that they brought her body from the Holy Land. A little later a monk from this community is said to have located an empty sarcophagus in a crypt at Saint Maximin in Provence, which was believed to have originally contained the relics of Mary Magdalene. It is from this time that the great Provençal traditions grew. Further investigation reveals that Mary Magdalene's story is paralleled by that of the penitent Mary of Egypt, who is believed to have lived in the fifth century.

Mardi-Gras is held the last day of the three-day Carnival preceding Lent. Each town has its own *bataille de fleurs* (battle of flowers), with flower-bedecked cars and floats moving for hours along the streets and boulevards. As friends and acquaintances meet, they pelt one another with showers of flowers.

In Paris, the city butchers observe Carnival with the *fête de Boeuf Gras* (Fat Ox). An ox garlanded with flowers, ribbons, and festoons of green is led through the streets in the procession. He draws a cart bearing a little boy known as the "King of the Butchers." Homage is paid the king by throwing confetti and flowers on him and by the constant blowing of horns.

The most noted observance of Carnival in France is held at Nice. Here an enormous effigy of His Majesty, King Carnival, surrounded by a train of buffoons and clowns, is formally presented the key of the city. On Shrove Tuesday night, having enjoyed a brief but gay reign and a torchlight procession, he perishes by fire at the stake. André Hallays, writing fifty years ago, apparently did not enjoy the occasion:

"It is Mardi Gras. Sensible people must flee from mirthful Nice. Nice, where all afternoon the people, dressed in linen and masked with wire netting —like bags surmounted by muzzles—are going to throw plaster in each other's faces. We must escape from the dust and noise of the carnival. So we have crossed the city before the traditional cannon shot gives the signal for the festivity. Already enormous trucks are rolling through the streets, loaded with

A collection of eggs from France including from left to center three Limoges china egg boxes; center, egg in stand, a confection made of Jordan almond paste colored with vegetable dye; above right, twentieth-century enameled and gold egg; below right, cloisonné egg, in coral and gold. (*From the collection of Priscilla Sawyer Lord; photo: Photographic Illustrators Corp.*)

bags of confetti; already, at the edge of the sidewalks, in the doorways of houses, hucksters are placing the stands from which they will sell the frightful projectiles and invite wayfarers to provide themselves with 'boms-boms.' We already see 'pleasure-seeking bands' occupied in choosing their dominoes (costumes) and trying on their masks: they are hideous."

In rural France the first Sunday of Lent was known as *Fête des brandons* (Feast of Torches) because young folk ran through the streets carrying firebrands to banish winter. In Lorraine, well in advance of the day, the peasants prepared torches made of hay, steeped in resin, to celebrate *Büre* or *Le feu des brandons et des Bures*. The torches were carried in a parade headed by a local band of fiddlers and pipers leading gaily decorated farm wagons filled with young people. They went house to house begging fuel, which they piled in the wagons and carried to the public square. After dark, when the fire was lighted, the villagers danced and sang folk songs. Then a master of ceremonies, a kind of *garcon d'honneur* selected by the young folk, read a list of the eligible couples of the village. As each pair of names was read with due ceremony, a musket was fired in salute, to the delight of the crowd. Afterward, each girl who fancied the partner selected for her invited him home for supper. This arrangement gave the parents an opportunity to appraise the young man who might well become a member of the family. Actually, the coupling of names, done in jest at the fete, was usually prearranged by the parents and often proved to be a very successful form of matchmaking.

In mid-Lent (*Mi-carême*), the gloom is lifted by a round of festivities. It is an occasion for popular celebrations, comparable to those of Shrove Tuesday, with disguises, parades, and costume balls. In Paris, the day is celebrated by the fete of the *blanchisseuses* (laundresses). The washerwomen of each district select a queen; from these the queen of the day is chosen and she, in turn, selects a king. In the evening she reigns over the colorful ball.

On Palm Sunday, which is known as Flower Sunday (*Pâsques Fleuris*), the French observe the custom of decorating graves and visiting cemeteries. The Procession of Penitents at Sangues during Holy Week dates from the twelfth century. On Maundy Thursday morning, the penitents proceed to their chapel, where Mass is celebrated. The evening procession, which is lighted by torches, lanterns, and candles, is watched by many. The cross is borne by two veiled, barefooted penitents dressed in red and girded with ropes. Children carry the symbols of the Passion while the other marchers shake rattles and chant psalms. The rattles replace the bells that have departed to Rome.

From Holy Thursday to Easter Sunday, the bells of the churches stop ringing as a sign of mourning. The children are told the traditional story that the bells have gone to Rome. An old lullaby goes something like this:

> *Do-do-ding, ding dong, sleep little man,*
> *Do-do-ding, ding dong,*
> *The bells have gone to Rome.*
> *It is time to sleep,*
> *The bells have flown away.*
> *They have gone to Rome,*
> *Down there, down there, far away, you see,*
> *To visit the Pope, a saintly man,*
> *An old man dressed in white is he.*
> *The bell of each church*
> *To him secretly speaks*
> *Of all the good little ones,*
> *And he himself* le Bon Dieu *tells*
> *The name of each good child.*
> *Do-do-ding, ding dong, sleep little man.*

During the days of the bells' silence, the choirboys call the villagers to church by using various types of instruments to make enough noise to summon the parishioners, or by shouting at the top of their lungs.

In the principality of Monaco, the Stations of the Cross are presented during Holy Week by an ancient brotherhood who use old-time costumes and properties. At each station a different actor takes the part of Christ, but all are garbed in scarlet. Curiously enough, the actors personifying Christ have white hair and white beards and wear a crown of thorns. An attendant holds an umbrella over Pontius Pilate, who is assisted by four gowned lawyers, their heads covered with the biretta of the French advocate. The basin in which Pilate washes his hands is held by a slave wearing a white satin cloak. King Herod makes his appearance attired in an eighteenth-century wig, flowered waistcoat, a scarlet gown, and a gilt paper crown. Even Adam and Eve are present dressed in the fashion of Louis XV. The entire pageant reflects the mode and manner of centuries-old tradition.

Easter-week visitors to Chartres Cathedral find townspeople in traditional peasant garb selling a variety of items in front of the cathedral. Following the service on Sunday, bagpipers are among the musicians leading the parade.

Jousting during Holy Week has long been the custom at Champagne. It can be traced back to the thirteenth century and is believed to be the only survival, in France, of this ancient form of mock combat. Before the event begins, the young men on horseback, carrying long lances, parade through town to church, accompanying a large wooden sculpture of Christ, set on a platform. After attending Mass, they ride to a hill outside town for the tournament.

On Holy Saturday, pace-egging, a means of collecting eggs, was practiced by the choirboys of the local churches. As they made the rounds of the village, they sang their own Easter carols:

> *Good women, who to God would fare,*
> *Bring us each of eggs a pair,*
> *A good ham, too, for a gift this day*
> *Makes sure, good women, that your hens will lay;*
> *And you'll go straight to your heavenly rest*
> *As the hen herself goes straight for the nest.*

Another French rhyme went like this:

> *Eggs for the little children, pray!*
> *Four for me and eight for my pal—*
> *And you'll go straight to Eternal Day*
> *As a stone to the bottom of the well.*

Some of the rhymes employ the traditional Easter exclamation of joy— "Alleluia!"

> *I've a little cock in my basket;*
> *It'll sing for you if you ask it*
> *With eggs red and white, Alleluia!*

In many villages, on the Saturday before Easter, the children used to assemble early in the morning on the steps of the church for a frolic. The last to arrive at the rendezvous was given the shameful job of following the others by dragging a plank on which was fastened a dead animal which they called the *"carmaigne."* The whole group ran through the streets singing:

> *Ah! Ah! Ah! the funeral service has begun.*
> *The "carmaigne"* is dead.*
> *It is Jack* (whoever is dragging it) *who is dragging him.*

* Represents any dead animal.

94

At Easter sunrise in France it is said that the rays of sunlight penetrating the dawn cold are the angels dancing for joy at the Resurrection. It is traditional to eat omelet for Easter breakfast, and everyone goes to church wearing something new. On Easter morning when the church bells begin to peal, the children rush out to see what the returning bells have brought them. In the fields, gardens, or in their homes they find the hidden Easter eggs—sugar and chocolate ones—Jordan almonds, almond-paste candies and all sorts of other goodies. In the eighteenth century, egg races were an important part of the Easter festival in many parts of France and a hogshead of cider was given as the prize.

In Provence it has long been the custom to present an egg to a newborn child, together with bread, salt, and a knitting needle. The wish is that the child will be whole as an egg (endowed with all his faculties), good as bread, sharp as salt, and straight as a needle.

Easter Sunday is a very special feast day in every part of France from Brittany and Normandy, on the one hand, to the Languedoc and Provence, on the other, and each province has its favorite dishes, particularly for feast days. These are cooked and served with pride, and fortunate indeed is the visitor who locates the "right" restaurant or, better still, is invited to dine in a French farmhouse. Crepes, oxtail soup, scallops with mushrooms in white wine sauce, Quiche Lorraine, sautéed chicken with shallots and artichoke hearts, braised veal chops with ham and parsley dressing, braised leeks, glazed carrots and chocolate mousse are but a few of the favorite dishes one might expect. Jambon persille, French Easter ham in parsley jelly, served as an appetizer is worth a try for those who enjoy commonplace food prepared in gourmet style.

Traditional and Regional Recipes

Jambon Persille
(French Easter Ham in Parsley Jelly)

1 8-pound precooked ham	½ teaspoon each dried tarragon and
1 cracked veal knuckle	chervil
1 calf's foot, cleaned and split	2 bottles dry white wine
Soup greens, cut up	1 tablespoon wine vinegar
(2 onions, 1 carrot, celery	White pepper to taste
tops)	2 cups chopped parsley
Bouquet garni (1 bay leaf, 1	
clove garlic, 2 cloves, 8	
peppercorns, 6 shallots, 6	
sprigs parsley, tied in	
cheesecloth)	

Put everything except the parsley into a large stew pot. Add enough water to just cover. Cover and simmer slowly for 3 hours or until ham is loose on the bones. Remove the ham and bone it. Strain, clarify, and cool the broth. Break the ham into small pieces with a fork and pack into a bowl. When the broth is slightly thickened, mix with parsley, pour over the ham, and mix well. There should be ½ inch of jelly over the ham. Chill well. Sprinkle with remaining parsley, serve and slice in the bowl. Serves 20 to 24 as an appetizer. If calf's foot is not available, add 1 envelope softened gelatin to each 2 cups warm clarified broth and let thicken slightly before adding parsley.

French Omelet

4 eggs	½ teaspoon salt
4 tablespoons milk or cream	⅛ teaspoon pepper
2 tablespoons butter	

Use a heavy pan of generous size. If used for omelets alone, it should not need washing each time. Instead, wipe carefully with a dry cloth.

Beat eggs slightly, just enough to blend yolks and whites; add milk and seasonings. Put butter in omelet pan; when melted, turn in mixture and reduce heat slightly. As omelet cooks, lift with spatula, letting uncooked part run underneath until whole is of creamy consistency. Increase heat to brown quickly underneath. Omelet should be creamy inside. Fold and turn onto hot platter. Do not try to make too large an omelet; make two or more smaller ones instead. Serves three.

Broiled Chops Provençale

Choose your favorite broiling chops to sauce in the Provençale manner. The secret of the sauce is to heat butter just to a thick creamy consistency; do not let it melt down to a thin liquid.

4 servings lean lamb chops for broiling	⅓ cup minced shallots
4 tomatoes, peeled, cut into sixths and seeded	½ cup dry white table wine
½ teaspoon sugar	3 cloves garlic, mashed
6 tablespoons butter or margarine	¼ cup minced parsley
	Salt
	Freshly ground black pepper

Grill or pan-broil chops to the doneness you prefer; keep warm. Sprinkle tomatoes with sugar; set aside. Melt 2 tablespoons butter over medium heat in a large skillet. Add shallots and just heat through. Add wine and cook, stirring, until slightly reduced. Add tomatoes and gently cook and turn until heated through (do not allow them to lose shape). Add remaining butter, garlic, and parsley. Gently shake and tilt pan over heat to mix ingredients and soften butter. Season sauce with salt and pepper. Pour over broiled chops and serve at once. Serves four.

Germany

ℳISCHIEF and merriment make good companions, especially at Shrovetide when Carnival is held. In cities, it tends to become an elaborate spectacle, often influenced by foreign customs, whereas in the small villages, particularly in Germany, this "last fling" before Lent usually expresses itself in a truly folksy manner, and is linked with one or more local historical events. Regional folklore enriched by local color, native costumes, music and pageantry, and a certain spontaneous spirit of performance gives these events their special charm and appeal.

Wooing a bride, *Brautel,* is a Carnival custom in Sigmaringen that dates back to 1648, at the close of the Thirty Years War. In this village in the State of Baden-Württemberg, bachelors who had the courage to become engaged were given a signal honor. Following the long war, hunger and pestilence became widespread, and the young men of the town became hesitant to assume the responsibilities of family life, to such an extent that the local population dwindled rapidly. The *Schultheiss* (mayor), forced to take drastic action, dreamed up a plan to make the idea of marriage attractive by a form of hero worship. Any bachelor who would consent to become engaged was to be carried on a platform at the head of a gala procession, culminating at the town pump in the village square. A festival with all the flourishes was launched, in true country fashion, and no efforts were spared to make this Shrove Tuesday event memorable. Even the most timid among the eligible young men were lured and the custom has continued. Over the years, changes have occurred so that now every man who has married within a year, or moved into the community, or celebrated his twenty-fifth or fiftieth wedding anniversary is accorded a similar reception. It is now a two-day affair with heralds dressed in tricorn hats, black breeches, white shirts and stockings who parade around Sigmaringen, accompanied by drummers and pipers, to invite the bachelors to the *brautel* by dancing in front of their doors. A refusal means that the victim must pay a ransom. As the procession makes its way to the town pump, the shouting crowd is treated to apples, pretzels, and sausages donated by the bachelors. An old *brautel* song goes like this:

> *And thus it always will be*
> *As long as laughing and kissing go on;*
> *As long as the Danube flows;*
> *As long as the girl gets her man, etc.*

No longer do the following words of an earlier verse have any significance. These probably alluded to the early days, according to Dorothy Spicer, who described the event in her *Festivals of Western Europe*:

> *Let's live long and be merry.*
> *Simmering girls set caps for the lads.*
> *But all, alas, is useless!*
> *Not a single girl gets a sweetheart.*

97

In Cologne, Prince Carnival presides over a Fools' Court, surrounded by advisers who wear high peaked hats as well as the badge of the Order of Fools. Members of his bodyguard, known as the "Sparks," are garbed in the uniform of this ancient city's guards and carry wooden muskets. Munich captures the flavor of the Middle Ages at this season with performers, dressed in court costumes, who present old-time guild dances. Both the attendant ceremonies and the colorful floats feature incidents related to the city's great history and development.

In *Festivals of Western Europe,* Dorothy Spicer has recorded several colorful events which take place in Lower Saxony and in Baden-Württemberg: "Eastern Saxony boasts some of the most charming carnival celebrations of all Germany. In this region a symbolic battle is fought between representatives of Winter and Spring. Winter always is vanquished and Spring welcomed with laughter, merrymaking, and song. In some localities this kind of carnival celebration occurs somewhat later than Fastnacht. The character of the spring drama varies from district to district. In Eisenach, for example, where the battle of the seasons has been observed since 1286, 'Summer is won' by burning Winter in effigy after his defeat by Dame Sun.

"People of Baden-Württemberg call Fastnacht *'Fastnet'* in local dialect. For over five hundred years Rottweil on the Neckar has celebrated a Fastnet parade with all kinds of traditional figures such as three huge cocks, known respectively as *Guller, Federhannes,* or Feathery John, and *Biss,* or Bite. Another feature of the parade are groups of Fools, wearing costumes decorated with ball-shaped bells, who dance about and recite verses of 'fools' wisdom' to the crowd."

In Lower Saxony, at Lüneburg, the Kope Festival takes place with the salt miners participating in a moving folk pageant that originated in 1471. The *Kope,* a wooden barrel filled with stones, used to be dragged through the narrow streets, pulled by horses and ridden by the *Salzjunker,* the journeymen saltmakers. The crowd that followed included not only the villagers, but also members of the local government and other public figures, all dressed in colorful outfits. Trumpets provided the deafening music, which with its loud blasts made the spirited horses jumpy. It took more than ordinary skill for the riders to handle the horses without trampling the excited children and townfolk. At the mouth of the salt mine, the barrel was dumped on a great pile of wood and set on fire.

When the burning pile was reduced to embers, the crowd paraded to the marketplace for the initiation of the journeymen into the Guild of Master Salters. Mining salt has been the mainstay of this town for a thousand years or more. The guild's importance demanded proper tribute which ended with an elaborate banquet. Like so many similar festivals, this one probably has pre-Christian roots, with the fire symbolizing the Sun God's victory over winter's darkness and the rolling of the *Kope,* "the relentless passage of time." For a time this ancient custom was forgotten, but, since tradition dies slowly, it was revived in 1950 as an annual event.

In southern Germany, the Thursday before Ash Wednesday has long been known as Wives' Night, when women used to run through the streets playing tricks on all the men they met, and danced in shops and offices, markets and railway stations. The days that immediately followed were called The Three Crazy Days, when almost anything could happen.

Palm Sunday is a heartening day in the German countryside when religious symbolism, blended with native folklore relating to the bursting springtime, gives rise to spontaneous folk art. In the Black Forest, tall poles are decorated with pussy willows, bits of foliage, heart and cross motifs and colorful streamers to be placed in the dooryard. Later they are carried in a procession to the church for the blessing, as in the ceremony of the palms. In a more elaborate way, the custom in Bavaria is to make trees of twelve kinds of wood that glitter with brightly colored glass beads. These, too, are taken to church for the ceremony of the day and then are set up in the fields to insure the success of the crops—a good yield and freedom from hail, drought, and insect damage. The spirit of the day is warmly conveyed by a wooden image, the palm *Esel* or donkey, symbolic of the humble animal on which Christ made his triumphal entry into Jerusalem. With ceremony and reverence, the image is carried into the church where the parishioners go forward and touch it to receive, as it were, the same mystic blessing bestowed on that eventful day, nearly two thousand years ago.

Holy Thursday is referred to as Green Thursday in Germany. The word "green" is a corruption of an old German word meaning to mourn; green was the traditional color of the vestments worn by the clergy on this day. An old saying had it that anyone who did not eat green salad on this day would become a donkey. Children, especially those in the country areas, made it a point to eat an entire meal of green things, raw and cooked. Beliefs associated with eggs are linked with this day also. An egg laid on Holy Thursday stays fresh for a year and if it is plowed into the ground as the first furrow is turned, the result will be an abundant harvest. To keep one in the house is to protect the property against lightning.

In a unique way the Passion Play held at Oberammergau dramatizes the story of Holy Week and the events that led up to it, with an unforgettable spirit of realism. Although it is presented in late spring and summer and cannot be considered a part of German Lent, the motive that made it a reality is basic to the spirit of the penitential season. It all began as the result of a vow made in 1633 that if their village was spared from the Black Plague then sweeping Europe, the inhabitants would perform a passion play every ten years. The village was spared and this promise has been kept for more than 300 years. To the villagers of Oberammergau, the drama remains a truly religious observance, but to most of the rest of the world it has become a great theatrical spectacle. Yet, a great many of the 500,000 spectators who journeyed thousands of miles to view the *Passions-Spiel* in 1970 found it a truly moving religious experience. In essence, the performers are reliving a way of life that was commonplace from the late Middle Ages through the early Renaissance when the

The cast of the Passion Play, presented at Oberammergau, Germany, every ten years, is made up of people from the village. Among the most prominent families connected with the play are the Langs. When not taking part in the play, they, like the other villagers, pursue their tasks as craftsmen.

Andreas Lang, shown at his wood-carving trade, portrayed Thomas in 1890, the Rabbi in 1900 and Peter in 1910 and 1922. (*Courtesy, Robert Edwards*)

Anton Lang is shown at his potter's wheel. (*Courtesy, Robert Edwards*)

Anton Lang as Christ in the Passion Play, Oberammergau, 1900. This portrait was one of several poses obtained by American tourists who attended. (*Courtesy Robert Edwards*)

miracle and mystery plays were presented in the churches and later in the public squares to teach the faithful the lessons of their faith. The approach to perfection attained in those remote centuries in the overall presentation of these plays is paralleled in many ways by the villagers of this little upland community which sits in a lonely valley in the Bavarian Alps. A sense of dedication, staunch faith, and, above all, a ringing sincerity are the earmarks of these thoroughgoing German countrymen. They have kept sacred and perpetuated a pledge made by their forefathers.

The cast requires nearly 1400 players, including understudies, of which about 250 are children, with about half the number in speaking parts. The actors are chosen from those who claim the village as their birthplace or have resided there for a given period, but exceptions are made by the committee. In 1970 Barabbas was played by a plumber who had fled from Czechoslovakia. In a small mountain town where practically everyone is on intimate terms with everyone else the task of casting is by no means easy. The play committee includes the sixteen village councillors, the mayor, the priest, the director, and six members of the community, who are elected by popular vote of all the men in the village eligible to take part in the play.

Actors are invited to try out for the various parts. Not only are their talents weighed but their private lives as well. It is considered of vital importance that all the principal actors be men and women of high personal integrity. All the adult female parts, with the exception of Mary, are filled by married women. The name of the Lang family is known the world over in conjunction with this beautiful village and its play. Anton was chosen to play the part of Christ in 1900 at the age of twenty-five. He performed again in 1910 and in 1922 (the change of date was occasioned by World War I). According to custom, when he stepped down from the leading role, he was assigned to read the prologue. Other members have added luster to the family name by their interpretive acting. Over the years, as the principal actors have changed, so, too, have the interpretations of the parts which they play. Spectators who have seen the play on more than one occasion enjoy making comparisons, all the while realizing that no two people would interpret a part in the same manner. Visitors have long enjoyed meeting the various performers in person, particularly out of season, when they are plying their trades as wood-carvers, hotel-keepers, pottery makers, shopkeepers, postmen and others. As one visitor put it, mingling with "apostles, saints and martyrs, publicans and sinners, Barabbas the robber and old Simeon 'waiting for the consolation of Israel' made the Bible story all the more real." Many are wood-carvers, for this is the leading industry of the village, long famed for its superb craftsmanship. The Christmas cribs are of exceptional quality.

Formerly the presentation was given in the churchyard, but at the turn of the century a theater was built which has been enlarged since, so that it accommodates more than 5000 people. It was designed somewhat like a great Quonset hut with no columns to impede one's view. The stage, with its three classical Roman buildings and a tree-studded hillside beyond, is open to the sky so that two sets of costumes are necessary, for the play is given rain or shine. Seven hundred people can be accommodated on the stage together with horses and donkeys. Performances are staged each day of the week except Tuesday and Saturday, beginning at 8:15 in the morning and continuing until 5:00 P.M., with a two-hour interval for lunch.

In 1970 there were 101 performances beginning in May and ending in September. More than 1,500,000 requests for seats were made, but only a third of that number could be accommodated. Some 800,000 Englishmen and Americans were among those eager to attend. The town plays host each year to skiers in the winter and hikers in the summer so that there are about thirty hotels and small inns. In addition, the villagers provide accommodations for as many visitors as possible in their homes. Others stay in the nearby villages of Ettal and Unterammergau. Although the ticket income from the 1970 performances exceeded $4,500,000, the cost to the village was an additional million or more which, as in the past, would be amortized over a ten-year period. The belief that the Oberammergau Passion Play is a great money-maker is without foundation. Furthermore, the performers are compensated so modestly that were it not for their trades and professions, they would be unable to devote the time required for rehearsing and performing. Weather limits the period during which the performances can be given. The present ten-year interval between performances has proved practical and there seems to be no tendency to televise the play. The sentiment of the natives is that it was born and must remain in Oberammergau.

Bonfires on Easter Eve are particularly common in Germany, where they are lighted not only in churchyards but upon hilltops, where the young people gather around and jump over them, dance, and sing Easter hymns. These are remnants of pagan and sacrificial rites in which quantities of tar-soaked barrel staves, branches and roots of trees were burned. For a time, in the early days of Christianity, these fires were banned by the Church fathers until the Irish bishops, who came to the European continent in the sixth and seventh centuries, declared that they had spiritual significance. St. Patrick, the founder of the Church in Ireland, had instituted the practice to supplant a long-established custom of the pagan Druids, who lighted fires as a salute to spring.

In the Harz Mountains, in the Rhineland, in Oldenburg, Westphalia and elsewhere, giant oak wheels, often seven feet in diameter and weighing as much as 800 pounds with straw-packed spokes, were placed at the top of a hill and set afire. The natives, having gathered around bonfires on neighboring hills, watched and shouted with joy as the great wheels rolled into the valleys below. The fields where the burning wheels finally came to rest were considered specially blessed, thus insuring a rich harvest to the farmer. Each family contributed its share of straw for the event. The flaming wheels, symbolic of the sun, were relics of early German fire worship which was observed in many parts of central Europe and elsewhere throughout the world. Sometimes barrels of pitch were substituted for the wheels.

In Bavaria on Easter Eve the practice of "burning the Easter Man" is also a time-worn custom. The fire, kindled on high ground near a village, was built around a tall cross wrapped in straw to make it look as though a man were upon it with his arms outstretched. It was set alight from a taper bearing New Fire from the church, and on Easter Monday the cold ashes were gathered and scattered on the fields as part of the spring fertility rites.

As with fire, so with water, special rites were carried out in rural areas not only in Germany but in many other countries on the Continent. Water was essential to life itself and to the crops that sustained the people. As Francis X. Weiser expressed it, "Water assumed in their minds a magic role of producing fertility, health and new life." Women washed their faces in brooks and rivers in Thuringia, where they believed that if they rose early Easter morning and so bathed, without uttering a word, they would be endowed with beauty for the coming year. Fresh dew served the same purpose.

Easter Saturday has long been the occasion for blessing the food to be served on Easter and the days following. No one attended church for any reason unless properly dressed and on this occasion those who owned them wore the old-style peasant costumes as finery. The basket containing the long braided holiday bread, colored eggs, bacon or ham, and butter molded in the shape of a lamb bedecked with ribbon was covered with clean linen.

Many spring flowers and several trees have a place in the Easter folklore tradition of Germany. In the Black Forest early spring blooms, as well as grasses and various kinds of foliage, were made into crosses and hearts and carried to church to be blessed. It was believed that the pear tree provided the wood of the Cross, and as a result the wood later developed roots and produced red flowers as well as leaves and fruit that were similarly veined. The glossy-leaved holly, commonly called English holly (*Ilex aquifolium*), had its white fruits changed to red when a drop of the blood of Christ fell on them. Actually, a white-fruited form of holly is grown in gardens, but it is not common; it is merely a variant or an albino form, a condition which occurs often in the plant world. Yet the facts do little to discount this folk belief. An old German myth had it that Judas, overtaken by remorse, ended his life by hanging himself from the branches of a tall brier rose. The red fruits of this thorny bush were called Judas berries, and presumably the bush was a small tree in form.

The Germans have a tradition that when Christ was crucified all the fish dived beneath the waters in terror, except the pike, which out of curiosity lifted its head and beheld the whole scene. Hence we have the fancy that in a pike's head all the parts of the Crucifixion are represented—a cross, three nails, and a sword being distinctly recognizable.

Easter is a bunny to most children. Yet nobody seems to know precisely the origin of the Easter bunny, except that it can be traced back to pre-Christian fertility lore. It has never had any connection with Christian religious symbolism. In Europe the bunny is actually the hare, which has shorter ears, longer hind legs, and a different kind of skull than the rabbit. Hares are born with their eyes open and always live aboveground. On the other hand, rabbits are born blind and live underground in burrows. Because the rabbit produces five

A cylindrical cardboard candy box is concealed beneath the original foreign dress of this Easter rabbit. It stands 6½″ high with head and hands of papier-mâché and legs of wood. It is probably of German origin and was made during the early twentieth century. (*From the collection of Madeline O. Merrill; photo: Richard Merrill*)

This Easter novelty rabbit doll made of celluloid by the German firm of Karl Standfuss, bears the mark "Juno" and was distributed in the United States by George Borgfeldt and Company during the early twentieth century. (*From the collection of Madeline O. Merrill; photo: Richard Merrill*)

A family of Easter Hares, carved from wood and neatly dressed for the delight of children in many parts of the world, is ready for shipment from Germany. (*Photo: Photographic Illustrators Corp.*)

or six litters a year, it is considered a fertility symbol. In common usage the term "rabbit" or "bunny" may actually be a reference to the hare.

In Germany, as important to children as St. Nicholas is to Christmas is the role that the rabbit plays at Easter time; in fact, some argue that the Easter bunny is the more important. The earliest recorded mention of the Easter rabbit and his eggs is a short admonition in a German book of the late sixteenth century. "Do not worry if the bunny escapes you; should we miss his eggs then we shall cook the nest." In a German book dated 1682, the story that the Easter bunny lays eggs and hides them in the garden is called "an old fable." Also from Germany comes the note that the Easter bunny was believed to lay red eggs on Maundy Thursday and eggs of other colors on Easter eve. Then, too, there are ancient folktales in which the stork, the fox, and the cuckoo rather than the rabbit or the hare were the creatures that brought the eggs.

In Swabian villages, little "rabbit gardens" are made so that an attractive setting will be ready for the longed-for-eggs. Near Hanover, in the Deister Mountains, nests made of moss are prepared. The eggs are concealed in unexpected places—in nooks and corners, under shrubs, in flowerpots, behind stones and in other sites.

Children's storybooks indicate that the legend of the hare became notably popular in England in the late nineteenth century. The Pennsylvania Germans had been telling the tale for generations to their children. The following verse, which was published in England about 1895, is believed to be a free translation from the German:

> *What is that in the grass out there?*
> *Look, oh, look, a hare, a hare!*
> *Peeping out, the long-eared puss,*
> *From his cosy nest at us.*
> *There he goes, away, away,*
> *Over earth and stones and clay.*
> *Quick, you children, come and see*
> *This glorious nest for you and me.*
> *The prettiest thing you ever saw,*
> *Grass and hay and moss and straw.*
> *Look inside, what have we found?*
> *Coloured eggs so smooth and round.*
> *See them lie each by his fellow,*
> *Blue and green and red and yellow.*
> *Little hare in yonder wood,*
> *Thank you, thank you, kind and good.*

In addition to the colored hens' eggs, there are those made of fondant with a chocolate coating; the delightful look-inside eggs with a molded landscape or a picture within which can be viewed from the open end; and the precious satin eggs, in soft colors, filled with sweets, perfume, small trinkets or tiny lace handkerchiefs.

Eggs, handsomely decorated, make the most acceptable of gifts at this season of the year. Hand-painted designs including those done by scratching on a coated surface are as traditional with their makers as is the custom itself. Names, verses, and sentimental messages are sometimes inscribed on the shells. As in other countries, the red egg is a symbol of affection bestowed by a girl on her suitor, and the girl who fails to have an expected egg ready gets a whack with a cane from her boyfriend.

Games with eggs are numerous. There are the usual contests to determine who can eat the greatest number of eggs. Cracking eggs with an opponent takes all the skill one would use in a duel. *Eier-spacken,* or *Eier-doppen,* call it what you will, is a sport for all ages, one which the menfolk enjoy. Gathering eggs becomes an involved game when bicycles and riding horses are part of the game, as in the Black Forest. Although it might not be an easy task to determine in which country egg-rolling contests were first started, German children enjoy it to the fullest. A game known as *Canningeln,* played usually by girls, requires rolling an egg through a ring.

Sometimes instead of eggs at Easter, an emblematic print was given as a gift. One of these is preserved in the Print Room of the British Museum. Three hens are shown upholding a basket in which are placed three eggs ornamented with representations illustrative of the Resurrection. Over the center egg is the Agnus Dei (or Lamb of God), with a chalice representing faith; the other eggs bear the emblems of hope and of charity. Beneath all are the following lines:

> *All good things are three,*
> *Therefore I present you three Easter Eggs:*
> *Faith and Hope together with Charity.*
> *Never lose from the Heart*
> *Faith to the Church; Hope in God,*
> *And love Him to thy death.*

A nineteenth-century traveler writing of German Easter customs observed that "Easter is another season for the interchange of civilities, when instead of the colored egg in other parts of Germany, and which is there merely a toy for children, the Vienna Easter egg is composed of silver, mother-of-pearl, bronze, or some other expensive material, and filled with jewels, trinkets, or ducats."

From the German writer Christoph von Schmid has come a legend relating to the coloring of eggs. A beautiful titled woman suddenly appeared in a mountain village, accompanied by her children and a single servant. Because of her many kindnesses the villagers came to love her, although her origin and her coming remained a complete mystery to them. At Easter she gave a party for the children of the village and presented each with a colored egg on which she had written a motto. One of these eggs finally reached her husband, who had been searching everywhere for her to take her back home to their castle, that he had finally regained from a villainous knight. The custom of coloring eggs is supposed to have started from this little party.

Toys for Easter were undoubtedly first made in quantity in Germany, the source of many of the finest toys ever produced. Pasteboard eggs made in varying sizes so that they could be opened and filled with candy were made in tremendous quantities in Germany after the middle of the nineteenth century. Sturdily molded and handsomely decorated, they now belong in the realm of collectors' items. Some were covered with brightly colored lithographed paper, with gilt lace edging; others had cloth coverings. Small candy boxes, some shaped like rabbits and other figures, were similarly produced.

In *Toys Through the Ages,* Leslie Daiken has described a marvelous mechanical rabbit probably made in Germany or Austria less than a century ago: "The Percy Muir Collection has one of the most elaborate constructions designed as an Easter toy. It is shaped faithfully like an egg, about twelve inches long and eight inches high, and covered with rich red plush. At the base is a musical movement which is wound by a key. When the spring is fully wound a tune is played and suddenly, following a few bars, the upper lid of the shell springs upwards like the lid of a Jack-in-the-box. After another few notes of the melody out pops the head of a white rabbit, covered in real fur, and with pink glass eyes. The effect is grotesque and likely to fill the average child with apprehension. Yet the toy is typical of something produced at the whim of a wealthy patron determined to have the most extravagant Easter egg that money and the latest mechanical devices could secure."

In medieval days when the miracle and mystery plays, dramatizing the life of Christ, were held in churches, a figure of the Savior was pulled up through a hole in the roof to indicate His Ascension. Stories were told to the faithful claiming that Christ had flown to Heaven, which eventually gave rise to the custom of serving fowl, usually associated with flying, on that day. Pigeons, pheasants, partridge, and even crows were considered suitable food. In Western Germany bakers made pastry in the shape of birds.

A fastnacht, or doughnut, is served on Shrove Tuesday. To be genuine, a *fastnacht kuche* is one made without yeast. Since Shrove Tuesday is a religious holiday preceding Lent, yeast was not used in cooking on this day in former times. Also, the *fastnacht kuche* is baked only once a year, either on Shrove Tuesday or on the Monday before. It was important that it be eaten on Shrove Tuesday, although generally a sufficient quantity was baked to last the rest of the week, provided the family appetite was not too great. Anything baked with raised dough was not considered a *fastnacht kuche,* regardless of when it was baked or how it was shaped.

Traditional and Regional Recipes

Genuine Fastnacht Kuche

¾ cup thick sour cream	¼ cup sugar
¾ cup thick sour milk	1 egg
1½ tsp. baking soda	

Stiffen with enough flour to roll. Roll about ¼ inch thick and cut into desired shape and size—two-inch squares are preferable. Fry in deep fat. The amount of sugar may be made larger, but this is not necessary if the fastnacht is eaten in the approved manner.

To eat, split the *fastnacht kuche* in half and fill the inside with *gwidde hunnich* (quince jam). To use anything as ordinary and common as molasses on a genuine *fastnacht kuche* was thought an abomination. In the absence of *gwidde hunnich,* crabapple jelly may be substituted.

Pretzels were made originally as a Lenten food in Austria, Germany, and Poland, and always made their appearance on Ash Wednesday. The name "pretzel" is the German contraction for the Latin word meaning "little arms." This form of baked dough was made to take the place of bread, since the use of milk, eggs, and fats was forbidden in Germany, as in other countries, during Lent. Pretzels, which are now enjoyed at any time of the year, were first made in the fifth century A.D. The dough, made of flour, salt, and water, is twisted in such a manner as to represent two arms crossed in the act of prayer. When pretzels were eaten, they served as a reminder of the reverence associated with the season of Lent, and for many years this was the only time they were eaten. It was customary to give them to the paupers of the town in place of bread on certain days during Lent.

Bread Pretzels

1¼ cups 85° water	1 egg yolk
1 cake compressed yeast	1 to 2 tbsp. water or milk
½ tsp. sugar	Coarse salt
4½ cups flour	

Let yeast and sugar dissolve in water for 1 hour. Mix in flour and other ingredients. Knead for 7 to 8 minutes. Let the dough rise in a greased, covered bowl until double in bulk. Form into pretzels. Place on a greased sheet. Bake in oven at 325° F. until brown.

Greece

ALTHOUGH the Greek Orthodox calendar is studded with feast days and holy days, Easter is the apex of the Greek festival year. In bygone days, Carnival covered a three-week period prior to Ash Wednesday. It was announced from a high place near a village by the firing of guns or the beating of drums by the town crier. Then followed "Meat Week," during which a pig was slaughtered and eaten. The final period, Cheese-Eating, or Cheese, Week, preceded Lent; during that week only cheese, milk, and eggs were eaten. The forty days ahead meant fasting in a truly rigid manner. There were no dances, fairs, or weddings and the women put their jewelry away.

At the beginning of Carnival season, on St. Anthony's Day, the women gathered at each other's homes to play games, to recite riddles and puns, and to chatter. A certain boldness of speech was permissible and even expected. Singing and dancing were the order of the day and the verses heard were both satirical and licentious. A popular Cretan saying had it: "During Carnival even old women go wild." By Thursday of the second week, *Tsiknopefti*, the Carnival spirit, was gathering momentum. First came a family meal, when even the poorest of families served the best they could afford, followed by a masquerade with singing and dancing. The masqueraders often dressed as a nuptial group, which included a bride and groom, the old matchmaker (a woman), the best man, and *Stachtiaris,* the ashman. The latter wore "the national white-pleated skirt with bells around his waist and a little bag filled with ash, with which to defend the bride and groom." A mock wedding took place, usually at the village square, as other colorful "characters" stood by with the laughing crowd. Plays, parodies, and satires acted out with great gusto provided more mirth. These included courtroom trials, the funeral of the miser, a gypsy wedding, robbing of the English lords, and the miller's story as well as a variety of incidents from seventeenth-century Cretan epics. Apart from the "official" program, spontaneous demonstrations by professional mummers were commonplace. Dressed as women, Moors, or in some outlandish fashion, they danced around a kind of Maypole, or a cardboard horse or camel, mounted by a man wearing a *foustanella,* the national white pleated skirt. Children added to the merriment with plenty of noise, and grown-ups tossed a few pennies into a tambourine, passed by one of the mummers.

At Vizyi in Thrace on Cheese Monday, a most unusual play, referred to as the *Kalogheroi* ceremony, which recalled the worship of Dionysós, was presented. Richard M. Dawkins described it in the *Journal of Hellenic Studies* as belonging "to the religious practices of the primitive ploughmen of Greece who sought, by means of homeopathic magic to influence the forces of nature, to assist the power which fertilizes the land—before that power had become personified under the name of Dionysós or Phallen, or the other gods of Vegetation."

A common belief among the Greeks was that during the first week of Carnival the souls of the dead were set free and wandered among the living. Accordingly, the first mouthful of meat and the first draught of wine taken at the Carnival meal were accompanied by the prayer: "May God forgive the souls of the dead."

In some places, such as Kydoniae in Asia Minor, it was customary to boil rice with meat on Thursday of Meat Week and to give to the poor in memory of the dead. The principal days consecrated to the dead were Meat Week Saturday, Cheese Week Saturday, and the first Saturday in Lent. Each of the three was called All Souls' Day. Housewives prepared a special dish which was distributed to neighbors so that the souls of dead relatives might be forgiven. Every family visited the graves of its dead. On All Souls' Day a long procession of black-clad women and girls went to the cemetery carrying dishes of *kollyva* decorated with powdered sugar, cinnamon, walnuts, sesame, pomegranate, parsley, and currants, which were placed on the graves as an offering to the dead; then relatives lighted candles and burned incense over the family tomb. On this day women abstained from work and remained unwashed.

The Cheese Week celebration came to a peak on the last Sunday of Carnival, with the day spent masquerading, visiting, eating, and drinking. Toward evening when the bells were rung for evensong, the noise quieted down, and the faithful made their way to church. About to enter Lent, they wished to be cleansed of sin. During the service, the priest and the congregation offered each other mutual forgiveness. The parishioners stood in a row, according to age; the younger members walked over to their elders, kissed their hands and said: "Forgive me," to which the older members replied: "May you be forgiven." This service was often followed by dancing on the village square, usually led by the parish priest. In Artotina, they sang a hymn which began: "Christ is the Tree, and Our Lady the Root."

In Northern Greece, in Western Macedonia, it was the custom on this evening to light large bonfires in the village square or in the streets. In Lakkovikia, near Mt. Panghaeon, children gathered armfuls of brambles and stacked them outside the village, "usually on the highest eminence." Then with slingshots, they shot stones at the stack of firewood saying: "Wherever the stone lands, may the fleas disappear." Near dusk, the fire was lighted and the children took turns leaping over it until it went out. In Vogatsiko, the children set a small tree in the ground and wrapped it with straw and dry branches so it would make an exploding noise when lighted. Later, the tree was burned and the single men of the village leaped over it, calling out the name of a favorite girl friend.

In some areas the feast held on Cheese Sunday evening included the whole village and the table was set at the mayor's house, as on the island of Carpathos. Traditional dishes included macaroni, eggs, cheese pies, milk pies, and a special dish called *tyrozoumi* (cheese broth). In Arcadia, *tyrozoumi* was placed on the table first. After a short family prayer, those present lifted the table "with their little fingers three times, saying: 'Holy broth, cheese broth—whoever drinks of it and does not laugh—shall not be bitten by fleas.'" Everyone had to drink three spoonfuls of broth, quickly and silently; then all burst out laughing in unison. With the eggs, served as the last dish, went a popular saying: "With an egg I close my mouth, with an egg I shall open it again," referring to the red eggs used at the end of Lent. In Eastern Rumelia, diners used to roll eggs across the table, saying: "May Lent roll by even as this egg rolls." In old days, the meal ended with a game called *Haskas* played with an egg. On the island of Skyros and elsewhere, the remaining egg from the meal was hung from the ceiling by string. Guests who sat around the table first tried to hit the egg with their foreheads to make it swing, and then tried to catch it with their lips. Singing and dancing followed. The "Pepper Dance" was a prime favorite, in which the performers made comical gestures imitating "the devil's monks grinding pepper."

III

At Katsidoni in Crete, it was customary to boil macaroni, meat, cheese, and other Easter foods in a large pot which was carried into fields and buried while the peasants burned incense over it. They lamented loudly that "Broadbean" had arrived and had sent "Macaroni" and "Meatman" into exile. When church bells were rung, merriment came to an end and Lent began.

Adherents of the Greek Orthodox Church observe a notably strict fast during Lent. Meat, fish, eggs, and milk are prohibited; on Wednesdays and Fridays and during the week preceding Easter, the same is true for wine and olive oil. Many Greeks, especially those living in villages, still follow these rules. During the first three days of Lent neither water nor bread is allowed, an observance usually kept by the women, who are later honored by other villagers when a special table is set for them. They partake of walnut cakes, bean soup, and *must* (sugar and water) syrup, and receive special gifts such as scarves and pillowcases as tokens of respect.

Since Lent passes slowly for those who fast, several methods of keeping time were devised in the days when there were neither calendars nor clocks. A curious figure of a nun, representing Lent, was cut out of paper. She was portrayed without a mouth, to denote abstinence from food; her hands were crossed in prayer and she had seven feet, one for each of the seven weeks of fasting. At the end of each week, one of the feet was torn off. In the Pontus provinces, an onion or a potato with seven feathers stuck in it was hung from the ceiling and served the same purpose. All-night prayer in church was common.

One of the most popular feast days was the Feast of the Two Saint Theodores, celebrated on the first Saturday of Lent to honor the dead. The faithful went to the cemetery to pay honor to dead relatives, carrying flowers, a laurel wreath, and a tray of *kollyva*. In large towns, this feast took on an official character, with civil and ecclesiastical authorities participating. At Korini in Messinia, it was customary to make a spinach pie or marrow pie for the occasion. Children went from house to house at Panormos in Asia Minor saying prayers for the dead and receiving buns in return. George A. Megas has described the folklore associated with this special feast in his *Greek Calendar Customs:*

"Being a day devoted to the dead, this feast is believed to have a special magical significance. The villagers on the island of Lesbos thread *kollyva* into wreaths, which they hang on the trees of their orchards to protect them against the evil eye. *Kollyva* are also the means by which unmarried girls hope to see their future husbands in their dreams; they place three or nine grains of boiled wheat in a piece of white cloth, tie it up with a black thread and put it under their pillow. The same effect can be achieved by sowing wheat according to a magic formula, by invoking the Fates, etc. For instance at Arachova the families in which there is a John or a Theodore hang a small bag of wheat at their front door on Friday evening. The unmarried girls who wish to see their future husbands in their dreams must visit two Theodores and one John, and try to take away a little wheat from all three houses. When they return home, they must bury the wheat in their garden. Then they must go to the

The risen Christ appears to Mary Magdalene,
a painting by Martin Schongauer which
hangs in the museum at Colmar, Germany.
(Photo: Richard Merrill)

A view of Jerusalem. (*Photo by George Taloumis*)

The Garden of Gethsemane showing some of the ancient olive trees.
(Photo by George Taloumis)

A mingling of the old and the new
in modern Palestine. The costume is
an echo of Christ's time. *(Photo by
George Taloumis)*

Fabergé obviously had a fondness for lilies of the valley. His imitator has used them effectively together with a cluster of lilies on the removable cover of this jewel-box egg, which suggests the possibility of placing a surprise within.

The custom of hanging decorated eggs on separate branches or on a small tree or shrub in the dooryard or indoors has long been a cherished Easter practice with Pennsylvania-German families. Helen Buzby used a manzanita branch for this table tree which she created for indoor decoration. *(From the collection of Priscilla Sawyer Lord)*

The lifelike quality of these flower-urn eggs, or egg-shaped baskets (as originally conceived by Fabergé), is surpassed only by the exquisite coloring and detail in each bloom. Ribbing and basket weave lend pleasing variations to the texture of the surfaces.

Flowers have been substituted for double-headed eagles in the design of this sugar version of a trellised imperial Russian Easter egg.

The Easter cakes on this page, triumphs in the art of baking and decorating, were made especially for this book by Mrs. John R. Burbidge, who, having steeped herself in the lore of Easter cookery, added the flourishes of decorating made possible by inherent skill and present-day equipment.

The hen's importance is based on its ability to produce eggs. Christ said of the hen, "...how often would I gathered thy children together, as a hen doth gather her brood under her wings . . ." (Luke 13:34). The inspiration for this cake creation came from Sweden, where the hen shape has been popular for centuries.

The sacrificial lamb of the Hebrews became the Christian symbol of Christ, the "Lamb of God, which taketh away the sin of the world" (John 1:29). The *beránek* (Easter lamb cake), of special significance to the Czechoslovakian Easter celebration, is popular in all the Slavic countries.

An Italian Easter basket filled with hard-boiled eggs, decorated
with pasta. At Easter many a girl has spent several hours preparing
this type of gift for the boy of her choice. *(From the collection of
Mr. and Mrs. John R. Burbidge)*

A collection of hen's eggs decorated in the Polish tradition by
Veronica Romanowicz, who learned the art in her native country
and brought it to America. Her children and grandchildren cherish
these ornaments and use them each year on their Easter dinner table.
(From the collection of Mrs. Joseph Bettencourt)

Left, a duck egg used to make a triptych for St. Francis; right, daffodils in decoupage.

Marble eggs from Turkey offered for sale to the tourist trade. Originally used as pacifiers, they were popular in the days of the Ottoman Empire and it is believed that they relate to similar objects of jade used by the Chinese. (*From the collection of Louise Alpers Bordaz*)

well or fountain and draw some 'speechless' water; as they bring the water home through the streets, they will hear names being whispered to them. Back home, they water the buried wheat with the 'speechless' water, uttering the following incantation: "I plant you and water you—may the man who is to marry me come soon—so that we may reap you together." They also try to remember the dreams they have seen after having planted the wheat grain.

"In some parts of Greece, women and girls gather in the morning to read the future; even though it is Lent, they often end up by dancing and making merry. Such is the case in the island of Skyros, where the village girls get together on the day of the two St. Theodores to cut the traditional 'salt-pie' (made of salt and flour). The pie is baked, on the eve of the feast, with flour and salt taken from three 'lucky' houses (i.e. houses which have suffered no loss for the last few years) with a Mary or a John in the family. With this dough, the housewife also fashions the letters of the alphabet, which she spreads out on vine-twigs on the terrace, where they will remain exposed to the starlight all night long, side by side with the salt-pie. The letters of the alphabet are covered with a red cloth; each unmarried girl slips her hand under the cloth and draws out a letter: that will be the first letter of her future husband's name. Unmarried girls also put a slice of salt-pie under their pillow at night in the hope of having revealing dreams."

The First Sunday of Lent (Sunday of Orthodoxy) commemorates the triumph of faith over heresy. It is an occasion for the children with plays and parties. At Aperi, on Carpathos, mothers of year-old children bake large buns, which are taken to church with other dishes, where the priest blesses them. A feast follows in the village square.

Since March is unofficially considered the first month of the year and the beginning of summer, winter must be banished on the first day of the month. February, represented as a lame man on a donkey, is escorted by the children, who bang tin cans and sing: "Out with you, lame February, and let March come to us with joy and flowers." Housewives clean house, throw out trash, and break an earthen jug against the front door, saying: "Bad year out—good year in—out with lame February—out with fleas and mice—in come March and Joy and the good housewife."

To counteract the March sun, likely to burn the tender faces of girls and small children, a "March" (flax thread of white and red or gold and red) is tied around the wrist or the big toe, after having been exposed to the stars all night on the branches of a rose bush, to protect the wearer from the sun and other harm. At Kydoniac in Asia Minor, this practice is believed to prevent stumbling. Placed around the handle of a water-jug, the "March thread" keeps water cool. In Carpathos, girls send one to their betrothed as a gift which is to be worn until Easter Sunday. Then it is tied to a rosebush so it will become rose-colored. In other areas, children wear the March thread until they see a swallow and a stork; then they take it off and put it under a stone. After forty days the stone is lifted; if ants are present, it is a sign of happiness and wealth; if worms appear, it means bad luck. This very ancient custom, mentioned by St. John Chrysostom, is probably linked with the Eleusinian mysteries, relating to the goddess Demeter.

In Athens housewives used to dip a handful of grass in freshly drawn water and sprinkle it on sleeping members of the household and the rooms of the house as well, chanting: "So you have come, March? Health has come with you, and a host of little insects. Come in, March, and bring us joy, etc." Green grass and water symbolize health, fertility, prosperity, growth, and youth. To transfer these gifts to animals and humans, one must touch them with a plant.

Perhaps the most imaginative custom of all that are linked with March is the Procession of the Swallow. At Metrae, in Thrace, two children fill a basket with ivy leaves, pass a rod through the handle and attach a wooden swallow, with tiny bells around its neck, to one end of the rod. With this novelty, they go from house to house singing a quaint verse similar in spirit to the ancient *Song of the Swallow*, written by Athenaeus, noted Greek writer of the third century:

See! see! the swallow is here!
She brings a good season, she brings a good year!
White is her breast and black is her crest;
See, the swallow is here.

Ho! roll a fruit cake from your well-filled cot,
Of cheese a fair round, of wine a full pot;
Porridge she'll take and a bite of hardbake;
She never despises good cheer.

Go we away empty to-day?
An thou wilt give us, we'll up and away;
But an thou deny us, O here we shall stay.

Shall we take your door and your lintel also,
Shall we take the good wife that is sitting below?
She's not so tall, but we'll lift her and all—
We can easily bear her away.

If you give us but a little, then God send you more;
The swallow is here! come, open the door;
No graybeards you'll see, but children are we;
So we pray you to give us good cheer.

The housewives who greet the children take a few ivy leaves from the basket and place them in a hen's nest so that they may be assured of an abundance of eggs. Then they give the children a few eggs before they move on to the next farm. Ivy, symbolic of evergreen vegetation, is believed to transfer fecundity and health to hens and other animals.

The Feast of the Forty Martyrs on March 9 memorializes forty Christian martyrs who were put to death in A.D. 320 in Sevastia. All the customs pertaining to this day have to do with the number 40, which has been considered sacred in Greek tradition for centuries. Special dishes prepared for this day use forty ingredients; pies are covered with forty thin layers of pastry; forty pancakes, or a dish including forty kinds of wild herbs, may be served. This food is distributed among the villagers in memory of the dead. A well-known Greek motto declares: "Eat forty, drink forty, and give forty to save your soul." In bygone days, at Mesimvria in Eastern Rumelia, girls wove or embroidered cloth with forty different kinds of thread; men had to drink forty glasses of wine and offer friends another forty; all had to tell forty lies. On the island of Lemnos it is customary to plant trees, vines, and flowers on this day; otherwise they may not thrive. Lambs are weaned on this day. In the same spirit, sweet basil is planted at Metrae in Thrace, so it will grow "green and thick—with forty shoots."

March 25, the Day of the Annunciation, has both religious and national significance. It is also Greek Independence Day, celebrated since 1821, when Greece revolted against Turkish rule. Since it is primarily a spring festival, and the swallows are expected to return from the south on this date, children remove the March threads from around their wrists and sing the swallow song. Shepherds in Crete lead their sheep to pasture saying: "Shear your sheep, ring your bells and go up to the mountains." It is also celebrated as a national feast, with patriotic decor, flags, and slogans. It is a day for a great parade with grown-ups and youngsters wearing national costumes. Soldiers killed in action are honored.

Few countries cherish more ardently a great number of religious and folk customs than does Greece. George A. Megas, noted scholar in the field of folklore, describes the prelude to Holy Week, which "is called Palm Week, and is commonly known as 'Dumb Week,' as no service is held in church throughout this period, except on Friday the eve of the Saturday of Lazarus, when a special evening service is sung. In some provinces the housewives bake special buns for the children; they knead them into the shape of a man in a winding-sheet, as Lazarus himself is traditionally represented. These buns are called 'lazaros,' and exceptional virtues are ascribed to them. In Lesbos the 'lazaros' buns are decorated with currants, walnuts and almonds. . . . The children climb a small hill and roll their buns down the slope. They believe that they will find a partridge's nest near the spot where the bun rolls to a stop.

"On Saturday the village children go from house to house singing special hymns known as 'Lazarakia,' which describe the resurrection of Lazarus. They usually hold a small picture depicting the scene. . . . In Cyprus, Lazarus used to be impersonated by a boy so heavily decked with yellow flowers that his face could hardly be seen. This child was led from house to house by a group of boys. As soon as the boys began to sing the Lazarus hymns, the child lay down on the ground pretending to be dead; he rose to his feet only upon hearing the group calling: 'Lazarus, come out!' It is obvious that this is the most ancient and authentic version of the custom of representing Lazarus' death and resurrection. This resurrection, according to popular conception, is the 'First Easter.'" In many ways a parallel exists between Lazarus in the Christian tradition and Adonis in the ancient Greek festivals.

Since palm trees grow in the warmer parts of Greece, the fronds are used abundantly to decorate the interiors and the exteriors of the churches for Palm Sunday. In the northern provinces sprigs of myrtle and bay are used, a practice that dates from the ninth century. The palm fronds are fashioned into small baskets, stars, half-moons, and crosses, and it is traditional, after the service, for the parish priest to present a *vaya,* a bit of bay or myrtle with a palm cross, to each parishioner. These are taken home and placed in the frame of one of the family icons as protection against harm and disease. Since these mementos of Palm Sunday have been furnished by the congregation for generations, fascinating customs of an elaborate ceremonial nature have evolved. Many of these are linked with ancient fertility rites which embrace not only people and animals but plant life as well.

It was believed that if a pregnant woman was touched with a *vaya* she would have easier confinement. In Skyros, families take their palm crosses home after the service and touch the animals, crops, and even the windmills with them. Those who own sheep tap them similarly and say, "Many happy returns of the day—*vaya, vaya,* happy Easter—next Sunday we shall have red eggs and soft white cheese." In some villages in Eastern Rumelia, village girls used to weave the palm crosses into wreaths, using red thread, and float them in a brook. The girl whose wreath floated by her group of friends first was considered the lucky girl of the year.

Holy Week was one of general solemnity and mourning. In some areas, church bells were silenced ("widowed") and the villagers were summoned to Mass by the town crier. On Good Friday practically all work was suspended. Since "Christ is on the Cross," even the handlooms were taken apart, but it was a day for general housecleaning inside and out. Church included two services daily, and strict fasting was observed by the women, who have always accepted religious discipline more readily than the men. On Tuesday evening of Holy Week, the Gospel passages referring to Mary Magdalene (in many lands, Mary of Bethany), who poured myrrh over the feet of Christ, were read and even "the women of the street" felt obligated to attend. On Wednesday, the faithful were anointed with holy oil, either at church or at home.

Eggs were dyed according to strict ritual on Maundy Thursday, often referred to as Red Thursday. "In many parts of Greece the number of Easter eggs to be dyed, and the methods of dyeing them, are restricted; for instance, they must be dyed with a special variety of red-wood, not with any other kind of coloring. The bowl which will contain the eggs must be new. The dye must not be thrown away or taken out of the house after use. In some villages it is the custom to draw various designs on the eggs, either before dyeing them, with melted wax, or after they have been dyed, with a needle. These eggs are called 'embroidered' or 'partridge' eggs." The first egg dipped into the dye was called the "egg of the Virgin Mary" and was believed to have miraculous powers. "Evangelized" eggs were those sent to the church to be blessed on Maundy Thursday. At Sinope in the Pontus area, it was customary to dye as many eggs as there were people in the house, plus one for the Virgin Mary.

In the evening, the eggs were put in a small box and taken to church where they were placed either behind the altar, or behind the bishop's throne until Easter. Later, when the eggs were eaten, the shells were placed beneath the fruit trees in the garden so that they would bear fruit. An old belief had it that eggs laid on Maundy Thursday, especially those from a black hen or a hen laying for the first time, had miraculous powers.

Easter buns were baked on Maundy Thursday. Each bun was studded with red eggs, dried fruit, and designs made with bits of dough. According to shape, they were called "dolls," "baskets," "bows," "eggs," etc. At Koroni in Messinia, buns were in the shape of a doll. Each housewife baked a large bun for the house, and smaller, doll-shaped ones for her children, nephews, nieces, and godchildren. New married girls prepared special buns for their mothers-in-law.

Despite the festivities in the kitchen, Maundy Thursday has always been a "sacred and austere" occasion in Greece. Services held in all the churches included the Gospel passages referring to the Last Supper. The children took Holy Communion. In the evening, the liturgy of the Twelve Gospels, an unusually long service, lasting well into the night, was read. After the fifth passage, referring to the Crucifixion, the priest placed a large wooden cross in the middle of the church, which the faithful adorned with wreaths of flowers. The women and girls mourned Christ as they would their own dead, with all-night services. Hymns and songs about the Passion included a long religious poem entitled "The Virgin's Lament." While the women carried on the singing, the young girls wove wreaths of flowers to decorate the *Epitaphion* (the wooden bier where Christ's body was to be laid symbolically on Good Friday). All objects used during the Maundy Thursday and Good Friday services were believed to be endowed with divine power.

"At Siyi, in Bithynia, when the time came for the priest to read the first Gospel passage, the children began writing down in all haste as many 'Credos' as they had time for before the priest had finished reading all twelve passages. Just before the end of the service, the children burst into the church shouting triumphantly 'Credos for sale! Credos!' These prayers were usually bought by old women and turned into talismans to be worn by the sick."

Among the faithful, Good Friday was a day of total fast; no work was done; most of the day was spent attending the Descent from the Cross and Christ's funeral (*Epitaphios*). Official participation in church ceremonies by government officials, the closing of stores and offices, and the flying of all flags at half-mast have long served to indicate the meaning of this day among the Greek people. In the villages of Phylia the faithful drank vinegar mixed with soot, since Christ was given vinegar to quench his thirst. The Cretans ate boiled food mixed with vinegar and boiled snails, since their juice resembled bile. In most villages the faithful did not light fires or eat.

Close to noon, the women of the parish decorated the pall, a piece of gold-embroidered cloth, representing His body. Each family sent flowers; "violets, roses, stocks, lemon-blossom—all the flowers of the spring"—were woven into wreaths or bunched. Eventually the pall was smothered in a bower of flowers. Then all flocked to the church to pay homage, and young girls sprinkled the bier with lemon leaves and rose petals. Devout tribute was paid to the dead Savior at the altars of neighboring churches also—a kind of Good Friday pilgrimage.

At dusk, the Epitaphion, or bier, is removed from the church and the funeral procession begins. In the larger cities, it is led by a band; in Athens the bier is followed by the Archbishop as well as representatives of the government and the king.

George A. Megas has described some of the touching tributes paid to Christ on this occasion: "In several parts of Greece the villagers burn incense and light bonfires during the procession; it is not infrequent to see the effigy of Judas hoisted over the bonfire. Bonfires are also lit at Meligala, in Messinia; when the church-bells ring for the Epitaphios, each housewife throws a handful of dry twigs across her threshold and sets fire to them. By the time the procession begins, the twigs have turned to ashes. As the holy Bier passes before her house, the housewife throws a handful of incense on the embers, and the priest—to reward her for having made the air smell sweetly for the passage of Christ's body—pauses to say a prayer for her. At Andritsaina, in the Peloponnese, it is the children's job to gather wood for the fire; they pile the wood in a heap before the church and light it at nightfall. . . . At Kios, in the Propontis, the housewives keep their front doors open during the procession, to let in the Divine Grace. At Metrae, in Thrace, the procession halts before a small country chapel, where an armful of firewood has been stacked with an effigy of Judas propped in the middle of it. While the priest reads the Gospel passage referring to Judas' repentance and death, the villagers light the fire and burn his effigy. . . . In the island of Lesbos there is a strong competitive spirit among the villagers as to who will build the largest fire. Once the fire is lit, they burn a Judas, beginning with his beard."

The women of Serres, and elsewhere in Greece, place an icon of Christ crucified along with a censer and a plate of green shoots of barley or lentils outside their doors. The green growth, started in a flowerpot earlier in Lent, recalls the "gardens of Adonis." During the feast of Adonis, Greek women, wearing mourning, used to display his image in wax on his deathbed, surrounded by flowers and pots of fennel and other herbs which grow and wither rapidly to symbolize either the premature death of the god or the fleeting glory of spring. Scores of other customs and beliefs relating to Good Friday including the Christ-candles, the Christ-flowers, the renewal of yeast and others are a meaningful part of Greek tradition.

On Holy Saturday, in Athens and other cities as well, the churches are decorated with bay leaves, and the priest tosses or scatters laurel leaves as he says: "Arise, O God, to judge the world." The women aim to catch the falling leaves that they may burn them as a talisman against the evil eye; some are used like lavender to put among woolens to keep out moths. At Koroni, in Messinia, villagers break a jug or a pan or shoot off firearms as the bell is rung for this service. The morning service on this day is referred to as the First Resurrection. Then household duties absorb the family. Cake and bread must be baked and the master of the house kills the Paschal lamb, either one chosen from his own flock, preferably a male with the whitest fleece possible, or the best one that he can purchase at market. A visit is made to the cemetery, where a service is held, after which those children who attend are given eggs, nuts, buns, and other goodies. It is a day for dispensing charity in the form of food to those who need it and to those recently bereaved. One who dies on Holy Saturday is especially blessed, for he is in the company of Christ. Faith among the devout is intense.

In the old days live wagtails (similar to warblers) were placed under the laurel leaves and when the priest cried, "Arise, O God . . ." the faithful kicked the leaves, and the birds flew away. As a result of these practices, "the phrase, 'Arise, O God' is often used in modern Greek to denote a loud noise, an uproar, a scene of great animation."

The Resurrection service, the most joyful festival of the Greek Orthodox Church, is observed by Greeks at home and abroad with great ceremony. In the old days it was held early Sunday morning, but as of recent date it is conducted on Saturday night, precisely at midnight. The church is decorated with greens; sprigs of rosemary, the herb sacred to remembrance, are scattered on the floor. People, especially the children, come to church wearing at least one article of new apparel, preferably the shoes. The faithful hold white candles with special ones for children, "decorated with white or blue ribbons, artificial flowers and gold thread." It is traditional for a young man to send his betrothed a candle decorated with white and pink ribbon—as well as new shoes to wear to the Resurrection service.

When the service begins the church is dimly lighted; then the lights are put out. Suddenly the door of the sanctuary swings open, and the priest appears holding a lighted candle: "Come ye, partake of the never-setting Light and glorify Christ, who is risen from the dead," he chants. Members of the congregation light their candles from the one held by the priest and pass the light on to their neighbors, until the entire church is ablaze with light. At Rapsomati, in Arcadia, newly married girls are the first to receive the Light; then they kiss the priest's hand. In Athens, girls attempt to light their candles from those held by the men present so that they will marry soon. After partaking of the Light, the congregation follows the priest outdoors where he reads the Gospel. Finally he intones the psalm: "Christos anesti" (Christ is risen"). The congregation swing their candles rhythmically as they accompany him, while church bells ring, guns and fireworks resound, and ships in the harbor blow their whistles. Then the faithful say to one another: "Christ is risen!" and the reply is, "He is risen indeed." Following this response, they exchange the "kiss of the Resurrection," sometimes called the "kiss of Love," which, in some places, takes place with great solemnity within the church. On the island of Chios it was customary also to exchange church pews as a sign of love. All feuds and quarrels are forgiven and forgotten.

The Blessing of Red Eggs, referred to as the "Eggs of the Resurrection" or the "Eggs of the Good Word," was an intimate part of this service since the eggs were believed to have miraculous qualities. At Sinope, the housewife placed as many eggs in a basket as there were members in her family and took them to church to be blessed. In Western Macedonia, the eggs were placed under the icon of Christ by the entrance to the sanctuary. At Hassia in Macedonia, after the service each parishioner broke his egg on a wooden clapper (which took the place of the bell) hanging outside the church. In some parts of Greece, Paschal lambs were blessed and distributed to the congregation by the priest, after which pieces were carried home and a portion was given to each member of the family "in a spirit of communion." It was considered a good omen to keep one's candle lighted all the way home.

Traditional and Regional Recipes

Spinch-and-Cheese Pie (Spanakopitta)

1 bunch scallions, chopped	8 oz. cottage cheese
1 cup plus 2 tbsp. butter	2 tbsp. farina
2 lbs. spinach, washed and drained	½ cup chopped parsley
	½ cup fresh dill
6 eggs, lightly beaten	Salt and pepper to taste
½ lb. feta cheese, crumbled	
¾ to 1 lb. phyllo pastry (purchase at a Greek bakery)	

Sauté the scallions in 2 tbsp. of butter until tender. Chop the spinach and place in a large pan. Cover and cook until wilted. Drain, pressing out as much moisture as possible. Preheat oven to 375° F. Place a small cooky sheet with edge or bottom round from a 10-inch spring from pan on the oven shelf.

Mix together the scallions, eggs, feta, cottage cheese, farina, parsley, dill, and spinach. Season lightly with salt and pepper. Melt the remaining butter, and butter a two-quart decorated ring mold. Unfold the phyllo pastry and place under a damp towel. Remove one sheet of pastry, brush with melted butter, cut into two, lengthwise, and place diagonally across the mold. Allow it to extend about one and one half inches over the sides of the pan; fit it down into the pan and over the center opening. Press against the sides of the mold. Repeat with other sheets of pastry, working around and around the mold with the strips to give even layers. Use a total of one half to three quarters of the pastry in successive layers.

Fill with the spinach mixture. Cut out and discard the disk of pastry covering the center hole. Brush another sheet of pastry with butter and cut into half-moons to fit over the filling. Repeat with several layers. Draw the overhanging pieces of dough up over covered filling. Place on the cooky sheet (to catch butter drips) and reduce the oven temperature to 350° F. Bake 1¼ hours or until golden brown and puffed. Let stand in the mold 5 to 15 minutes before unmolding onto a warm platter. Yield: 10 to 12 servings.

Stuffed Lamb (Arni Yemesto)

Although raisins and chestnuts or blanched almonds are often used to stuff lamb in Greece, this recipe is a favorite in the Dodecanese Islands.

1 cup uncooked regular or processed white rice	1 cup light or dark raisins
½ cup hot butter or margarine	1 4-lb. cushion shoulder lamb roast
1 lb. chuck beef, ground once	½ tsp. salt
½ lb. calf liver, ground once	¼ tsp. pepper
1 large onion, peeled, grated	¼ cup butter or margarine
2 tsp. salt	⅓ cup lemon juice
¾ tsp. pepper	6 fringed leek stalks
1 tsp. powdered cinnamon	1 large onion, in rings
2 tbsp. snipped mint leaves	1¾ oz. bottle green olives
	9 or 10 lemon wedges
	Fresh dill

Start heating oven to 325° F. Cook rice as label directs. Meanwhile, in ½ cup butter or margarine, heated in large skillet, sauté beef, calf liver, and grated onion till onion is golden. Remove from heat; add 2 tsp. salt, ¾ tsp. pepper, cinnamon, mint, raisins, and cooked rice. Rub pocket of lamb shoulder with ½ tsp. salt, ¼ tsp. pepper; fill with meat and rice stuffing; skewer in place. Place lamb in shallow roasting pan; dot with ¼ cup butter; sprinkle with lemon juice. Roast, basting often, for 2 to 2½ hours, or to 182° F. on meat thermometer. Place rest of stuffing in baking dish; cover with sheet of foil. Bake along with lamb, last half hour of roasting. When lamb is done, arrange it on heated large platter with extra stuffing heaped near pocket in lamb. If desired, garnish with leek stalks, onion in rings, green olives, lemon wedges, and fresh dill. Makes 6 servings.

Roast Lamb, Roman Style (Abbaccio Al Forno)

1 5-lb. leg of baby lamb	2 tbsp. dried rosemary
6 cloves garlic	1 tsp. black pepper
1 tbsp. salt	½ to ¾ cup olive oil

Remove skin from lamb. Cut 2 cloves garlic into thin slivers. Make several gashes in lamb with sharp pointed knife and insert a garlic sliver in each. Crush remaining garlic and combine with salt, rosemary, and pepper. Pound to a paste, adding olive oil gradually to make a fairly thick, spreadable paste. Spread over lamb, rubbing in well, and let stand at room temperature for 3 hours. Roast in a preheated 375° F. oven for one to 1½ hours. Baste frequently with olive oil. Slice and serve with skimmed pan juices. Serves 6 to 8.

Baklava

1¾ cups sugar	3 cups coarsely ground walnuts or slivered blanched almonds
Juice of ½ lemon	
2 tbsp. rose water	1 recipe Puff Pastry or 1 package frozen phyllo pastry, thawed
⅔ cup butter, melted, or peanut oil	

Bring 1½ cups sugar and ½ cup water to a boil and simmer until very thick and sugar spins a thread (215° F. on a candy thermometer). Add the lemon juice, simmer for 5 minutes, skimming carefully. Flavor with 1 tbsp. rose water and cool. Add half the melted butter, cooled, to the nuts and mix to a paste with remaining sugar and remaining rose water. If using puff pastry, roll out to a large square 16 by 16 inches, ⅛ inch thick. Cut the pastry into 4 8-by-8 pieces. Butter or oil an 8-by-8-inch cake pan. Line cake pan with 1 piece of pastry. Spread with a layer of nut mixture. Repeat layers, ending with pastry. If using the phyllo pastry, brush each leaf with melted butter or oil. Use 10 leaves for each layer; spread with squares or diamonds with a very sharp knife. Pour on remaining butter and bake in a preheated 425° F. oven for 10 minutes. Lower heat to 375° F. and bake for 35 to 40 minutes or until well puffed and golden. Remove and pour on the syrup. Cool before serving.

Puff Pastry

2 cups sweet butter	1 teaspoon salt
4 cups flour	

Knead the butter until waxy. Shape into a flat, square cake, wrap in foil, and refrigerate. Sift the flour with the salt into a bowl. Gradually add about 1½ cups water (not all may be needed) and knead on a lightly floured board until dough is smooth and elastic—about 20 to 30 minutes. Wrap the dough in foil or in a cloth well wrung out in cold water; chill for 30 minutes. Roll it out on a well-floured board into a ½-inch thick square. Roll edges a little thinner than center. Lightly flour the square of butter and place in the center of the dough. Fold the 4 edges of the dough to completely cover the butter, sealing edges. Roll out with a floured rolling pin, rolling forward only, until a long rectangle is obtained. Should dough tear, take a little dough from the edges and mend immediately to entrap air. Strip should be about 8 inches wide and 16 inches long. Fold a third of the strip over and bring opposite end over this so as to have 3 layers of dough. Pass rolling pin lightly over edges to seal. Turn the pastry a quarter turn and repeat rolling and folding. Wrap, chill for 30 minutes, unwrap, and repeat rolling, folding, and chilling 4 times more, always keeping edges of dough facing you when rolling out. The last 2 "turns" should be made just before pastry is used.

Grecian Feast Bread

1 pkg. hot roll mix	2 eggs
⅓ cup each raisins, chopped citron, candied cherries, chopped almonds	¾ cup sifted confectioners' sugar mixed with 1½ tbsp. cream

Sprinkle yeast from roll-mix package over ¾ cup warm water; dissolve; add an unbeaten egg, an egg yolk, and the dry mix. Let rise at 85 to 90° temperature until doubled in size, taking 30 to 60 minutes. Turn out on floured surface and knead in raisins, candied cherries, citron, and almonds.

122

Divide dough into three parts. Shape each into smooth ball shape and place on greased baking sheet 1 inch apart, in a 3-leaf clover design. Let rise in warm place until doubled in size, again 30 to 60 minutes. Brush tops with beaten egg white. Bake at 375° F. 25 to 30 minutes until golden brown. Glaze while still warm with confectioners' sugar combined with cream. Decorate with blanched almonds and candied cherries.

Greek Easter Eggs (Kokina Avga)

Carefully wash and dry each egg. Set a large pot of water to boil. Add a red dye or food coloring and ¾ cup of vinegar to the water, and boil for a few minutes. Slowly lower the eggs into the pot, and when the water comes to a boil, lower the heat. Let the eggs simmer for 15 minutes, then remove them carefully from the pot. If you plan to cook more eggs, add 2 more tablespoons vinegar to the water. Wipe cooked eggs with an oil-soaked cotton ball, then wipe each egg with a clean dry cloth. Place on a platter. Serve cold.

Hungary

At Carnival season, young Hungarian men go about the villages deriding those girls whom they consider "too proud," particulary those who, in their minds, have refused a suitor for insufficient reasons. They stand outside the culprit's door singing a mocking little song, which can be mere teasing, as it is supposed to be, or actually spiteful.

Probably a survival of a pre-Christian ritual, the traditional battles between Prince Cibere and King Bone are acted out in Hungary, typifying the strict Lenten season and its joyous ending. Prince Cibere, representing winter, is a straw-and-rag figure who fights the good King Bone on Shrove Tuesday and overcomes him. While Prince Cibere reigns, all go hungry, but on Palm Sunday there is another battle, and this one King Bone wins. The vanquished prince is carried around the village by the crowd, singing and shouting, and then is either burned or drowned, or thrown over the parish boundary. With him go hunger, illness, personal sorrows, and the danger of hail and storms, according to an old belief.

The Hungarians call Lent the "great Fast" (*Nag y böyt*). "Tomorrow is Ash Wednesday," sing the Hungarians. "Tomorrow it won't be as it is today," they lament.

Centuries ago, on Palm Sunday, it was customary to bless not only branches but also the various flowers of the season. In fact, the flowers are still mentioned in the antiphons after the prayer of blessing. Thus, the name "Flower Sunday" (*Virágvasarnap*) is used in Hungary.

Easter is referred to as the "Feast of Meat" (*Husvet*) because the eating of meat is resumed after the long fast. A meat loaf, served on the great feast day, is made of chopped pork, ham, eggs, bread, and spices.

Easter eggs, like those of neighboring countries, prepared weeks in advance of the day, are beautifully hand-painted—carrying messages, quotes from Scripture, or figures of a man and a woman in costume—and are outstanding examples of eggcraft. Many of the simpler eggs are white with a red flower pattern drawn on them. Hungarian children exchange painted eggs with each other as tokens of friendship.

Easter Monday, *Loscolkodas* (Dousing Day) in Hungary, provides for plenty of mischief. Boys surprise their girl friends by dousing them thoroughly with buckets or bottles of water, all the while reciting a little rhyme:

Water for your health,
Water for your home,
Water for your land:
Here's water, water!
Don't shriek and cry and run away;
It's good for you on Dyngus day.

Formerly this practice was much rougher, for young men literally dragged girls to ponds or streams at dawn and threw them in. It was expected that the girls would accept it all good-naturedly and reward their tormentors with Easter eggs, hard rolls, or a glass of brandy—or all three. The dousing was supposed to make them good future wives.

Two views of an Easter wedding egg from Hungary decorated about 1912. This elaborately painted goose egg portrays the bride on one side and the groom on the other, both wearing traditional Hungarian wedding garments. It was considered the most important gift for those married at Eastertide. (*From the collection of Priscilla Sawyer Lord; photos: Photographic Illustrators Corp.*)

Ireland

*I*N a small country largely devoted to agriculture where memories are long and folklore is a part of everyday life, the storytelling tradition has helped materially to keep ancient customs alive together with a speech pattern that has made them all the more meaningful. Until a decade ago, the life of the rural Irish was truly pictured in their speech. Gaelic thinking and the Gaelic idiom, superimposed on the English speech which they adopted centuries ago, made their drama and their ability at storytelling unique. As a consequence, when William Butler Yeats, John Millington Synge, Lady Gregory, Douglas Hyde, and a host of others launched the Irish literary renaissance at the turn of the century, they brought to life pure Elizabethan English in the Irish idiom. The patter of the "stage Irishman," so familiar to the American ear, is not only gross exaggeration of true Irish speech, but woefully inaccurate as tourists in recent years have discovered. This little country—a great island some 300 miles long and only 170 miles wide—is pecularly homogeneous because of its predominantly Catholic population, dispersed in countless small villages. It is in these intimate communities that folklore has been cherished and kept alive, more so than in the cities. However, like the rest of the world, Ireland has undergone great change during the past twenty years, and many of the old folkways have largely disappeared or been forgotten. Fortunately, many of them have been carefully documented by the Irish Folklore Commission at University College, Dublin.

Romance and marriage are closely linked with the Easter season in Ireland. Ancient conviction and ecclesiastical decree held that marriages were not solemnized during Lent. Accordingly, Shrovetide was a favorite marrying time and the period prior to it was a busy one for the matchmakers. (Matches made during the penitential season resulted in marriages after Easter.) A wedding in the village provided the last fling before the forty-day observance of Lent began. Dancing, feasting, and drinking and "all the other jollifications" that attended the occasion were greatly enjoyed, but woe to the confirmed bachelor or old maid who would not budge from the family hearth. Talk was one thing and talk the neighbors did when the object of derision was the "boy" or the "girl" still under the thumb of domineering parents.

"Drawing the log," as recorded by Mr. and Mrs. C. S. Hall more than a century ago, took place in the city of Waterford on Ash Wednesday. "It was instituted as a penitential exercise to the bachelors and maidens who permitted Lent to arrive without 'joining in the holy bands.' The log was a large piece of timber, to which a long rope was attached; it was drawn through the streets of the city, followed by a crowd of men and boys of the lowest grade armed with bludgeons, shouting and hollering 'Come draw the log, come draw the log; bachelors and maids, come draw the log.' The party had generally a piper, who squeezed from his bags the most noted of the national airs; and it was no small part of the frolic to see the poor minstrel upset in the mire by the jolting of the unwieldy piece of timber over the rugged stones with which the streets were paved." Like many another rough-and-tumble custom, drawing the log fell into oblivion in the nineteenth century.

In the county of Waterford and elsewhere, the whitewashed walls of the homes of bachelors were daubed with tar and inscribed with graffiti; on occasion, the unlucky lad was ducked in a nearby pond or horse trough by his friends. Donegal boys had a way of putting a rough effigy of a woman near a bachelor's gate to embarrass him. On market day, the Thursday after Ash Wednesday, salt was shaken on the derelict who had failed to marry, to keep him fresh and healthy until the next Shrovetide. It was in parts of Galway and Mayo, as well as at Mullingar in Westmeath, that they threw the salt. Ashes were used in a similar way. Tricks of every kind including the blowing of horns, beating on buckets and cans, stopping up chimneys, removing gates, and tying cartwheels to the roof were typical shenanigans reserved for those who failed to marry. Chalk Sunday, the first in the Lenten season, provided an occasion for great mirth for the small boys of the village, who marked eligible lads and lasses alike with chalk on their way to or from church. Raddling was a more offensive practice since it referred to being marked with the permanent color used in identifying sheep. Chalking was a practice well understood especially in Clare, Kerry, Limerick, and Tipperary.

Tossing pancakes over the open fire was a highlight of Shrove Tuesday. The family gathered around the fireside together with the young boys and girls, their older brothers and sisters, and friends in the neighborhood for an evening of fun and eating. Each in turn tried his skill at tossing. The first performance was given by the "eldest unmarried daughter of the host," who was usually a bit shaken since her "luck" for the coming year depended on the success with which she turned over the batter cake in the air and reversed it "without a ruffle on its surface." The girl who failed usually dropped her cake among the turf ashes and, consequently, would have no chance to marry for a year at least. The winner, on the other hand, could have her "pick of the boys" whenever she liked. Some of the "boys" were in their thirties and others a bit older. The cake she tossed was cut and shared with all present and, if her mother's wedding ring turned up in a piece of it, the recipient would surely be the first married and would have doubly good fortune in his mate. A lad whose elbow was jogged in tossing was likely to "toss the cake crooked."

The fact that palm was hard to come by in Ireland failed to dampen the ardor of the countryfolk in their observance of Palm Sunday. Branches of spruce, cypress, and silver fir sufficed; "sprigeens" of yew, often worn by the men in their hats, led to the habit of calling these conifers palms, which they do not remotely resemble. Some kinds of palm have been introduced to the subtropical climate of Killarney, where they flourish. Palm distributed in the city churches came from the warm parts of Europe. As elsewhere in Europe, a piece of palm was hung in the best room or placed over a religious picture and usually a bit of it found its way into the cattle byre as a symbol of protection from harm.

126

Good Friday was the day of the black fast as Kevin O'Danaher, noted Irish folklore scholar, reminds us: "Women and girls did not do up their hair, but let it hang loose over their shoulders. A most rigorous black fast was kept, in which no milk, butter, sauce or condiment of any kind was taken with food. In many seaside places it was customary not even to eat fish on this day, but to substitute for it limpets, periwinkles, and other shellfish gathered on the shore. People walked barefoot to visit the church and do reverence to the crucifix, and very commonly, people went to the churchyard on this day to pray at the graves of their dead relatives."

On Easter Saturday every household was represented at the village church since water was blessed on this day and distributed. Each member of the household was besprinkled with holy water, and the usual sprinkler was a little frond of the Palm Sunday "palm." Following this ceremony, the water was used to bless the house and the cattle as well. Then each member of the family took three sips in the name of the Holy Trinity. Faith is an integral part of Irish family life, and this custom is still observed.

The ceremony of the Paschal fire, first kindled on Easter Saturday night A.D. 433 by St. Patrick, took place on Slane Hill in the valley of the Boyne River, some twenty-eight miles from Dublin. At the time he is said to have proclaimed the establishment of Christianity throughout Ireland. The practice of a spring bonfire had its roots deep in Druidic rites which Patrick was eager to supplant. The Germanic nations had a similar tradition of spring bonfires, obviously pagan in origin, which the Church frowned upon and eventually suppressed. However, the fact that Irish clerics were present on the Continent in the Dark Ages and brought their customs with them resulted in the rite's being accepted by the Church fathers as a part of the Easter observance.

Easter Sunday in Ireland, as in all predominantly Catholic countries, is one of the greatest feasts of the year, equaled in importance only by Christmas. According to a pious old legend dating back to the Middle Ages, the rising sun danced or made "three cheerful jumps" on the morning of the Resurrection. The rays of light which penetrated the clouds were believed to be angels dancing for joy. Grown-ups and children alike used to rise early on Easter Sunday morning in the hope of seeing this marvelous performance. In some households, youngsters set a mirror or a pan of water in an east window to catch the sun's rays and by rocking either one would cause the reflection to dance on the wall or the ceiling.

Kevin O'Danaher again reminds us: "Eggs in large quantities must appear on the breakfast table, and everybody should eat as many of them as possible. Failure to consume at least four or five is looked upon as a very poor effort, while some heroes put away a dozen or more. And someone is sure to tell how, in his grandfather's time, a stout servant boy lowered the most incredible numbers of them, for no housewife would venture to call a halt for reasons of economy to such a spirited observance of the time honoured ritual. Sometimes the children had been collecting eggs on their own account, and had a private feast on them, boiled over a little fire in a quiet corner in the open."

The "better-off" farmers sent presents of eggs to their poorer neighbors. An ancient saying among Irish countryfolk went like this: "One egg for the true gentleman; two eggs for the gentleman; three eggs for the churl (have-not); four eggs for the lowest churl (tramp)."

Gifts included meat also, for Easter Sunday was one day when even the poorest of the poor had meat for dinner according to ancient custom. Those who could do so slaughtered a bullock, a sheep, or a pig for the occasion. Fruit cakes filled with raisins and citron and other dainties were on hand, and no caller would go hungry when tea was served. Spring housecleaning had to be completed by Easter so that there was a freshness about everything.

From the *Journal of the Cork Historical and Archaeological Society* we learn that it was the custom on Easter Sunday to decorate the trees outside the cottage door with eggshells, hanging them on the branches like blossoms in honor of the occasion. From this custom, a small townland in the parish of Kilbolane, in Orrery and Kilmore barony, is said to derive its name of Bally-nablay ("The Town of the Blossoms"), sometimes written "Blossomville." Ballynablay townland is now merged into that of Gortnagoul—"The Field or Garden at the Fork" of the Deel River.

In some Irish villages, on Easter eve, Whitsunday, and the feast day of the patron saint of the parish, the cake dance was the order of the day. Sir William Robert Wilde described it in an issue of the *Dublin University Magazine,* published in 1850. It was usually held on a Sunday evening at a crossroads or a public house. A large cake—similar to barmbrack (speckled bread), a fruit loaf—decorated with "a variety of apocryphal birds, fabulous fishes, and outlandish quadrupeds, such as are only known in heraldic zoology, raised in bold relief on its upper crust, was placed on the top of a churn-dash, and tied over with a clean white cloth; the staff of the churn-dash was then planted outside the door as a sign of the fun and amusement going on within." The man judged to be the best dancer was awarded the cake, which he presented to his partner, usually the girl of his choice for a bride. It was then divided among the guests, and the festivities continued. From this custom came the expression "He takes the cake." A similar custom prevailed in ancient Greece. The famous "cakewalk," a dance popular with southern American Negros, ended with the awarding of a cake to the most graceful pair of strutters.

Dubliners celebrate the Easter season at Fairyhouse on the rolling plains of Meath, some fifteen miles outside their fair city, by attending the annual steeplechase meeting of the Ward Union Staghounds. The Irish Grand National is run on Easter Monday. The gorse bushes are a blaze of yellow and when the weather is not capricious the clear blue sky complements the setting. Cardsharpers and tic-tac men add to the noise and the liveliness of the day as they compete for attention with the bookies, the tinkers (or gypsies), and the "white-aproned women out from Dublin's Moore Street" peddling baskets of oranges and chocolates.

Ireland is as full of stories as there are stars in the sky on a clear winter's night and not the least of them is one concerning a recipe for a Lenten soup that was the favorite of St. Columba, who lived in the sixth century. In those days rigid fasting was an integral part of Lent, and this man of the cloth gave orders to his cook to make a broth of nettles and water with a touch of salt added on Sundays. The cook, a lay brother, was concerned about the meagerness of the ingredients and questioned Columba, who replied that nothing more was to be added "except what comes out of the potstick." After a few weeks of this rigid diet, the saint grew so thin and weak that the cook became alarmed. Then, suddenly, the saintly man improved in appearance and weight since the cook had made himself a hollow potstick into which he poured milk and oatmeal. Thus, he saved his master's life, for he could honestly declare that nothing went into the broth but what came out of the potstick. Maura Laverty in her book *Feasting Galore* gives this glorified version of "Brothchán Buidhe," which is pronounced "Brohawn Bwee," meaning yellow broth:

4 cups chicken stock	1 small carrot
4 tbsp. butter	1¾ cups spinach
¼ cup flour	2 tbsp. cream
2 tbsp. flake oatmeal	Pepper and salt to taste
1 medium onion	1 tbsp. parsley
1 stalk celery	

To stock add onion, chopped celery, carrot, and salt and pepper to taste. Cook 30 minutes. Knead butter and flour together and add to stock. Sprinkle in oatmeal and add chopped spinach. Simmer 15 minutes. Pass through a sieve, correct seasoning, stir in cream. Sprinkle with minced parsley.

Irish pancakes made with buttermilk, served with sweet butter and powdered sugar, are hard to beat, but buttermilk is not easy to come by these days. Every age has its delights and delicacies and ours is one that enjoys the flavor of liquor in cookery. Here is a contemporary recipe which appeared in *Ireland of the Welcomes,* the official organ of the Irish Tourist Board, that speaks for itself. It is obviously a twentieth-century recipe since no self-respecting Irish cook, at the turn of the century, would have wasted Irish whiskey on diced peaches:

Cailín Deas (Pretty Girl) Pancakes

Batter	*Filling*
½ lb. flour	Diced peaches soaked in Irish
1 egg	whiskey, topped with whipped
2 egg yolks	cream to which Irish whiskey has
¾ pint milk	been added.

Place batter in cold place to settle for 2 hours. Place diced peaches in saucepan with Irish whiskey and heat gently. Make very thin pancakes; leave open on plates; add filling and cream.

Italy

In Italy, Carnevale begins January 17 and continues until Ash Wednesday. As with carnivals the world over, the Italians accelerate their ceremonies during the last three days prior to Lent, especially on Martedi Grasso (Shrove Tuesday). Masquerades, dancing—especially the tarantella—pageants, and music all add to the merriment. Each town and hamlet has its own interpretation of the season and each elects its own "King of the Carnival," with one important stipulation—the king must be fat, since he symbolizes eating and drinking, the essence of pre-Lenten revelry. Each king is attended by four harlequins. In Venice the king is actually a straw body, stuffed with firecrackers and explosives. When his reign has terminated, he is burned at midnight in the Piazza San Marco—a demise that is as loud as it is exciting.

On the fourth Sunday of Lent (Mezza Quaresima), a witchlike hag, *Quaresima*, is the center of attraction. In Venice the young people dance around her rag-stuffed effigy ecstatically to celebrate the fact that Lent is half gone. Children are given toys on this day in the guise of a lean, old woman with seven legs, each leg representing a week of the seven weeks of Lent.

Fronds from the date palms, grown in Bordighera, are shipped all over Italy for Holy Week. On Palm Sunday, in some communities, fronds are plaited into crosses and trimmed with roses, lilies, and other flowers; in others they are unadorned. It is also a favorite practice to apply silver and gold paint to olive branches. Both are blessed at the morning Mass. To dramatize the event, the officiating priests leave the church in procession and knock at a closed door, representing the gate of Jerusalem. When it is thrown open, they make their triumphal entry amid the waving of palms and glorious music.

Rome is the city where many tourists as well as native Italians wish to be during Holy Week. Hence, there are many pilgrimages to Saint Peter's and the Vatican at this season of the year. On the eve of Passion Sunday, it used to be the custom in churches, not only in Rome but throughout the world, to drape all crucifixes, statues, and pictures in deep purple cloth as a sign of mourning. This old practice originated in Rome, where the images in the papal chapel in the Vatican were shrouded simultaneously as the deacon chanted the concluding words of the Sunday Gospel, "Jesus hid himself and went out of the temple."

Ceremonies at St. Peter's Basilica are especially colorful. On Palm Sunday, the Pope is borne aloft in an elaborate procession for the blessing of the palms. This ceremony marks the beginning of Holy Week in Rome.

Holy Thursday, also known as Maundy Thursday, marks the feast of the Last Supper, the washing of the feet of His disciples by Christ, and the message of brotherly love which He gave to His disciples: "A new commandment I give unto you, that ye love one another." This was a new mandate, which in the French is spelled *maunde,* one explanation for the name Maundy Thursday. Each year, the Pope washes the feet of thirteen men in St. Peter's. Twelve represent the apostles, and the thirteenth symbolizes the angel who came to the table, according to tradition, when Gregory the Great was officiating at the Last Supper ceremony in the sixth century. In monasteries, each member of the order performed this act for as many men as he was years old.

Sometimes this day is also referred to as Green Thursday, or the Day of the Green Ones, in reference to the old custom of readmitting penitents to the church. (In the early days of the Roman Church, those who had committed serious sins appeared at church on Ash Wednesday to beg forgiveness and receive penance which they carried out during the Lenten fast.) The penitents wore sprigs of green herbs to express their joy and were referred to as the "green ones." Green vestments were worn by the priests for the same reason.

On this day, the Sepulcher of Christ is prepared for the Good Friday services. The Host is ceremoniously placed on the altar of a side chapel, which, on the following day, represents the sepulcher. On Easter Sunday, before High Mass, the Pope embraces the three youngest cardinals, who meet him as he approaches the altar. In the seventeenth century, the Benedictines at Bobbio augmented a ceremony for the blessing of the lambs which was adopted in Rome. For many centuries the main course served to the Pope on Easter Sunday was roast lamb.

On the evening of Easter Sunday, one of the most impressive sights in Rome is the illumination of St. Peter's. The entire majestic cathedral becomes a mass of flickering lights which are fixed against the dark sky and outline every architectural detail. After an hour or two, the lights slowly change to a reddish hue, gradually fading, and it is only then that the thousands of spectators leave.

The solemnity of Good Friday is acted out in every corner of Italy. Dramatic processions of men carrying crosses and wearing crowns of thorns, and boys carrying large candles, are true expressions of pathos. In Italy the common barberry (*Berberis vulgaris*) is considered the source of Christ's crown. For generations the memory of Judas was kept alive at the church at St. Croce in Florence, Italy. On Good Friday morning, it was the custom for the boys to obtain bunches of willow tied with colored ribbons which they took to church. At a point in the service, they beat the pews with the willow rods and gave vent to their feelings as they "thrashed Judas."

In Rome and elsewhere, Easter Saturday, or Easter Eve, is often referred to as a day of preparation for the "Lord's Day of Joy." The ceremonies, which include the blessing of the water, the Paschal candle, and the new fire, are traditional among Catholics. When blessing the water for baptism took place, it was the custom to bless the rivers, the wells, and the brooks also. In both Catholic and Episcopal churches, new fire used to be kindled at midnight by striking a flint against steel. People gathered in a darkened church to remind them of Christ in the tomb as they witnessed the making of light. Once the flint was struck against steel and flame was made, the Paschal candle was lighted, and then followed the lighting of all the other candles in the church, including those carried by the congregation. The church bells are silent from Holy Thursday until Easter eve, when they are rung at noon, following the Mass of Glory.

Perhaps the most impressive ceremony of all held in Italy at Easter takes place in Florence with the Scoppio del Carro, the "Bursting of the Cart," which takes place at noon on Easter Sunday in the Piazza del Duomo, fronting the Cathedral of Santa Maria del Fiore. Since thousands attend this spectacle, the noise is deafening and viewing space is at a premium. This festival commemorates not only the blessing of the new fire, but also a historic event in which Jerusalem's walls were stormed during the Crusades by a band of soldiers that included one Florentine citizen named Pazzi. Later, his family, residing in Florence, inaugurated this annual ceremony, the story of which has been perpetuated in a legend, *The Sacred Flame,* by Selma Lagerlöf. Long before midday an oxcart is drawn into the square. Halting it immediately before the church door, the driver leads the oxen away leaving the cart with its conelike structure for all to see. Spiraling up the cone are rows of bright red pompons. As soon as the cart is ready, uniformed men perform a flag-tossing routine, preliminary fanfare for the ending of the High Mass, within the cathedral. There, as the priest strikes the revered historic flint, a miniature skyrocket shaped like a dove suddenly shoots from the altar along a previously arranged wire, out through the door and into the square, setting ablaze the red pompons. Actually there are timed fireworks tastefully draped over the cart and as they go off like clockwork, ascending the structure, the crowd watches eagerly. If one misfires, it means that Florence and the Florentines will not have a good year, but if all ignite, the peasants believe that the crops will be not only good, but abundant. When the fireworks have faded, the flag-throwers repeat their drill amid a hubbub of shouts, following which a joyous celebration takes place.

In the early days of Christianity, the Easter eve vigil was observed in the midst of great illumination. Rulers set up and ignited great pillars of wax to make their cities as bright as day. Candles, lamps, and torches were used by private citizens in front of their homes. In the churches, the great Paschal candle and quantities of smaller tapers, symbols of Christ as the maker of light, provided the gleam and glory that must have made a profound impression on the faithful as they waited through the night of watching for the dawn.

The chocolate factory in Perugia, where the world-famous chocolates are made, is a busy place in the months prior to Easter. It is here that the hollow Easter eggs are made. An Easter egg with a surprise inside is a part of every Italian home—the bigger the egg, the better. Not all the eggs are made for children; grown-ups enjoy surprises, too, and one designed for an

Each year on Easter Sunday, thousands of believers crowd St. Peter's Square in Rome. Pope Paul VI is shown imparting his blessings from the center of the Basilica, while a sculpted figure bearing a cross looks down on the crowd. (*Photo: United Press International*)

Clemente Cardinal Micara, Prefect of the Holy Congregation of Rites, leads a procession of hooded priests through the Roman Colosseum. This Way of the Cross ceremony, which is celebrated yearly during the week preceding Easter, is one of the few remaining ceremonies in which the Hooded Brotherhood of Death still appears in public. (*Acme Photograph by Albert Blasetti*)

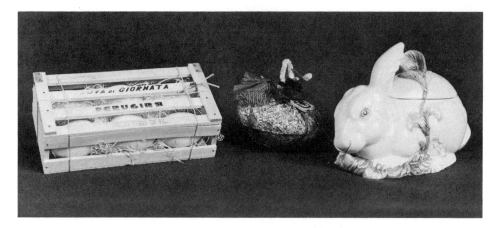

Miniature hens' eggs made of sugar, a foil-wrapped chocolate egg, and a small ceramic rabbit tureen are all from Italy. (*Photo: Photographic Illustrators Corp.*)

adult may cost as much as 60,000 lire ($100)! They are attractively wrapped in fancy gilt wrappings and colored cellophane and tied with beautiful ribbons There is an egg to fit everyone's pocketbook.

The importance of wearing new clothes at Easter is older than the dictates of fashion or high-powered advertising. In the early days of the Church, baptism was administered to converts at Easter, and after the ceremony they put on white garments as a sign of joy. However small or insignificant, a bit of new wearing apparel had to be worn on Easter Day—even a pair of shoelaces, a bit of ribbon, or a fresh feather. Woe to him who did not heed this custom, for the crows (or the pigeons or some other bird) would single out the culprit and put their mark on him! For centuries, even in pagan times, it had been the custom to put on new clothes for the spring festivals. A pair of gloves sent to a girl on Easter eve meant that her suitor had serious intentions and, if the recipient wore them, marriage was more or less assured.

Foods have a special part in all Italian holidays and celebrations, and Easter time is no exception. All over Italy the children enjoy a rich bread shaped like a crown and studded with colored Easter egg candies. Other cakes made for the young are molded in the shape of either a cock or a lamb.

Hertha Pauli has written a beguiling young children's story, *The First Easter Rabbit*. Its setting is an island in the middle of an Italian lake and its two principal characters are Saint Francis of Assisi and the first Easter rabbit.

In Genoa at Easter time the *torta pasqualina* is one of the famous dishes. It is composed of chopped artichoke, greens, green peas, egg, milk, and cheese baked in flaky piecrust. In this same town, in the Cathedral of San Lorenzo, built in the year 1100, one may see an emerald cup which the Crusaders had brought from Caesarea, the cup our Lord was said to have used at the Last Supper.

134

A homemade tart made especially for Good Friday is the accomplishment of cooks in Apuli. *Focaccia piena* consists of black olives, onions, capers, chicory, and anchovies between two layers of pastry. Figs grown in the garden of the Cistercian Convent in Rome, when cut through, reveal a green cross inlaid on white pulp. At Easter, the *columba pasquale,* an Easter bread shaped like a dove, makes its appearance in Lombardy. In Rome, *caprelto,* a milk-fed kid, is the traditional Easter meat, and stuffed artichokes are baked until they are so tender every bit of them may be eaten:

Stuffed Artichokes Baked (Carciofi Arrostiti)

Soak and trim artichokes. Drain them well. Make a dressing of:

Bread crumbs	Grated Parmesan cheese
Minced garlic or onion	Chopped parsley
Chopped celery	Salt and paprika

Chopped anchovies or anchovy paste

Push the dressing down between the leaves. The choke may be removed if desired and the center filled with the dressing. Pour a little olive oil over the artichokes. Place them in a baking dish and cover the bottom of the dish with ¼ inch boiling water or stock. Bake them covered in a moderate oven until they are done—about 1 hour. Baste frequently with olive oil or stock.

Traditional since the Middle Ages, Italian Easter Pie has been considered a kind of cheesecake, yet it differs from the fluffy variety known in America in that it has substantial texture. The crust, *Pasta Frolla,* is light, tender and quite like a rolled cooky dough. The two combine in this modern version of a favorite last course for the Easter feast.

Italian Easter Pie

7 tbsp. quick-cooking tapioca	1 cup sugar
¾ tsp. salt	4 eggs, separated
1 tbsp. sugar	½ tsp. grated lemon rind
½ tsp. ground cinnamon	2 tbsp. lemon juice
2 cups milk	½ cup chopped mixed
2½ cups creamed	candied fruit
cottage cheese	Pasta Frolla (see following recipe)

Mix tapioca, ¼ tsp. salt, 1 tbsp. sugar, ½ tsp. cinnamon in saucepan. Gradually stir in milk. Cook to full boil (6 to 8 minutes), stirring. Remove from heat; cool 15 minutes. Stir well; chill.

Pasta Frolla

Meanwhile sift together 1½ cups sifted flour, ¼ tsp. salt and ¾ tsp. baking powder. Cream ⅓ cup butter; add ⅓ cup sugar and ½ tsp. grated lemon rind. Add 1 egg; beat well. Gradually stir in sifted dry ingredients; mix well. Reserve ⅓ of the Pasta; line a 9-inch spring-form pan with the remainder. Press Pasta evenly over bottom and up sides of pan to within

½ inch of the top. Bake at 400° F. for 18 minutes. Beat the cottage cheese with a rotary beater until smooth. Add the remaining sugar and egg yolks one at a time, beating well after each addition. Add remaining ½ tsp. salt, ¼ tsp. cinnamon and the grated lemon rind and juice. Gradually add chilled tapioca mixture, blending. Fold in fruits, then the 4 stiffly beaten egg whites. Pour into cooled Pasta-lined pan. Roll the reserved Pasta on a lightly floured board to a 6x10-inch rectangle. Cut into 6 (10-inch-long) strips. With these make a lattice top for the pie, folding strips over outside edge to seal. Bake at 350° F. for 80 minutes. Turn oven off; cool cake with door partly open for 1 hour. Chill before serving. Makes 12 servings.

Samuel and Narcissa Chamberlain offer these two recipes:

Pitte con Niepita—Easter Turnovers (Calabria)

Make a pastry dough with 2 cups flour, a pinch of salt, 8 tablespoons butter (½ cup), and 4 tablespoons sugar. Add ⅓ cup ice water, or enough to make a manageable dough, and roll it out thin on a floured board. Or use your own favorite pastry recipe.

For the filling, mix 1 cup firm grape marmalade or jam, ¼ cup sugar, ⅛ teaspoon cinnamon, ½ cup ground walnut meats, 6 tablespoons cocoa, and 1 tablespoon rum or brandy. If your grape marmalade is not truly firm, heat the mixture and thicken it with 1 tablespoon potato starch dissolved in a few drops of water. Cool before adding the rum.

Cut the dough into rounds 3 to 3½ inches in diameter, place a spoonful of filling in the center of each, fold the rounds in half, moisten the edges, and press them firmly together. Prick the tops with a pointed knife, brush with egg yolk, and bake the turnovers on a floured baking sheet for 15 minutes in a hot oven (400° F.), or until they are golden. These are good either hot or cold.

Pizza Pasquale alla Triestina—Trieste Easter Bread (Friuli-Venezia Giulia)

1 cup flour	1 tsp. salt
1 envelope dry yeast	¾ cup sugar
⅔ cup tepid water	⅔ cup warm milk
3 cups flour	¼ lb. melted butter
3 eggs plus 1 egg white	1 tsp. vanilla
2 tbsp. rum	

The following rich and delicious bread resembles brioche, and keeps better.

Make a sponge with 1 cup flour and 1 envelope of dry yeast dissolved in about ⅔ cup tepid water. Work it well with a wooden spoon and let it stand in a warm place to rise to double its bulk.

In a bowl put 3 cups flour sifted with 1 teaspoon salt and stir in 3 eggs and 1 egg white, ¾ cup sugar dissolved in ⅔ cup warm milk, ¼ pound melted butter, 1 teaspoon vanilla, and 2 tablespoons rum. Add the sponge. Mix all well together and let the dough rise again to double its bulk. Stir it down and put it in a round buttered and lightly floured baking pan or in 2 bread loaf pans, half filling each pan. Let it rise again to double its bulk. Brush the cake with melted butter and bake it in a moderate oven (350° F.) for about 40 minutes, or until it is browned and firm.

Lithuania

N the eve of Ash Wednesday in Lithuania, a play is given, in which a very plump figure (Lasininis) and a very thin one (Kanapinis) go through the motions of a great struggle. The thin man, representing Lent, wins the fight over his opponent, who impersonates the Carnival days, by throwing him to the ground and stepping on him, thus indicating that the lush days of Carnival are over and Lent has arrived.

On Holy Saturday, the Lithuanians take two baskets of food to church to be blessed. One is a small basket containing tiny portions of the food to be eaten the next day at breakfast; and the second basket, a large one, contains bread, meat, rye or wheat, to be distributed among the poor who wait near the church. Also taken home from the service of blessing are vials and bottles of holy water to be used in the sickroom. The water is sprinkled about the house during electrical storms for protection; some is poured into wall fonts hung on the kitchen door so that members of the family may dip two fingers into it and bless themselves before they leave the house. Sips of holy water are taken by some before Easter breakfast as a surety against illness and disease for the current year.

Holy Saturday afternoon, dozens of brown eggs are simmered in onion skins to be colored for the children. The white eggs that have been boiled are decorated by using beeswax and are prepared for the adults. Everyone waits expectantly for the *lelouninkai,* a chorus of young men who go from house to house greeting the family with: "Little father, little mother, shall we gladden your humble home? Which of these two songs shall we sing— 'Christ Our Lord rose from the dead' or 'The joyful day has now begun to shine'?"

If the first song is requested, the singers receive three eggs; if the second is sung, they get four eggs, because the hymn has sixteen verses. Still more eggs are lavished upon the singers if they are accompanied by an accordionist or a violinist. Naturally, the children want the songs with instrumental accompaniment, but the host and hostess hope for singers only, so that the Easter egg supply will not diminish too quickly. Brown eggs are given to the singers since they wish to eat them, but *margučiai,* the eggs decorated by using beeswax, are reserved for the family and for friends.

After Mass on Easter Sunday, members of the congregation hum and sing an old Lithuanian Easter hymn as they make their way home, happy to be singing once again, for singing is not permitted out of doors during Lent.

Before partaking of the Easter feast, each person sprinkles salt liberally over everything he is to eat, for, "Sprinkle salt on Easter bread, and there will always be bread on the family table." In the afternoon, friends, neighbors, and relatives call at each other's homes to exchange Easter eggs and to admire those on display. An old verse of this season often repeated in Lithuania reads:

That if one is good on Easter day,
Then he will be deserving throughout the year.
But if one is bad in any way,
Then he will be bad the rest of the year.

No one seems to be certain whether the "look-inside" Easter egg originated in Lithuania or in Latvia; however, there is no question as to its popularity with all ages in many countries of the world. The "look-inside" egg is made of fondant with a round opening at one end through which one looks at a landscape modeled of fondant. In size, it usually resembles a turkey or duck egg, but may be even two or three times larger, depending on the maker. The sculptured landscape includes trees, shrubs, hills, houses, rabbits, chickens, and perhaps tiny eggs. In short, it is a whim of its creator. The outside is elaborately decorated with flowers and lacy borders. Carolyn Sherwin Bailey has woven a charming legend around the "look-inside" Easter egg, which she entitles *The Sugar Egg*. It is as much a favorite of small children as are the eggs themselves.

The decorated Lithuanian Easter egg differs considerably from other European eggs in that it contains designs either scratched onto the surface with a knife or laid on with beeswax. This type of decoration on Easter eggs dates back to the sixteenth century. Eggshells are painted not only at Easter, but also on St. George's Day and at Whitsuntide. Some of the eggs are plunged into colored dye, and the design is then engraved or scratched on with a knife; or, in imitation of Javanese batik, the figures are designed by the application of beeswax, and the egg is soaked afterward in a dye. When the wax is removed, the ornament or decoration appears white. In general, the background is dark: black or dark brown, blue or red.

Luxembourg

 HE Grand Duchy of Luxembourg, bounded by Germany, Belgium, and France, is predominantly Roman Catholic. Family pride is centered in the young, and church activities are planned carefully to include them. On Shrove Tuesday, children go about seeking pancakes and waffles and any other delectable bit that a housewife will offer them. As they go from door to door in little bands, they sing this ditty:

Here come the Good Lord's little singers,
Give us some bacon and peas,
A book, maybe two.
Then you'll have good health throughout the year.
If you don't give anything, you'll slip on the ice;
If you don't give anything at all,
You'll be like a sack of nuts!

The last line implies that they will pound miserly people with their fists, just as they pound nuts in a sack! Fantastic costumes, similar to those worn by American children for "trick or treat" purposes at Halloween, lend color and a touch of pageantry to the impish performance.

In Luxembourg, the fourth or middle Sunday of Lent is known as *Bretzel-sonndeg* (Pretzel Sunday). The boys give their girl friends beautifully decorated cakes, resembling pretzels. If she wishes to encourage the boy, the girl, in turn, gives him a decorated Easter egg and on Easter Sunday walks with him in the park. If the pretzel cake received is large, the young lady responds with a large egg, usually made of chocolate. Being hollow, the egg will be filled with bonbons. A small cake merits a small egg. When leap year occurs, the custom is reversed; the girl offers the pretzel cake on *Bretzelsonndeg* and the boy reciprocates with an egg at Easter. Married people usually observe this custom also.

In Luxembourg, Holland and several other European countries, the "palms" used on Palm Sunday are actually branches of boxwood which remain green and fragrant throughout the year. Children carry them to the priest to be blessed; then, holding them above their heads, they form a procession as though to welcome Jesus on His triumphal entry into Jerusalem. The procession is led by the young folks, followed by the choirboys, who bear a large crucifix decorated with palms. Church dignitaries and priests bring up the rear as the procession moves up and down the aisles of the church and then out of doors. All chant in Latin:

Glory, praise, honor to Thee,
Christ our King and Savior,
To whom this child chorus sings reverent hosannas.

Since the bells have "flown to Rome" on Good Friday, schoolboys go through the streets shaking wooden rattles to call the villagers to worship. The air is heavy with sadness and the churches are draped in black.

On Holy Saturday, it is customary for the choirboys to go from house to house where they are received warmly and presented with eggs and money.

The money received is pooled to defray the expenses of an excursion made with the priest to some historical site. Midnight Mass is preceded by the ceremony of blessing holy water, to be used for baptism, and the blessing of fire. Each parishioner carries a wax candle which is lighted, during the ceremony, from the great Paschal candle on the altar until the entire church is bathed in candlelight. The service continues until midnight, the traditional hour of Christ's Resurrection. Then the organ resounds with notes of joy as the church bell peals out the arrival of Easter.

Easter morning is always exciting for the small children since they are told that the Easter Hare has been romping outside in the tall grass, and the hunt for eggs is on. These include some colorfully dyed eggs, those made of sugar and, best of all, the chocolate eggs for which Luxembourg is noted. Dessert for the family dinner is usually a cake or an ice, always made in a Paschal-lamb mold.

The Netherlands

ONE of the most curious customs of the Easter season is a practice observed by the farmers on the island of Zeeland on Shrove Tuesday. In the afternoon, at Schouwen-en-Duiveland, they gather at the village green with their horses, forming a procession. Having been groomed carefully, their manes and tails combed out, the horses have their heads decorated with gaily colored paper roses. To halt the procession, the leader toots his horn, which is also the signal for each rider to lead his horse down to the beach to get his feet wet. In primitive times, horns were blown to drive away the evil spirits of winter and it was held that wetting the horses' feet was a symbolic cleansing act. Upon returning to the village, the farmers are toasted by the burgomaster and the evening ends with dancing and merry-making.

On Palm Sunday the children go from farm to farm carrying a Palmpass, or Easter "palm." Actually, the Palmpass is a curiously decorated staff, covered with Easter emblems, which varies in appearance from district to district. It is made of a hoop attached to a stick which may be from eighteen to fifty-four inches long. The hoop is entwined with boxwood and decorated with eggshells, paper flags, sugar rings, oranges, raisins, figs, the famous Dutch chocolate eggs, and small cakes. At the top, little dough figures in the shape of cocks or swans are placed. Sometimes competitions are held and awards are made for the most distinctive Palmpass, provided that all the correct symbols are displayed. Carrying these Palmpass sticks, and empty baskets as well, the children roam through streets and lanes singing:

> *One more Sunday*
> *And we'll get an egg,*
> *And we'll get an egg.*
> *One egg is no egg;*
> *Two eggs are half an egg;*
> *Three eggs are an Easter egg.*

Obviously, they expect at least three eggs!

140

In many towns, on Palm Sunday, a man chosen to personify Judas, accompanied by his assistant, travels from farm to farm, begging for money and eggs. Both carry baskets for the eggs and sing Easter songs as they make their pleas. The eggs are then sold to help defray the expenses of the pine wood that must be purchased for the Easter fires.

On Easter Eve, in some rural districts in Holland, the boys chase the girls around the Easter Eve bonfires and throw soot at them. This lively and messy practice is not resented by the victims because it is supposed to bring good luck. In fact, it is a direct survival of an ancient fertility rite, but probably few of the onlookers, or the young people directly concerned, realize it.

Easter Sunday is anticipated eagerly by the Dutch. In preparation, they clean their yards, recut and trim the topiary trees or bushes, an art in which they are skilled, and make their houses clean and tidy. Throughout the house they place vases of flowers, tastefully arranged. The dining table boasts a basket of colored Easter eggs, including some made of Dutch chocolate, as well as nosegays of spring blooms. *Paasbrood*, the special Easter bread, deliciously stuffed with raisins and currants, is ready to be served to callers.

A strange and ancient custom observed in Denekamp takes place on Easter afternoon. The "Judas" and his aide who had collected eggs and money for the Easter fire, accompanied by men and boys from the village, walk down the long, beech-lined avenues leading out of the town to the site of the celebration. There they search for a tree to serve as the Easter pole for the Easter night bonfire. Judas climbs the chosen tree and securely ties a rope to the top of it, after which it is stripped of all side branches except for the "feathery" top. When Judas descends, the tree is cut down and dragged, top foremost, to the Church of Saint Nicholas in the village, where it is dropped outside the door. After Easter vespers, it is dragged up the Easter hill, located on the edge of the town, and erected close to the spot where the huge fire will burn. Again, Judas climbs the tree using a ladder and tries to auction the tree to the highest bidder, only to be hissed and ridiculed. He relinquishes his place to his aide, "Iscariot," who is also repulsed by the crowd. Finally, Judas announces the great bonfire will be lighted at eight o'clock that evening. Then the people disperse to their homes for Easter supper, returning at the appropriate hour for the great Easter fire. As the bonfire burns, the villagers enjoy folk dances and sing an old song, the original words of which exist only in their native dialect.

The Easter egg hunt, held on Easter Monday, features hard-cooked, colored eggs, which are hidden in a meadow or some other suitable outdoor spot where children can frolic. As the eggs are discovered, they are packed in a basket by each hunter. When all the eggs have been found, each child seeks a partner with whom he may have an egg-knocking contest. The opponents must first match egg colors before knocking eggs. The winner is the holder of an unbroken shell and he keeps all the eggs, his own and his adversary's.

The adults dance the Vlöggelen, meaning to "go as with wings." Undoubtedly a survival of an early spring fertility rite, this dance is a slow ritualistic performance. The participants form a line on the narrow, cobbled streets.

Each person puts his right hand behind his back and clasps the left hand of the person directly following him, thus forming a human chain. Advancing gradually, "like birds on the wing," they keep time to the song they sing, an ancient Easter hymn which ends in an Alleluia refrain. A seemingly endless chain of dancers zigzags through the winding streets, along country roads, in and out of inns, farmhouses, and barns, entering by the front door and leaving by the back door, all the while keeping a line formation and singing joyously to boot.

The Easter "lifting" custom, familiar throughout Europe, obviously refers to Christ's Resurrection from the tomb. Lifting consists of raising a woman three times into the air, which must be done between 9 A.M. and noon on Easter Monday. The usual "payment" expected of a woman is to give a kiss to every man in the group which has done the lifting. The next day, the women do the lifting.

During the first week of May, Holland holds its annual tulip festivals. Thousands upon tens of thousands of tulip blossoms bob and dance in the spring sunshine and all of Holland seems literally to be carpeted with the rainbow blooms of the almost countless varieties for which the Dutch are famous. Tourists come from the world over to see this breathtaking sight and to pay homage to the country that has perfected and given to the world one of the spring's most welcome flowers. Coming as it does in early May, this group of festivals has become one of the Netherlands' Easter customs, since it takes place during Eastertide, which terminates on Whitsunday.

Norway

In Norway, five of the days in Holy Week have become a long national holiday combining religious observances with sports activities. In addition to participating in church services at this season, the Norwegians in great numbers enjoy skiing in the mountains. Along the ski trails near Oslo there are convenient open-air chapels for the worshipers, who spend many of their Sundays in the rolling countryside just outside their national capital.

At this time, Lapp weddings take place at Karasjok in the northernmost province of Finnmark. Some of the nomadic Lapps still make their living as reindeer herders on the mountain plateau of Finnmarksvidda and elsewhere in northern Norway. At Easter, they convene in the villages of Karasjok and Kautokeino for the usual church services and marriage ceremonies as well. Young Lapps are wed in their colorful costumes; children are baptized; then, for two or three days, there are celebrations. A recent innovation is reindeer racing. Sitting in their wobbly "pulkas," sleds shaped like shallow canoes, the Lapps drive their reindeer across the snowy plains at a very fast pace.

The Sunday before Lent in Norway is an exciting day for the children, for it is the day that they may use the *fastelavnsris,* birch branches which they have decorated gaily with paper streamers of red, yellow, orange, or green and with tinsel. Sometimes, a small doll, with skirts that are stiff and outstanding, is tied to the topmost branch of the switch; or the top may be decorated with a bunch of gaily colored paper flowers. Armed with their branches, the children, who rise at the crack of dawn, scurry from one bedroom to another, eager to catch the occupant sleeping so that they may switch the "lazy" person awake. They go about this switching with great zest, for custom decrees that they receive a delicious hot cross bun for each sleeping victim they spank. Many a grown-up feigns sleep; thus, the children's appetites are whetted by this early morning game. Plenty of hot cross buns disappear from the breakfast table.

During Carnival time, the days preceding Lent, *Fastelavnsboller* are sold in great quantities. These buns, which resemble muffins, are sold throughout the year. But, at Carnival time, they are filled with whipped cream and coated with sugar and frosting, an "extra-special *boller."*

Good Friday is known as Long Friday. One of the customs for this special day in northwestern Europe is the gathering of the branches of the mountain ash, which are placed on the doorposts of homes as protection against evil. The mountain ash, or rowan tree, is thought to have special powers against witches, ague, and snakebite, for it is believed to be a sacred tree and the conqueror of the serpent of evil. This custom can be traced back to the Norse mythology of Yggdrasil. It was believed that the fabulous ash tree, which was at the center of the world with branches that reached to heaven, had roots which lay in the underworld, gnawed by the worm Nidling. Odin, or Wotan, the Norse supreme God-All-Father, learned the secrets of divination by spearing himself to this tree in a sort of crucifixion. The following rhyme states:

> *I know that I hung*
> *On a wind-rocked tree*
> *Nine whole nights,*
> *With a spear wounded,*
> *And to Odin offered*
> *Myself to myself;*
> *On that tree*
> *Of which no one knows*
> *From what root it springs.*

Although a great number of Norwegians are out of doors enjoying God's open spaces at Easter time, those at home adhere to worldwide customs. The children have been busy dyeing and decorating eggshells which they have been hoarding for weeks. Often the shells are cut in half and filled with small candies, after which they are fastened together again. Paper cutouts are pasted on the shells. Egg-hunting time is Easter morning. Parents take time to hide eggs in all sorts of strange places—in dolls' beds, in flowerpots, or in mother's sewing basket. It is a real scramble and a hard search, for the youngsters must look practically everywhere to find their treasure. Church services are held throughout the country, and the attendance is large.

About fifty years ago, breweries in Norway started to make a special Easter beer (*Paskelbrygg*). A blend of the best beers made in Norway, it is now very popular and a favorite addition to traditional Easter fare in Scandinavia.

Poland

THE Easter feast in Poland is probably the most complete and elaborate served in all the countries that celebrate Easter. First, the table itself is decorated with foliage. A lamb made of sugar, or a cake made in a lamb's mold, with the standard of the sacred flag, dominates the center of the table. Around the figure of the lamb are placed platters of ham, sausages, cold roast pork, various kinds of salads, a dish of horseradish with its vinegar as a reminder of Christ's suffering on the Cross and the "water" which He was given to drink when He asked for it. The lamb symbol is repeated again in the mold of butter. There is also a loaf of high-rising *babka* bread, and *chrusciki,* Polish love knots. On a china plate (the very best china is used on this special day) are replicas, in miniature, of all the main dishes, fashioned out of colored marzipan.

Of great importance to this feast is the display of Easter eggs, *pisanki* (or *pysanki*) as they are called. As famed for it as for their cooking, the Polish people excel in Easter egg decoration and, together with the Ukrainians, are the acknowledged masters of this particular art. Hours upon hours go into a single decoration, which may be of geometrical or abstract pattern. Christian symbols such as the fish and the cross are also used. To produce such superbly decorated eggs requires not only patience and skill, but also native ability and technical know-how. To the blown egg, wax is applied by means of a needle or a tiny metal tube. Sometimes the tip of a shoelace is used! Parts of the egg are coated so that they will not absorb color when the eggs are dipped into a particular dye. To achieve the multicolored effect, the egg is waxed and dipped repeatedly. Each color has its own particular source. To get the most delicate light green shade, one must use moss that has been taken from underneath a stone. An infusion of crocuses supplies the orange tone, and black is brewed from alder bark and cones. These eggs are presented as gifts and are always kept for a long time.

Easter eggs are not usually given to one's parents or children; rather, these special gifts are presented to godparents and to friends. A gift of an Easter egg from a girl to a young man is a sign that his attentions will not be unwelcome. In years gone by, Polish girls gave their favored suitors anywhere from thirty to a hundred eggs, which they decorated themselves; or, if they were not skilled in the art, they patronized women who were. (This generous giving is no longer practiced.) If the girl had to "purchase" her eggs, she might perform housekeeping chores, thus releasing the artist for egg-making. When the eggs were finished, the young lady, eager to please her suitor, wrapped the eggs carefully in a fine lawn handkerchief, tucked in a handful of nuts and a packet of tobacco, and offered it to her chosen one. He was expected to reciprocate with a piece of dress material, a kerchief, or ribbons of many colors, or all three! This custom, too, is fading away.

Several legends and cherished beliefs surround the Easter eggs and their importance in the life of the Poles. One of the fables concerning the presence of *pisanki* at the Easter table relates to Mary Magdalene. She and her companions went to the sepulcher with sweet spices with which to anoint Christ's body and took a few cooked eggs with them in a basket to eat when they had completed this sad mission. On their arrival at the tomb, they found that their eggs had miraculously taken on all the colors of the rainbow. Another tale relates that the first *pisanki* were made by Mary the mother of Jesus in the peaceful days at Nazareth, long before the shadows of Calvary fell across her life. To amuse the infant Jesus, she took eggs from her household store, boiled them until they were hard and then painted them red and green and yellow.

The *pisanki* are thought to have the power of protecting the house from all evil. Always a few of them are kept, since they will bring good luck to the house. A few are planted in the vineyard to guard the vines against hail, wind, and destructive storms.

The passing of winter is dramatized by presenting a pageant in which a straw personage, Marzanna, is drowned. This ceremony may take place anytime from Shrovetide to the fourth Sunday in Lent, depending on the calendar of each village. Nowhere else in the world is there such strict adherence to Lent. The Polish people do not indulge themselves or relinquish the Lenten fare for even a single meal. They are determined to adhere to "lean" meals, awaiting patiently the Easter feast for which they are famous.

The Shrovetide Carnival shows up the mischief latent in the Pole. Marriageable young men and women who have failed to choose a mate during the preceding season are punished on Shrove Tuesday. Chicken feet, turkey windpipes, herring skeletons and anything else that is equally unattractive and odorous are pinned onto these unwilling "victims" as they come to church, dressed in their best, to be shriven.

The following verse is often pinned upon them too:

> *If, gracious maiden, you walked in a pair*
> *You would not now carry this block of wood—*
> *In penance for your spinsterhood*
> *Bear as your badge this turkey foot.*

On Shrove Tuesday there is the auctioning of the girls. Toward evening, the young men herd the young women into a tavern where with much merriment and joking the men bid for the girls much as they would bid at a cattle

An ornamental figure
on a Polish Easter card.

auction. The men laughingly examine the girls' eyes and teeth with an exchange of humorous bickerings. For the youth who has rescued her by "buying" her, a "bartered" girl usually has a reward—a gift of colored eggs when Easter arrives. Should a girl not be bartered for, she is shown the door and put out of doors in disgrace.

The married women gather in a tavern and are asked to dance the Shrove Tuesday dance "to make the hemp grow tall." The women leap as high into the air as they can; their husbands, if they think the leap can be bettered, give them another mugful and ask them to leap higher. It is an evening of great merriment. Huge quantities of doughnuts are consumed in this "hemp" ceremony.

In Poland, Palm Sunday is known as Flower Sunday. The "palms" are long sprigs of pussy willow that have been blessed by the priest. These are placed in water to assure the maturing of the catkins, for on Easter Sunday it is believed that swallowing a catkin will give protection against a sore throat. In some villages it is held that the "palms" stuck in molehills will drive those pests away and save the crops.

Flogging is practiced on Palm Sunday, for the beating of a man will make his crops grow, and the beating of a woman will make her fertile.

The willow smites, but does not kill—
The great day is but a week away—
And cuts the flesh but once a year.

146

Holy Week is an especially busy one for the Polish family. Besides attending church services all week long—for the Poles are people of intense faith—the husband must make his yard, buildings, and animals clean and sweet for Easter. His wife works tirelessly making her home spotless, decorating the *pisanki* and cooking the traditional foods. These activities are much more important than the customs and traditions that surround Christmas. This week is considered a lucky time for a person to die, for it is the belief that if all the graves are open, they and the earth will lie lightly upon him who passes and he will rest in peace.

The blessing of the food on Holy Saturday is a ceremony of signal importance and each household awaits eagerly the arrival of the priest or pastor at their home.

Easter Monday, known as Dyngus, is the occasion for the men to drench the girls with water. Turn about being fair play, the ladies drench the men on the following day, all in good-natured play.

TRADITIONAL RECIPE

Postna Zupa—Lenten Soup

4 carrots	2 sprigs parsley
4 stalks celery	2 tbsp. butter
1 onion	2 qts. cold water

Salt and pepper

Wash vegetables, cut into small pieces, and sauté in butter under cover until they turn yellow. Add water and simmer for half hour. Strain before serving.

Portugal

SWEET sadness prevails in Portugal, where the attitude toward life is coupled with a philosophic outlook tempered by strong faith, yet blended with a curious mixture of beliefs, supernatural and superstitious. The accumulation of centuries of seafaring which involved the establishment of rich sources of trade—spices in particular—and of tilling the soil in a small country where land is precious has created for the Portuguese a life filled with uncertainties, disasters and struggles. Thus, *Se Deus quizer* ("If God wills") is an expression heard so frequently in Portugal that nothing is accomplished without uttering it. In similar fashion, there is always the occasion for a song, a dance, a reason to make noise, and a smile in which God is thanked for some favor. Consequently, it is easy to understand why these people can attend Mass and march in a religious procession on Sunday morning and spend the rest of the day dancing, singing, and feasting or attending a bullfight. Christian symbols and all that they represent go hand in hand with a way of life that puts the Portuguese on such intimate terms with the Holy Family that, on a feast day, they salute the Virgin Mary with a sign which says, "Welcome, Maria." It has been claimed that St. Peter, the patron of fishermen, long a favorite with the Portuguese, holds not only the keys to Heaven but those of Portugal as well.

The last three days prior to Ash Wednesday culminate the pre-Lenten festivities which began several weeks earlier. Throughout the country masked balls, parties, confetti battles, and dances are held. A century or more ago the Lisbon carnival was characterized as a time of license, with obscene jokes, coarse horseplay, and battles with eggs, oranges, flour, and water predominating. However, public festivities in Lisbon today are restricted, for the most part, to processions of gay flower-decked cars, music, dancing, and parades of revelers in fancy costumes. In rural areas Carnival continues to be celebrated with much of its old-time gaiety and abandon. Battles of flowers, the frolicking of mummers and musicians, the burial in effigy of King Carnival, and old folk plays are features of the festivities.

On the Madeira Islands, famed for processions and pageants, the natives dance to the music of the *machetes* and the *rajoes*. Outdoor festivals called *espetadas,* in which roasted spiced meats are skewered on laurel branches, are especially popular.

At Loulé in Algarve, the annual Mardi Gras begins while the almond trees are flowering. The fragrance of almond blossoms fills the air. In fact, few fruit trees bear flowers more fragile than those of the almond, which burst forth in great beauty each year in late January, the branches spreading like thin, low clouds over the landscape. These flowers of romantic legend are much loved in Portugal and each year when the buds unfold, the event is announced in the local papers. All the festivities of the season are staged against a setting of Moorish architecture, for which the old city of Loulé is famous. These include a battle of flowers, a parade of floats, and spirited folk dancing—all enjoyed in an atmosphere of sunshine, fragrance, and birdsong. The days prior to Ash Wednesday are devoted to a fair.

In Estoril, and elsewhere in Portugal, illumination is a feature of all the processions and festivities, and none of these would be complete without fireworks. In this town, a great Carnival ball is held at the Cassino.

Perhaps the most impressive of all the Holy Week observances is that held in Braga. Statuary used in the churches and the figures carried in the processions are extraordinary for their lifelike qualities. Facial expressions are animated with glass eyes, real hair, and ornate garb including numerous jewels. In their hands they hold familiar objects such as little boats or bunches of grapes which make them almost human in appearance. The large candles carried in the processions may be dyed one of several colors; some are ornamented with gilt or richly carved; others are embellished with garlands of flowers. Carpets of flowers in elaborate patterns are worked out on the pavements. The exteriors of houses decorated with four-foot palm leaves and other greens add to the setting and the glory of the day. Here, as everywhere else in this tiny country, folklore and folk art are alive, bursting with color and pageantry. In Barcelos there is a Festival of Crosses. In Bussaco, in the same province, during Holy Week the women dress in deep mourning and carry little bouquets of rosemary as they pay their visits to seven different churches. This herb, symbolic of remembrance, recalls for them the sorrows of the Passion.

On Maundy Thursday and Good Friday practically everyone in Lisbon makes a trip to the seashore to gather clams and other shellfish, which are brought home and made into clam soup. This traditional outing affords a pleasant bit of recreation as Lent comes to a close.

Diego de Sousa, noted Bishop of Braga in the sixteenth century, created a town so distinguished for its architectural beauty that the years in which he was active have been referred to as a "golden age." Braga has long been known for its Holy Week processions, considered the finest in all Portugal and comparable to those of Seville. Located in the province of Minho, the gayest and most colorful region of Portugal, the area shows its lively spirit in the costumes the people wear, the festivals they conduct, and the manner in which they combine pleasure and labor. The potters of Barcelos are noted for their pink ceramic roosters and flower-dotted chickens which make Easter party tables gay and colorful. Here in northern Portugal, visitors delight in the way in which the natives announce forthcoming fairs and festivals by building fragile arches of reeds decorated with paper flowers. At night when these *arraial minhoto* are lighted, they create an atmosphere of rare delight.

During the Lenten season, in northern Portugal, people take *ramos* to church to be blessed. These are branches bent into half loops and decorated with a profusion of spring flowers which later are carried in the processions. Once used, like the palms, they are preserved carefully in homes, but are burned during storms as a protection against lightning.

During Holy Week, sometimes even throughout Lent, there are exhibits in the churches as well as the processions through the village streets featuring scenes from the Passion of Jesus to remind the faithful of the significance of the solemn season. For example, in the church of *Senhor dos Passos,* Our Lord of the Way of the Cross, in the city of Guimaraea, a different Passion tableau is presented each day of Holy Week. Two of the most famous Passion processions are those held in the city of Covilhã on the slope of the Serra da Estrella, and in the town of Vila do Conde. In many places these processions are attended by bands of *anjinhos,* children dressed as little angels, with crowns on their heads and fluffy eiderdown wings attached to their shoulders. The figures of Jesus, which have real eyelashes and hair, as well as tears made of crystal, are sumptuously clad in robes of purple velvet. Similarly, the clergy's vestments and all the processional properties are violet in color. Even more dramatic are the bunches of violets tossed to their suffering Lord by those who line the *via dolorosa.*

In Portugal, the bullfighting season opens in April, usually coinciding with the Easter holidays. Although the best arena is in Lisbon, Vila Franca de Xira in the province of Rabatejo is the bullfighting capital of Portugal, whose combat bulls and horses are raised in a province noted for its green pastures. This ancient sport holds a strange fascination for young and old on every level of society. The bull is fought on horseback, and the highly bred stallions used for this purpose are as skillfully trained as polo ponies. Unlike the practice in Spain, neither the bull nor the horses are killed in Portugal, and after each round, the bull is led out of the ring by oxen. Each horn is protected by a ball placed at the tip and held in place by a leather sheath. Before each fight the bulls are led through the main streets of the town (there are thirty or more arenas in Portugal) by mounted *campinos* in natty uniforms. The curious watch with great excitement to see who will test his luck by braving one of the bulls as they gallop freely up the street. Often the foolhardy are forced to scale a lamppost, a wall, or a balcony to escape, but seldom are there any serious accidents. It is a costly sport; the bulls bred for the ring are carefully observed and cared for and are allowed to participate only once in a *festa brava,* or bullfight.

Early map makers described the land mass of Southwest Europe which lay beyond the Pyrenees as "the bull's hide." A quick glance at the map of Europe indicates that their image was apt, for the Iberian Peninsula truly resembles the stretched hide of a great bull. It is significant, too, that this huge shape reaching, nose to tail, from Portugal's southwest tip to Spain's northeast edge, should comprise the only two countries in Europe where bullfighting prevails.

Old and young, rich and poor, dressed in their best, attend the Easter Masses, which are truly impressive, greatly enhanced by magnificent Resurrection music. Many of the churches are decorated with an abundance of white flowers. After the services, families eat a holiday meal and visit among friends and neighbors.

Folar is a popular Easter bread in Portugal. Made of sweet dough, it is baked in a round flat shape and decorated on top with hard-boiled eggs. At this season it is customary to give presents of little colored-paper cornucopias filled with sugar-covered almonds.

TRADITIONAL AND REGIONAL RECIPES

Folar (Sweet Bread)

¾ lb. melted butter	¾ lb. sugar
2 cups evaporated milk	Pinch of salt
4 oz. yeast	Lemon to flavor
2 cups water (to be put in kneading pan)	1½ lbs. flour

Mix together milk, melted butter, and yeast. To this add water and beat. Then add sugar, a pinch of salt, and lemon. Mix in about 1½ lbs. of flour,

Folar, the traditional Easter bread of Portugal. (*Photo: Richard Merrill*)

then knead. While kneading, add just enough flour to keep dough from sticking to hands and to the pan. Cover dough and let rise at room temperature about ¾ of an hour. Remove dough from pan and put on floured table. Divide into three parts and roll out by hand. Braid the three rolls together and join the ends, thus forming a round braid. Let stand for ½ hour in buttered pan which has been dusted lightly with flour. Add hard-boiled plain or colored eggs in shell onto top of loaf and put into preheated oven at 250° F. to 275° F. and cook about 1 hour.

Marzipan

1 egg white	1½ cups sifted
1 cup almond paste	confectioners' sugar
Lemon juice	

Whip egg white until fluffy. Work in almond paste gradually. Add confectioners' sugar; use more if necessary to make paste easy to handle. If it becomes too thick, work in lemon juice drop by drop. Should it become too oily, work it in a dish over ice. In any case, knead the paste. Mold into any desired shape. A cup of marzipan usually contains 8 oz.

Russia

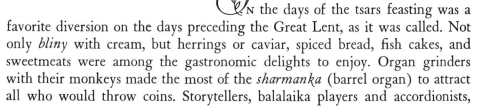

In the days of the tsars feasting was a favorite diversion on the days preceding the Great Lent, as it was called. Not only *bliny* with cream, but herrings or caviar, spiced bread, fish cakes, and sweetmeats were among the gastronomic delights to enjoy. Organ grinders with their monkeys made the most of the *sharmanka* (barrel organ) to attract all who would throw coins. Storytellers, balalaika players and accordionists, "theatrical companies in motley costumes—the whole multitude swirled about, gesticulated and bawled in the frail framework of planks and painted canvas." Such was Russian Carnival in Moscow. On the Taganka side of the city, the merchants rode out in their elegant carriages drawn by horses whose harnesses were bedecked with paper flowers and ribbons. Wives and daughters resplendent in their jewels nodded to and greeted their friends as the carriages passed one another. On the Saturday prior to Shrovetide, business was unusually brisk with crowds filling the restaurants and liquor shops, the circuses and theaters.

Then, come Sunday, all was quiet; but, at twilight, the peasants hauling their produce to market began to arrive at their site on the banks of the Moskva; enormous quantities of fast-day food were needed for the long Lenten season in the teeming city of Moscow. Pickled cabbage in barrels, baskets of dried mushrooms, salted cucumbers, all other kinds of pickles, chick-peas and countless other items were unloaded in the merchants' huts. During the first week of Lent, neither butter nor milk nor white cheese was eaten by those who adhered to church rules. Even in raw weather, a festive air prevailed as the crowds made their way to the riverbank to view the market and its provisions. Henri Troyat has painted a vivid picture of the occasion in *Daily Life in Russia Under the Last Tsar:*

"Garlands of white, yellow and brown mushrooms hung between the shafts of the sleighs. Nimble hands plunged into casks of brine where gherkins floated among fennel branches and currant leaves. At the end of a vigorous arm swung a whole family of glazed cracknel biscuits, strewn with poppy-seed. Honey oozed from rows of wax. Between two piles of potatoes an artist was selling wood-carvings representing scenes from the holy scriptures, and a colporteur was offering ikons and cheap bibles. . . . The Muscovite housewives hurriedly bought the strict foodstuffs which they would need during the long weeks of the Orthodox Great Lent. Then, laden with bundles, baskets and jars, they returned home. But they left again at once so as not to miss the solemn penitential mass, during which the singing of the choirs is always so sad and so beautiful. The bells no longer sounded except at long intervals, deep and funereal. In the nave the priests, in their chasubles of mourning, black with silver embroidery, knelt three times while repeating: 'Lord and Master of my life . . .' "

During the first week of Great Lent, the imperial theaters were closed, but the public rushed to see performances by foreign actors who poured into the city at this time. The following Sunday an impressive ceremony led by the bishop took place in the Cathedral of the Assumption in the heart of the Kremlin. Against a background of solemn liturgy, after much genuflecting and tribute to the bishop, the assisting priests surrounded him, and the first deacon took his place in the center. Facing the congregation, he uttered in sonorous tones the solemn warning meted out to the laggards and the heretics, to "those who did not believe in the resurrection of the dead, the immortality of the soul and the illuminating omnipotence of the Lord, those who scoffed at the Church, who did not observe the fast. . . ." There were a dozen categories of great sinners. Every time he mentioned one, the first deacon paused and then cried in a voice of thunder:

"A-nath-ema!"

The windows shook. Three times the priests answered in chorus:

"Anathema! Anathema! Anathema!"

In these few words more was said than is often bespoken in a dozen sermons. Thus it was with the old religion in Russia.

As the weeks passed and the days lengthened, signs of spring began to arrive, even though snow flurries continued. The arrival of the larks on March 9, the Day of the Forty Martyrs, was the occasion for serving little loaves "shaped like birds, with folded wings and eyes made of dried raisins." On the Friday and Saturday before Palm Sunday, people cut branches of willow. As one observer noted: "A forest of branches with their soft silver-gray catkins moved in convoys in the direction of Moscow and poured into the Red Square. The crenelated fortress walls, the Minin and Pojarsky monuments, and the Cathedral of St. Basil were surrounded by fluffy, moving thickets." Balloon sellers made their appearance to the delight of youngsters who, with their toy trumpets and their rattles, gave the impression that a fair was beginning. The pussy willows were carefully examined by the housewives, who bought them as if they had been cut from some exotic plant—but, after all, they were the "palms" which would be blessed in church the following day. On that day, the native willow replaced the consecrated boxwood trees which the Russians revered.

On Palm Sunday, after Mass, a willow branch was placed on every icon, from those in humble homes to those in the finest mansions. For the most part, during Holy Week, the city squares were deserted; the bells everywhere were silent; the faithful attended church constantly and observed a strict fast. Yet, in the midst of all this solemnity, housewives began their culinary preparations for the Easter feast, making dough for the *kulich,* sugared white cheese for the *paska,* and dyes for the countless Easter eggs that would be needed. To color the shells, dye in powder form was mixed with boiling water and vinegar. The eggs were plunged into the liquid one by one and emerged red, green, blue, or yellow, according to the dye used, but always there was an abundance of red. When greased with a scrap of bacon fat, they shone like jewels, after which they were decorated or inscribed.

At this time of year, housecleaning, polishing brass, and removing storm windows were a part of the humdrum of life, but news that the ice was breaking on the Moskva was the kind of music to the ears that everyone wanted to hear. There would be floods, and they could be serious, but such a threat came every spring. There were new garments in the making and finery to be purchased so that even the "news" of the ice was soon forgotten.

On Holy Thursday every churchgoer took home a little taper which had been lighted during Mass. A screw of paper protected the flame on the way. "Innumerable flickering glow-worms thus hurried at the same time through the twilit Moscow streets." Upon arriving home, the worshiper customarily made the sign of the cross above the door with the black smoke from the taper. Then the candles at the icons were relighted. On Easter Saturday almost everyone on the street was laden with baskets and boxes containing bread and sweetmeats. At home, the icons were decorated with paper roses by dear old *nyanya*, who always tended to such matters, and housewives carried their *paska*, eggs, and *kulich* to church to be blessed.

In those days it was fashionable to go into the Kremlin to attend midnight Mass on Easter Eve at the Cathedral of the Assumption. Practically every person in that great milling crowd held a wax taper in his hand—"a light for every face. The flames flickered in the wind. All classes of the population were represented. . . . Some carried coloured eggs and *paska* wrapped in paper. . . ." Everyone was joyful; "people were not praying; they were whispering and jostling with feverish impatience, as they awaited permission to give free expression to their gladness. Distant singing floated out through the cathedral doors. A misty glimmer floated above the entrance. All the candelabra were lit inside." This was the way Henri Troyat recalled it.

Within the cathedral, the psalms having been sung, the priest approached the sepulcher (a special altar) and with a ceremonial flourish raised the shroud to discover that the Saviour was no longer in the tomb. Then he turned and, accompanied by the clergy and the faithful, went out into the square in search of Christ. Not finding him and convinced of the truth of the miracle, he reentered the cathedral and announced to the congregation: "Christ is risen." With a burst of joy, they replied, "Truly, He is risen." Following this, friends, relatives, and strangers alike exchanged the triple Easter kiss.

The religious processions, colorful with banners, tapers, and the golden chasubles of the priests, moved forward through the crowd shedding the light of what seemed like thousands of flickering flames. The joyous singing of the choir poured forth with such volume that it seemed as if it could be heard at the ends of the earth. Then came the fireworks, showering golden rain upon the domes of the great cathedral.

In the country churches, following the night service, the congregation, with the lighted tapers still in their hands, moved to the cemetery to take the Easter greeting to their dead. Little eggs of colored porcelain were hung upon the arms of the crosses so that the dead would not be excluded from the joy of celebrating Easter.

But life has changed in Russia. Although the ancient vigil is still held each Easter Eve in the Patriarchal Church of the Transfiguration of Our Lord in the village of Peredelkino, the Soviet authorities discourage the practice of traditional religion; but they still tolerate this rite. As described in 1969, people began to arrive half an hour before midnight, when the procession was due to begin, but the scene resembled a dance hall more than a religious gathering. Gaudily dressed young girls, most wearing slacks, arrived in small groups and pushed their way into the church. The older women were already seated, having arrived early. Not wishing the company of their elders, the girls sauntered out into the courtyard, milling around and shouting insolently at one another. The boys, roughly dressed, were even coarser in their conduct. To the Russian writer who made these observations, the milling crowd seemed more oppressive than the Tartars. The young had come to watch with contempt rather than devotion.

The procession from the church into the churchyard consisted of a mere handful of priests and ten women, most of them old. All marched in a spirit of devotion, but the expression on the face of the elderly verger, carrying a cut-glass lantern, was one of fear. There was no hooliganism. Apparently it had been worse in other years.

Following the midnight church service, it was the fashion in the old days to serve an elaborate supper for friends and family. "Egg fights," as they were referred to, proved to be an ideal way to get better acquainted. Each of the guests took a colored egg and struck it lightly against one held by his partner. The holder of the unbroken egg kept his trophy for a hoped-for later encounter and proceeded with the rest of the guests to eat his share of the eggs, with salt sprinkled on them. The coloring used gave the effect of marbling—pink, red, yellow, or green—to the plump white surfaces of the shelled eggs. Then followed hot and cold *zakuski* (roasted suckling pig) and many other delicacies, along with glasses of vodka, zubrovka, and pertzovka. Toasts to the hostess, to persons present and absent, to Great Britain, to Russia, and to beautiful women added to the gala occasion. The *paska,* shaped like a truncated pyramid and packed with preserved fruits marked with "XB," the symbol of the risen Christ, has been the traditional Easter cheese dessert in Russia for generations. In evidence, too, was the delicious bread, *kulich,* with its topping of melted sugar. Supper ended at four in the morning!

On Easter morning a thousand bells rang the good news across the city. Anybody in Russia who desired could go to the church and ring the church bells on this day. In every dining room, tables were spread for the Easter feast. In the afternoon everyone went to visit friends; to forget even a single one was considered discourteous. Every table held the same fare, and the greeting was the same: "How kind of you! Come in! *Christohs voskress* (Christ is risen)!" All then kissed one another three times and proceeded to the feast. Every dish had to be sampled to please the hostess.

The whole city was in festival array as the crowds, all dressed in their Sunday best, paraded through the streets. Even the men displayed their vanity in brightly colored shirts of every hue. Their hair shone with pomade and their boots shone as well. For the women, flowered skirts and brilliantly colored scarves gave them the glamor they desired. As they met, they embraced, chatted, and exchanged Easter eggs, many of which vied with their owners in color and beauty of design. It was, in short, a day of great joy and merriment, one on which small presents were given to household servants and other employees. The parish priests, called "popes" because of their high caps and flowing beards, which gave them a venerable look, went around blessing food, exchanging pleasantries, eating, and enjoying a glass of cheer, usually vodka.

The dowager empress joined her son each year for Easter at Alexander Palace, where his entourage gathered to pay him tribute. These court receptions, resplendent with military uniforms, Arabs in turbans with shawls over their shoulders, ceremonial robes worn by the clergy, and the high fashion of royalty, included every level of Russian society. The gardeners with baskets of fruit and flowers, the blacksmiths, the cooks, the butlers, the scullions, the coachmen, the stablemen, and all the rest joined with the hundreds of visitors who gathered for the occasion. The fragrance of roses and lilacs filled the room. Protocol demanded that the emperor receive every employee, to whom he gave the traditional kisses and offered an Easter egg. Persons of lower rank were given large porcelain eggs made in the imperial factories while the dignitaries received smaller eggs made of stones from the Urals which were cut in the imperial factories.

On Easter weekend young ladies are given Easter charms shaped like eggs which may be any one of several semiprecious stones, such as lepidolite, quartz, jade and the like. The more charms a girl receives, the more popular she is. These charms are worn on a necklace rather than a bracelet.

In Russian religious art a portrayal of the head of Christ, crowned with thorns, painted on a scarf or handkerchief, is sometimes seen. The story behind it, known as the legend of *St. Veronica's Handkerchief,* was written more than fifty years ago by Selma Lagerlöf, the distinguished Swedish folklorist. As Jesus was on His way to Calvary, He passed the home of a humble woman, and sank to the ground under the weight of the heavy Cross, which He was carrying. She gave Him her veil to wipe His brow, and according to tradition, His image was imprinted on the cloth. From the sweat that fell to the ground, there sprang up a blue-flowering plant with a tiny image in each floret which has the name Veronica. Derived from the Greek, it means "true image."

At Richmond, Maine, a colony of 300 or more Russian families celebrates Easter according to the calendar of the Eastern rite in a New World replica of an old Russian Orthodox church. Here in the United States, these Russian Americans and those in other communities practice their age-old religion in freedom. On Easter Eve, carrying icons, bright banners, censers, and the traditional Easter foods, the parishioners file in procession to the church. There, after a ceremony of old Slavonic church songs and readings, the Easter foods are blessed. These foods to be eaten on Easter Day itself are oddly shaped. There is the tall cylinder-shaped *kulich* (a rich coffee cake); the *paska,* a pyramid-shaped cheese enriched with eggs, raisins, and butter; there are also fruits, preserves, honey in the comb, meats and many, many colorful Easter eggs. Many of the foods are marked "XB" (*Christohs Voskress*).

Easter Day, wrote the Abbé d'Auteroche, in his *Journey to Siberia,* written in the late eighteenth century, was set apart for visiting in Russia. "A Russian came into my room, offered me his hand, and gave me, at the same time, an egg. Another followed, who also embraced [me], and gave me an egg. I gave him, in return, the egg which I had just before received. The men go to each other's houses in the morning, and introduce themselves by saying, 'Jesus Christ is risen.' The answer is, 'Yes, He is risen.' The people then embrace, give each other eggs, and drink brandy." Eggs were colored red with Brazilwood, and it was the custom for each parishioner to present one to the parish priest on Easter morning. They were also carried for several days following Easter. Persons of high station usually displayed gilded eggs, and greetings and eggs were exchanged in the home, in the marketplace or wherever friends met.

On Easter morning in Russia, in the Ukraine, and in Poland, the egg plays a significant part in the beginning of a joyful day. Before breakfast is served, the father of the household cuts an egg that has been previously blessed and distributes pieces to all the members of his family, wishing them a happy and holy Easter. Then the family sits down to a hearty breakfast with eggs aplenty.

"Nothing," observes Kohl, a nineteenth-century writer on customs and manners, in his book *Russia,* "is more amusing than to visit the markets and stalls where the painted eggs are sold. Some are painted in a variety of patterns; some have verses inscribed on them, but the more usual inscription is the general Easter greeting, 'Christohs voskress'—'Christ is risen'; or 'Eat and think of me,' etc. The wealthier do not, of course, content themselves with veritable eggs, dyed with Brazilwood, but profit by the custom to show their taste and gallantry. Scarcely any material is to be named that is not made into Easter eggs. At the imperial glass-cutting manufactory we saw two halls filled with workmen, employed in nothing else but in cutting flowers and figures on eggs of crystal. Part of them were for the Emperor and Empress to give away as presents to the courtiers."

The Easter egg tradition is deeply rooted in Russian culture and in no country in the world has the egg been glorified in a more creative and enduring manner than by Carl Fabergé, the great goldsmith and jeweler of the late nineteenth and early twentieth centuries. Fabergé eggs are perhaps the most sought-after jewels of the Easter tradition in the twentieth century. They are often illustrated in newspapers and magazines, and in the spring of 1961 an exhibition of "Easter Eggs and Other Precious Objects" by Carl Fabergé held at the Corcoran Art Gallery in Washington, D.C., attracted international attention among art lovers and all who enjoy distinguished craftsmanship, so seldom seen in our machine age.

In the catalog of the exhibition, A. Kenneth Snowman, noted English authority on Fabergé, wrote: "Social historians of the future may well wonder how it was that, in the years following the second great World War, the popularity of certain precious objects designed and made by a pre-Revolution Russian craftsman should have increased and spread so prodigiously. The answer is not far to seek. Carl Gustavovitch Fabergé's philosophy was a simple and uncompromising one summed up in the word 'quality.' It has been said that as much as twenty per cent of his firm's output never left the St. Petersburg workshops where close to two hundred craftsmen worked. Every single article was submitted to Carl Fabergé before completion, for his approval, and, if he felt that the work fell short in any respect of the exacting standard he had set, it had to be scrapped and restarted."

A Fabergé egg enameled in translucent lime green with a green gold laurel-leaf trellis and doubleheaded eagles in black enamel and rose diamonds. Dated 1897, it served as a case for a replica of the Imperial coach used at the coronation of Nicholas II and Empress Alexandra Feodorovna at Moscow. Height of egg, 5 inches; length of coach, 3¹¹⁄₁₆ inches. (*From the collection of Messrs. Wartski, London*)

Of French Huguenot extraction, the Fabergé family left their homeland in the seventeenth century and moved to Russia to escape persecution in their own land. It was in St. Petersburg that Peter Carl was born, in 1846. Four years earlier, his father, Gustav, a goldsmith and jeweler, had established a small business in a basement. After study in Europe, young Carl returned to St. Petersburg to find that his father's jewelry business was thriving. He was in a position to supply jewelry and precious objects of art to members of Russian royal families, and they were eager for his output.

The young craftsman set forth the standard that "in the matter of objects of *vertu* and jewels generally, the emphasis previously placed squarely on sheer value should be shifted to craftsmanship. The sincerity of a gift was to be measured rather by the amount of imagination shown in its conception than by a noisy demonstration of wealth. So he switched from the production of conventional articles of jewelry to the designing of decorative objects composed of materials of considerable beauty, but of no great intrinsic value."

The tsar became one of his chief patrons and each year Fabergé designed the fabulous jeweled Easter eggs, contrived with the utmost skill and imagination, which contained ingenious surprises. These were presented to the tsarina as gifts by her husband. The English Prince Consort, Albert, was another of Fabergé's patrons, who commissioned carvings in various semiprecious stones depicting many of the domestic animals at Sandringham. Fabergé was as adept in selecting suitable materials for his pieces as he was in choosing a particular craftsman to execute his design. He assembled craftsmen from Russia, Finland, Sweden, Germany, and other countries, and was able, by his own extraordinary skill, to inspire his men to create masterpieces which were first and foremost of distinction and true originality. Great artist that he was, Carl Fabergé had the ability to train each new craftsman to share the joy and the responsibility involved in his craft.

For his precious stones, Fabergé had the vivid Siberian emerald, the gray jasper of Kalgan, and the abundant mineral deposits found in the Urals, the Caucasus, Siberia, and elsewhere in Russia, from which to draw. Here was a truly great artist and craftsman who chose the right location for his business and assembled the best available skills to produce, for a receptive public, work of incomparable beauty. But it all came to an end with the outbreak of World War I in 1914. "When the Communists took over control of private business houses, Fabergé is said to have asked, with a characteristic absence of ceremony, for ten minutes' grace 'to put on my hat and coat.' He died in Lausanne in 1920, an exile both from his country and his work."

One of Fabergé's Imperial Russian Easter eggs, in pink enamel quartered by rose diamonds. Lilies of the valley are fashioned of pearls and rose diamonds with leaves of green gold and green enamel. The egg, which measures 6½ inches high, was presented by Tsar Nicholas II to the Tsarina on April 5, 1898. (*From the collection of Messrs. Wartski, London*)

Pasha (Easter Cheese "Cake")

1 lb. pot cheese or dry cottage cheese	½ cup commercial sour cream
½ cup butter or margarine	½ cup shelled almonds, chopped
½ cup granulated sugar	½ cup mixed glacéed fruit
1 egg yolk	1 tsp. vanilla extract
Glacéed cherries	Heavy cream

Day before serving:

Pass cheese through a fine sieve. In large bowl, with electric mixer at medium speed, beat butter with sugar until fluffy. Then beat in egg yolk, cheese, sour cream, almonds, glacéed fruit, and vanilla extract. Now carefully blend in ½ cup heavy cream, whipped. Line a sieve or colander with cheesecloth. Spoon in cheese mixture, then fold ends of cheesecloth over top. Set in larger bowl to catch any drippings; refrigerate.

Just before serving:

Unfold ends of cheesecloth, invert cheese mixture on serving dish; remove cheesecloth. Decorate with a little whipped cream, then some glacéed cheeries. Makes 8 to 10 dessert servings.

Kulich (Russian Easter Bread)

2 pkg. active dry, or cakes, yeast	2 tbsp. grated lemon rind
½ cup warm water	3 eggs, beaten
½ cup milk, scalded	¾ cup canned, toasted, slivered almonds
¾ cup granulated sugar	¾ cup mixed glacéed fruit
¾ cup melted butter or margarine	6 cups sifted all-purpose flour
1 tsp. vanilla extract	1 cup sifted confectioners' sugar
¼ tsp. powdered cardamon	5 tsp. lemon juice
1 tsp. salt	Glacéed cherries

Day before serving:

Sprinkle yeast onto warm water to dissolve. In large bowl combine milk, granulated sugar, butter or margarine, vanilla extract, cardamon, salt, lemon rind; when lukewarm add yeast, eggs, stirring until well blended. Add almonds (reserving about 2 tbsp. for later use) and glacéed fruit. Now gradually beat in flour, then turn onto a floured board and knead until smooth and satiny. Place in greased bowl, cover with towel and let rise in warm place (80° to 85° F.) until doubled, about 2 hours. Punch down dough, divide in half, then place each half in a well-greased 1½-qt. casserole, or a 3-lb. shortening can. Cover and let rise in a warm place until doubled. Start heating oven to 350° F. Bake loaves 35 to 40 minutes, or until golden.

Remove to rack; let cool; remove from casseroles. Combine confectioners' sugar and lemon juice, blending until smooth. Spoon over tops of *kulich,* sprinkle with reserved almonds, then decorate with glacéed cherries. Cover with wax paper until serving time. If desired, freeze one for later use. Nice for Easter breakfast, cut into wedges. Makes 2 loaves.

Scotland

ASTER in Scotland is not nearly so significant as New Year's Day. To be sure, in certain regions of Scotland where the natives are members of the Catholic Church and the Church of England, many of the Easter customs popular elsewhere in the British Isles are observed. The Church of Scotland, being Presbyterian, naturally frowned on any of the folklore that smacked of papistry. Yet, tradition to those who cherish it manifests itself with an undying spirit in many a remote village and in some of the towns as well. In Aberdeenshire on Shrove Tuesday— also called Fasten's E'en and Eve of the Fast—children would scribble on the blackboard these words:

> *Beef-brose and bannock day,*
> *Please gie's a half-holiday.*

"Beef-brose" was a kind of brewis (broth) made with milk, water, oatmeal, and beef, and the term "bannock" referred to a cake made with oatmeal cooked on a griddle, a type of pancake.

Mock skirmishes reputed to commemorate a historic battle between the English and the invading Danes used to take place annually on the Scottish border on Fasten's E'en. The event was also considered a memorial of a fierce struggle between the English and the Scots at Ferniehurst Castle. More recently it has become a football match. At Stitrig in Scotland the opposing teams were composed of men on the western and eastern banks of the river. In Edinburgh the rivalry was between the "uppies" and the "downies," so called because of their location on the river. At Scone, bachelors challenged the married men on Shrove Tuesday.

A truly ancient rite of spring, known as Whuppity Scoorie, is observed on March 1 in Lanark. The details of its origin are unknown, but it is presumed to be a pre-Christian custom involving the making of noise to ward off those evil spirits bent on damaging crops. Another explanation centered around the annual bath given to prisoners in the local jail on this day when they were taken to the River Clyde and given a good scrubbing. In the Scottish vernacular they were "whupped and scoored," hence the musical name, Whuppity Scoorie.

For a period of four months beginning October 31 and ending February 28, the Lanark town bell in the steeple of the old parish church is not tolled in the usual manner at six each evening, but on March 1 the daily custom is renewed each year. The event calls for a celebration with hundreds of boys and girls from the area gathering at the Lanark Cross in the late afternoon, armed with paper balls with string attached. As the bell is rung the youngsters run around the church three times pelting one another with the paper balls. In recent years, coins tossed to the crowd by the town fathers have made for even more of a scramble as well as added merriment. The old kirk dates back to the very beginning of the twelfth century and the bell, one of the oldest in Europe, was recast in 1659 and again nearly a century later.

An old record of the parish at Lanark described "a gala kept by the boys of the grammar school . . . on the Saturday before Palm Sunday." They paraded through the streets with palms or their substitute, willow branches covered with catkins and decorated with daffodils, February daphne, and boxwood. As described, the custom was considered a "Popish relic of very ancient standing."

The Easter Saturday fires, which date back to pagan times, have been described vividly in old documents. The great midwinter fire at Burghead and the ceremony in Shetland, where a spurious Viking ship was sent blazing out to sea from Lerwick, undoubtedly relate to sun worship. In the days of the Druids, in both Scotland and Ireland, there were many festival tributes held in honor of the sun god, Baal, including a spring bonfire. On Easter Sunday morning, it was held that the sun whirled around like a cartwheel and gave three leaps.

Egg rolling on Easter Sunday has been a way of celebrating the occasion for centuries. Folklore scholars have documented the custom in many parts of Scotland where, as in England, special sites were set apart for the fun. In Dundee the practice is so widespread that the nationally distributed comic strips in the local newspapers depict the custom in cartoons. Picnics held on this day always include hard-boiled eggs.

Sicily

*T*HE Sicilian is the most enigmatic of Europeans. During the 2700 years of its recorded history, Sicily was invaded by the Phoenicians, Greeks, Romans, Byzantines, Vandals, Normans, Spaniards, Italians, Nazis, and the Allies of World War II. The Sicilian's religion, having evolved from so many races and cultures, is a unique form of Christianity which, to a high degree, incorporated rather than displaced the ancient paganism of his ancestors.

Of all Sicily's pagan-Christian festivals, Easter Week is celebrated with more color, more emotion, and more spontaneity than any other. Before Christianity came, the springtime fertility rites had been the principal festival of the year; thus, when the Christian religion was adopted, Easter became

Holy Week is celebrated with great color and festivity in Sicily. This little girl in Albanesi is dressed in her special native costume for this high point of the Christian year. During Holy Week, the Sicilian women dress in dark shawls for mourning, but on Easter Sunday they appear in their finest regalia.

the climax of the ecclesiastical year, although the Sicilians abandoned neither their pagan deities nor their symbols of springtime fertility. Families start the holy season by planting wheat in small clay pots which they place on window ledges. By Palm Sunday the boxes are full of the delicate blades of this fertility symbol. The Christian Trinity was simply added to the pagan goddesses. It was no problem for the legend-loving Sicilians to continue worshiping their earth goddess and to render adoration to the Virgin Mother too. Since they venerate motherhood above all else, they believe that all sons, even Jesus, are unworthy of their mothers.

During Holy Week, some towns present an Easter play on a puppet stage. The dialogue deals mostly with the Saracen-Christian wars of Sicilian history. The puppets, which are three feet tall and weigh from fifty to seventy pounds each, are operated by steel poles from the top of the stage. The stage is so perfectly proportioned and the puppets have such convincing and strong personalities that, at times, they seem human. Some of the scenes are heart-rending—a kind knight is slain by the villain and is mourned by his dog. At the end of the violent battle, Jesus, wearing a pink gown and long wig (among Latin people Christ is always portrayed as fair), drops onto the stage from heaven. Seeing the aftermath of the violence, He expresses sorrow at the evil of men and then wafts heavenward, carrying the dead knight in his arms.

In Castelmola, a tiny village "suspended like an eagle's lair on a mountain-top" above Taormina, the Last Supper is celebrated in an earthy, hearty manner. The twelve disciples, dressed in their brightly colored togas, consume enormous quantities of wine, macaroni with meat sauce, roast beef, vegetables, cakes, and cheese, all topped off with a round of cigars. The foot washing, carried out on a platform covered with red velvet, has its humorous elements.

The disciples, mostly elderly men, struggle with bootlaces and gaiters and, at times, must be assisted when they are unable to bend far enough to reach their own shoes. The monsignor, concerned about personal hygiene, uses twelve separate pieces of cotton for the washing.

On Good Friday, Christ is depicted riding on a box of green fertility wheat, no doubt a symbol of the pagan celebration of spring, the season of fertility. The great procession is accompanied by a slow, plaintive waltz tune. Conspicuous among the black-veiled matrons and the young men wearing crowns of thorns and rope lassos around their necks are little girls, dressed in white, who carry toy ladders, symbols of those used to mount the Cross.

The Resurrection is celebrated on Saturday, so the story goes, because Sicily, being so close to Palestine, received the news a day before the rest of the world. One might suspect, however, that it is because the people want to leave sorrow behind and get on with the merrymaking.

In Sicily, wisteria has a special meaning, for buried inside each tiny blossom is the hand of Christ—five tiny stamens which can be seen only when the blossom is pulled apart.

In the town of Palermo the Resurrection egg is lavishly decorated. Adorned with gold and silver and hollowed out to display toys or clocks inside, the eggs range from chicken size to as much as 33 pounds of chocolate. The Paschal lamb candies are the most delicate and artistic symbols of Christ. Made from sugar with tiny chocolate hoofs and pink noses, they come in all sizes and are decorated with green feathers and a tiny gold bell. Each one has a red spot under the neck to represent the blood of the Crucifixion. Some wear insipid expressions; others are made to look dead and lie prostrate with simulated blood splattered over their tiny bodies.

The Sicilians observe a custom most familiar to Americans, using Easter Sunday as the time for a "spring fashion show." Piana delgi Albanese is a hill town noted for its elaborate Greek Easter celebration although it is observed on the Roman Easter date. When Turkey captured Albania in the sixteenth century, the prosperous Greeks who moved to Sicily retained their own customs. Here butcher and pastry shops are open on Easter Sunday and whole lambs may be seen roasting on spits. Easter is the women's day, for hardly any of the men appear at church. During the week prior to Easter, the women dress in dark shawls in mourning for the Crucifixion, but on Easter Sunday they come forth in all their glory wearing rich colorful fabrics, lace bodices, and lace aprons. Older women wear black or Burgundy shawls; the young, a uniform of blue; and many little girls wear white hair ribbons. Affluent women wear small gold caps called "keze," and all the women wear an abundance of jewelry.

The square in Piana delgi Albanese is decorated with orange and lemon leaves entwined on the balconies and strung up the utility poles, making them look like Maypoles. Seats are provided for tourists on the town-hall balcony and on the numerous stands near the church and inside it. Girls and women wearing gorgeous costumes fill the stands, wearing red silk damask skirts richly embroidered in gold and silver, with rose and other floral designs; white blouses trimmed with handmade lace, wide pleated sleeves, and collars pleated in the back. The red bodices are also embroidered. There is a wide variety of headdress—flat, wide embroidered bands, sheer veils, and the little caps, or keze. Occasionally a black velvet bodice is seen. Most of the women carry a Madonna-blue head square trimmed with gold lace. Each of these has a green cross in back. Some wear black silk head squares and these women wear patterned olive-green skirts with black or green bodices. A few of the men who serve as heralds are garbed in white wool pantaloons, red vests embroidered in gold, white shirts with pleated sleeves with cuffs, red tasseled caps and shoes.

The clergy dress in white with richly embroidered robes and vast head-dresses. All the young assistants are clothed in black. Amplifiers carry the intoned chanting and responses of the choir outdoors. The music rendered during the two-hour service is truly elevating, but the almost continuous movement of the crowds and the quick actions of the photographers interfere with the solemnity of the occasion. After the communion, great baskets of red dyed Easter eggs are brought out and tossed high in the air for the assembled crowd. The hotel nearby serves free pastries and vermouth; then comes the parade of costumes with great merrymaking and feasting afterward.

The emotions aroused at Easter are more closely bound to the suffering of the Madonna than to the agony of Christ. When a Sicilian is asked, "Whose festa is Easter—Mary's or Jesus'?" the answer is, "It is a festa for both, but of course it was her Son who was crucified." Some think it was inconsiderate of Jesus to allow Himself to be crucified and bring such anguish upon His mother. If He could perform miracles, He could have saved Himself. Not everyone feels this way, but it is true that the heroic figure of the Sicilian Easter processions is the Virgin Mother.

Spain

In a land filled with architectural marvels, where the trappings of religion are rich in pomp and color, and the emotions of the populace are pitched high, pageantry has its most appropriate setting. Such a country is Spain, where soldiers and martyrs have rated their due measure of glory, recorded in a thousand different tales. For generations, year in and year out, countless religious processions held in the great cities and the remote villages have preserved the regional spirit of the country. The strong adherence to tradition maintained for nearly twenty centuries, by the Catholic Church, an institution slow to change its ceremonials and its dogmatic attitudes, has, nonetheless kept alive a plethora of customs that otherwise would have been forgotten, particularly in Spain.

The last three days of Carnival, which culminate the pre-Lenten period of merrymaking and amusement, are devoted to eating and all kinds of entertainment. Every town and village celebrates with bullfights, parades, feasting, masquerades, and dancing. Valencia, like many other cities, is the scene of picturesque revelry at this season when the orange trees are in bloom and the air is filled with fragrance.

Not only in Spain and in Portugal but also in many parts of Central and South America where the cultural influence of these two countries has been introduced, an old-time Carnival custom known as the "burial of the sardine" (*enterrando la sardina*) is observed, usually at the end of Carnival. In the eighteenth century the noted Spanish painter Goya used it as the subject of one of his cartoons. In bygone days, the lowly sardine was an important part of the lean Lenten diet, served so frequently that everyone wearied when it was placed on the table. Thus evolved the practice of the mock burial of something disliked, and sorrow was expressed by the participants, who drowned themselves with drink.

Each year in mid-Lent, Valencia celebrates the Fallas of San José with more than ordinary vitality. It is an occasion not only to commemorate the Feast of St. Joseph, March 19, but also to welcome spring. Parades, bonfires, fireworks, music, dancing, and general frivolity prevail for nearly a week. The Guild of Carpenters, whose guardian is St. Joseph, use this occasion to pay tribute to their patron with a parade of effigies and a huge bonfire. Using pasteboard and wood, they spend weeks creating grotesque images of animals and caricatures of prominent public figures which portray a spirit of criticism and sarcasm seldom equaled elsewhere. So extraordinary are these *fallas* that the best are saved for display in a local museum, since the carpenters in every section of the city vie with one another to produce something original and very special. Great secrecy surrounds the production of these effigies and when completed they are displayed in a public square, sometimes a week prior to the parade. As the preparations for the big event continue, bands play everywhere and the noise of fireworks fills the air periodically. On the night of March 19, the Cremá is held in the Plaza de Emilio Castelor, and the sky becomes brilliant with the flames of the huge bonfire which consumes most of the effigies.

In Spain at mid-Lent, a puppet made to represent the oldest woman in town was paraded noisily through the streets and then sawed through the middle. The ceremony, called "Sawing the Old Woman," was taken to symbolize the final dispatch of the dying year as the winter ended. At Barcelona, it was a common thing, in the early part of the nineteenth century, to see large groups of boys racing through the thoroughfares armed with saws and billets of wood. As they ran, they would sing a song declaring that they were looking for the oldest woman in the place and intended to saw her in half. In due course they would pretend to have found her, and would start sawing the billets. The latter would then be consigned to the flames.

In Spain, Palm Sunday is known as *Pascua Florida,* a name which has come to refer to all of Holy Week. The state of Florida in the United States took its name from the day of its discovery in 1513, when Ponce de León first saw land on Easter Sunday and so named the peninsula.

With Spanish Catholics, this day has long been the occasion for administering the sacrament of confirmation. The palm fronds were duly blessed, carried home and placed on balconies to serve as lightning conductors for the coming year.

On the Spanish Mediterranean coast at Elche in the Province of Alicante is located the famous palm forest which supplies the greater part of Europe with palm fronds for Palm Sunday rites. When cut, they often measure six feet long. An ancient mystery play is presented each year at midsummer in the palm forest.

On the Friday following Passion Sunday (fifth of Lent), the Feast of the Seven Sorrows of the Blessed Virgin is observed with great devotion since the Spaniards are known for their dedication to Mary. It is a day when all the shrines are decorated lavishly with greens, flowers, and clusters of young wheat.

In Hijar near Alcañiz in Aragon, a strange drum-beating ceremony takes place on Holy Thursday at midnight and lasts until late on Easter Eve. Every able-bodied man in town becomes involved, each dressed in a long robe. Some use *bombos,* big brass drums; big or little, the constant beating of hundreds of drums to the same simple march tune for hours on end becomes not only deafening and deadly monotonous but disturbing to a marked degree. Young men serenade their fiancées; some compete in groups to show their skill; others just drum away contentedly as they wander up and down the streets. Whence came the custom, no one seems to know, but it probably stemmed from an old Moslem belief that evil spirits could be driven away with drums.

Formerly, in many parts of Spain, the presentation of a miracle play was an old tradition of this solemn day. The characters included Joseph with his lily-crowned staff, Mary Magdalene wearing black curls which hung down to her knees, Pilate as a kindly old gentleman, the Wandering Jew and, at the end, the Mother of Sorrows, sitting alone in her grief.

Another curious tradition of Spain was the making of a weird effigy of a woman with seven legs. The legs represented the seven weeks of Lent, and the strange figure, made of cardboard, was known as the Queen of Lent. She was paraded about and each week one of her legs was removed; finally in Passion Week she was burned on a pyre.

In some towns in Castilla in the central northern portion of Spain, a life-sized straw image of Judas is made during Holy Week. This effigy is suspended over the street by means of a heavy rope extending from a window on one side of the street to one on the opposite side, and remains there throughout Holy Week, to be burned at a celebration on Easter Monday.

Semana Santa, Holy Week, in Spain is known throughout the world for its magnificent processions, numbering more than three thousand. In addition to the great spectacles in cities like Seville, Cartagena, Murcia, Granada, Málaga,

Pasos, heavy platforms bearing life-sized sculptured images depicting episodes in the Passion story, are brought out of the churches and paraded through Spain's city streets during *Semana Santa* (Holy Week). These processions were photographed in Murcia. The *paso* is escorted by confradías, ancient religious lay brotherhoods or trade guilds, wearing purple robes and tall pointed hoods.

Valladolid and others, every village in the country has its own demonstration of devotion and religious fervor in the form of a procession.

Seville tops them all in splendor and display. During the seven days from Palm Sunday through Easter Saturday, processions are held daily. Every parish in Seville has its day and each provides its own floats. The entire performance evolves as a huge spectacle which outshines any similar portrayal of Easter Week anywhere in Europe. Business is largely forgotten as every segment of life in this teeming old city turns out and stays out for endless hours either to participate or to watch. It is a long day for all the participants—they require twelve hours to gather at the church, remove the *pasos* (floats), organize the marches, parade the long route, and return to the parish church for the restoration to the sanctuary of the Savior's image or that of the Virgin Mary. There are always spectators every step of the way who watch, pray, and express their love and devotion for their patron virgin. She is very real to them with all the human virtues they admire and their hearts are moved deeply as she passes. Conducted by *confradías,* or confraternities of men stemming from the various guilds of earlier days, these religious processions are well organized and well directed. Members of the *confradías* wear long purple robes or tunics, tapered hoods with slits cut in them for vision, heavy shoes and white capes. A six-foot candle, carried throughout the procession, completes the costume. Participation by the members in this annual event is intimately associated with their personal lives, particularly those who march barefoot, their ankles shackled with chains, as they carry a heavy wooden cross. This voluntary performance takes the form of either penance or gratitude for a favor granted. In addition, the military and the police together with all the local politicians help to comprise the body of the marchers.

What gives these processions their great eye appeal is the floats depicting Christ at the Crucifixion with the Roman soldiers, or some variation of this theme, and Mary in glory. On the one hand, the gaunt figure of Christ in wood stands in marked contrast to the elaborately dressed Roman soldiers in the tableau; on the other hand, the Virgin Mary, with real eyebrows and hair, glass tears on her rouged cheeks and the elaborate gown she wears, is all the more regal with her glittering jewels.

A richly ornate canopy, together with masses of flowers and hundreds of lighted tapers surrounding her, inspires the crowds to shout, *"Viva la Macarena"* when Seville's Virgin of Good Hope, the city's best-loved symbol of the Queen of Heaven, appears on Good Friday night. Women along the way weep openly and occasionally the weird moving sounds of a *saeta* are heard—a wailing song of sorrow and repentance, done in low key. Later that night, before La Macarena is returned to her altar inside the church, the bearers of the *paso* tip the platform from side to side, rocking it "to make their Virgin dance." Each float is roughly nine feet wide, twenty feet long and fifteen feet high—an enormous platform weighing nearly half a ton. Sturdy stevedores hired by the confraternity bear the platforms on their heads, using a bag of sawdust and sand to cushion the weight. They take rests at

Soldiers in full military regalia escort La Macarena during a *Semana Santa* (Holy Week) procession in Seville. In Spain, these parades are military as well as religious processions, for one of the principal jobs of the army has been the protection of the church.

The *pasos* in Seville are the most ornate and elaborate in Spain. Many are masterpieces of fifteenth- or sixteenth-century wood carving. This scene, depicting Christ before Pontius Pilate, is remarkable in its workmanship and realistic detail.

The Virgin Mary plays a central role in the Holy Week
processions in Spain. Many floats depict her, throned in
glory. One of the most eminent is Seville's La Macarena
(the Virgin of Good Hope). When the procession ends at
her church, hidden bearers under the *paso* rock it from side
to side "to make their Virgin dance."

s detail of Christ and Judas from the Museo de Salzillo in Murcia
ws the lifelike qualities of these famous figures used in the Holy
ek processions.

frequent intervals, emerging from their curtained tunnels for air and a drink. A few extras follow along to relieve the burden of those overcome with fatigue. A leader walks in front of each float to give orders for stopping and starting. As they move along, the floats sway gently with the movements of the stevedores, giving the wooden figures an almost lifelike effect. Some of these figures date back to the seventeenth century while others were carved at a later time. Not only have they been restored frequently, but embellished, repainted and rejeweled from time to time so that the local spectators are fully aware of these changes.

The joy of the Easter message bursts forth on Easter Saturday in Seville and elsewhere in Spain. The mourning clothes worn by the women are discarded for the gala attire which will be worn not only on Sunday but for the fairs and fiestas which begin on Easter Monday, and the bullfights as well. Bells in the churches peal forth as all the traffic noise builds up and the babble of voices rises in the air. Preparations are made for the Easter feast complete with good wines, and the spirit of the hour is festive. Seville's fair will open in a matter of hours and so will those at Jerez, Murcia Ronda, and dozens of smaller towns. The Seville fair (*fería*) is known for its display of beautiful costumes which both men and women flaunt with pride as they stroll or ride horseback. Trading cattle is part of the event, but sociability takes over as everyone enjoys himself eating, drinking, dancing, visiting with friends, and watching the sights of the fair. These holidays become one mad whirl of uninhibited gaiety.

An old Eastertide custom associated with the cathedral at Seville was known as the dance of the Seises. The presentation was made before the high altar in the presence of the archbishop and the assembled clergy, who wore blue and white vestments. Similarly, the boy dancers, wearing blue and white doublets, white stockings and hats with plumes, performed to music in the tradition of Palestrina, marking time with castanets.

Murcia, a city with a population of a quarter of a million, is noted for its Holy Week procession as well as its *Bando de la Huerta,* battle of flowers, which begins on Easter Monday as a salute to spring. For nearly two weeks this ancient city is a constant stream of excitement, and celebration runs the gamut of human emotions. Holy Week with all its religious solemnity gives way to the gayest of gay celebrations. The *pasos* used in the Holy Week procession, carved in the eighteenth century by Francisco de Zalcillo, are noted for their conspicuous realism displaying the suffering connected with Christ's Passion so vividly that these wooden images seem almost real. Come Easter Monday, the atmosphere is vibrant with all the bursting force of spring in Spain. For five full days the revels continue with processions, costumes, fireworks, singing, dancing, and picnics galore. Villagers from the nearby countryside descend on the city to conduct a curious ceremony involving proclamations which are read with great gusto as the orators enumerate their praises and their complaints—some in earnest, some in jest. The girls in their brilliant shawls and colorful dresses rival the brilliant profusion of flowers seen everywhere and especially when the procession featuring the battle of flowers takes place. At this time the Murcians bury the sardine with a torchlight parade. Lent and winter are forgotten.

Customs associated with Easter eggs are practically nonexistent in Spain, with the exception of a fiesta held each year on Easter Tuesday in the little town of Pola de Siero in the province of Asturias in northern Spain. People from all over the province as well as from other regions of Spain flock to Pola for the occasion. The origins of this "painted eggs" festival are obscure; some say it came from the Orient, others that its roots were in an early religion which had godparents and godchildren exchanging eggs at Easter.

An old German legend, often told in Asturias, offers another clue to the source of this custom. A young duchess named Rosalinda had two suitors asking for her hand. One was the Count Arno de Lindemburgo; the other was a gallant young man named Hanno. She chose the count, which made Hanno very sad. Later, several years after the marriage, he invaded the palace in a fit of rage while the count was away; Rosalinda was forced to flee to a small town with her children. To entertain the children, she gave them colored eggs which she told them a hare from the nearby woods had laid. In truth, the duchess herself was painting the eggs to pass the time and to amuse the children. One of the children decided to go to the woods to hunt for eggs himself. In a ravine he came across a young man who had been hurt and was dying of hunger. The child gave him one of the eggs to eat and led him back to town. The young man turned out to be Arno de Lindemburgo. The duchess, happily reunited with her husband, returned home.

Before the advent of modern stoves, the eggs were cooked in the hot ashes on the hearth which gave their shells a blackish color—*prieto* in Spanish; hence the name *huevos prietos*. Late in the nineteenth century, after the discovery of aniline, the natives of Pola began to dye their Easter eggs and to paint names, verses, and flowers on them with a small stick.

It takes one hour to decorate each *huevo prieto*. Two months before Easter Tuesday, local homes are turned into workshops. Parents instruct their children in the technique of egg decoration and thus the tradition is handed down to each new generation. First the egg is scrubbed clean with soap, lye and sometimes even sand. A design is then painted on with a pencil, either directly on the eggshell or on tracing paper to be transferred. The egg is cooked for two minutes, and then, while the egg is still warm, the colors are painted on. A final touch is sometimes added—a layer of varnish. These painted eggs will last many years if the shell doesn't crack during the first few days after being painted; eventually, the inside turns to a fine powder.

One heirloom egg, decorated with an Asturian type barn, bore this inscription:

A les pascues de la Pola vienen muchos forasteros
Con intencion de comprar por poques perres los güevos.

which translated freely means:

At Eastertime many strangers come to Pola
Wishing to buy eggs with a few pesetas.

173

Dressed in their Easter finery, these young Spanish children eagerly await the fiesta held in Pola de Siero each year on Easter Tuesday. The little town in Asturias province in northern Spain is one of the few places in that country where real Easter eggs are painted. Whole families work for weeks decorating dozens of eggs which will be sold to tourists or given to families and friends during the fiesta. People from many different regions of Spain flock to Pola for the festivities. Farmers in sturdy wooden shoes come with their oxcarts. Children and adults, dressed in native costume, participate in the parade, some marching proudly along, others riding gaily on the floats. The streets are decorated with branches fastened to wires, and the thirst of marchers and spectators alike may be quenched by the large barrels of cider that are set up along the way. Bands, complete with bagpipers, and colorfully costumed dancers, displaying their talent in regional steps, add to the gaiety. (*Courtesy, House of Culture, Pola de Siero*)

These eggs are individual creations, since each painter designs the eggs and writes the verses according to his own whim and imagination. In a single family with three young people working, as many as 75 dozen eggs may be painted. Chicken, duck, and goose eggs are used. The eggs, which cost the family 35 pesetas per dozen, sell for 35 or 40 pesetas (50 to 60 cents) each. Goose eggs usually bring at least 50 pesetas.

On the day of the festival, the streets are decorated with branches fastened to wires strung from one side to the other, and large barrels of cider are provided so that spectators may have a free drink whenever they wish. All who take part wear folk costumes for the parade, which, complete with bagpipers and typical regional dances, makes a truly gala occasion. Some of the marchers wear enormous egg-shaped headgear.

In other parts of Spain the only Easter eggs found are those made of chocolate, elaborately decorated, and sold in candy shops. They are packed in fancy baskets and frequently are attached to fluffy stuffed animals, such as dogs, bunnies or chicks. An interesting contest is held each year in Cataluña, where a prize is awarded for the best chocolate sculpture. Both candy stores and individuals vie with one another to see who can produce the most elegant figure; many of them are of animals.

In some families at Easter the grandmother of the family makes a special treat for the children. She fashions a round bun or roll with a whole egg in the middle, surrounded by pieces of sausage.

Spanish tradition lays claim to close association with the true Cross. The Good Friday service in Catholic churches everywhere included the adoration or veneration of the Cross in which the members of the congregation came to the altar rail and kissed a crucifix which had been carved by the officiating priest. In Old World churches, relics related to the life of Christ were venerated similarly. The practice stemmed from one carried out in Jerusalem as early as the fourth century. The Roman province of Spain was the home of a lady named Egeria, who recorded it in a diary of a pilgrimage which she made to the Holy Land A.D. 380. Francis X. Weiser gives us this account: "According to her report, not only the Cross but also the title board bearing the inscription (John 19: 19–22) was presented to the pilgrims. They were allowed to kiss, but not to touch, the sacred objects. When the Mohammedans conquered Jerusalem under Sultan Saladin, in 1187, they took the relics away, and no trace of them was ever found. Fortunately, a piece of the true Cross was brought to Rome in the fourth century, and from it many churches in all countries have received small particles as relics."

In the cathedral at Valencia may be seen the *Santo Cáliz* or *Santo Grial*— the Holy Grail. It is claimed to be the very cup that Jesus used in the Last Supper. Made of agate, adorned with gold, it is embellished with twenty-six pearls (originally twenty-eight), two rubies and two emeralds. Tracing its provenance back to the Virgin Mary, whose property it was, this jeweled cup has been in Spain for centuries and in Valancia for more than 500 years. Tradition has it that Mary visited Spain to give Saint James a pillar (now in the church at Zaragoza). Other relics including fragments of the Savior's cloak, thorns from His crown, one of Saint Peter's sandals, a lock of Mary Magdalene's hair and several hundred small pieces of the Holy Cross are to be found in Spanish churches. In this country where scores of saints once lived are to be found countless records and relics of their lives.

Toledo is almost as well known for its intriguingly shaped marzipan sweets as for its delicate damascene work and its keen blades used in bullfighting. Almonds, the gift of the Moslems, are crushed to a paste and combined with sugar and egg to make this toothsome confection which the Spanish call *mazapán*.

Even today in Spanish markets rabbit is often displayed with the furry paws left on to prove that it is not cat. But hare, that larger cousin of the rabbit, has never been too well liked, for it is feared to be rabid.

TRADITIONAL RECIPE

Paella Valenciana

1 tsp. dried saffron	2 cups rice
4 to 5 cups broth, half chicken, half clam	2 large tomatoes, peeled, seeded, and diced
1 cup olive oil	2 small lobsters, cut into chunks
2 cloves garlic	12 mussels or clams or both, scrubbed
1 3-lb. chicken, cut into 2-inch pieces	2 chorizos, or Italian sausages
Salt and pepper	1 small jar pimentos
1 large onion, finely chopped	½ cup cooked green peas

Bring saffron and broth to a boil and keep hot. In a 12- to 14-cup casserole or paella pan heat half the oil and fry the garlic until brown; remove and discard it. Fry the chicken pieces until golden. Season with salt and peper, turn, and add oil as needed. Add the onion and cook until brown; add more oil and rice, and cook, stirring about 3 minutes or until slightly browned. Add tomatoes and simmer over low heat for 2 to 3 minutes. Add 4 cups broth to rice mixture and stir once. Bury lobster pieces, mussels, and clams in the rice and cover and simmer for 12 to 15 minutes or until rice is done and fish is cooked. Discard any unopened shells. If rice needs more cooking, add broth as needed. Put paella in a preheated 450° F. oven for 10 minutes, uncovered. Meanwhile, slice and fry the chorizos in 2 tbsp. olive oil, reserve. Cut the pimentos in even sections and heat slightly in oil. Mix peas and chorizos into paella. Arrange pimentos in a decorative circle over rice. Serve very hot. Serves 8 to 10.

Any cooked vegetables may be added (artichoke hearts, zucchini, yellow squash). The paella may also be made with chunks of fish. Heat oil and garlic, discard garlic, cook until golden brown 2 pounds solid fish and continue recipe as above, minus shellfish.

Sweden

WEDEN'S contribution to Easter lore may well rest in the great collection of folk tales written by Selma Lagerlöf, who was born in Sweden in 1858 and became one of the world's most distinguished collectors and writers of legends. Her best-known work is her *Christ Legends*. Her legend of robin redbreast is known the world over. She tells us that when God created the world, He made not only heaven and earth, but all the animals and plants as well, giving each of them its name. As He painted the birds, He turned to a little creature with gray feathers and said, "Your name will be Robin Redbreast. Although there is no red among your feathers now, you must earn this name, for red is the badge of courage."

Wondering what he might do to earn his feathers, the robin flew into a nearby rose thicket to build his nest. To the other birds of the air, it looked as though he were waiting for a rose petal to fall which would cling to his throat and breast and thus give him the colored vest he so desired. For a long time he and his fledglings tried in every way possible to earn their promised red breasts. Neither the swelling of the robin's breast in song nor the encounters he had in fighting other birds would spark the color in his breast. All efforts seemed to end in sheer despair.

Then, one world-shaking morning, when the universe seemed in a state of confusion, a courageous robin decided that it was his destiny to earn the coveted red breast so that all who followed him might bear the desired plumage. Determined in his quest, he flew to a hill near Golgotha in the Holy Land. It was shortly after noon, the day Christ was crucified. Happy and hopeful that his mission would be a success, he was soon overwhelmed with sorrow as he witnessed Jesus suffering on the Cross, made from the trunk of a hawthorn. His heart was filled with sadness when he saw the crown of thorns that the cruel soldiers had placed on Christ's brow. Finally he became so engulfed with pity that, forgetting his timidity and his reluctance to be near people, he flew above the crowd and circled around the Cross again and again until, at last, darting down in a sudden burst of courage, he pulled a large thorn from the brow of Christ.

As Robin performed this impulsive act in full view of the soldiers, the blood from the wound made by the thorn oozed out of Christ's brow and stained the bird's breast so deeply that when he flew away he was marked with a splash of bright red. There was no mistaking the color or what had made it. When he reached his nest, his family welcomed him, exclaiming as they fluttered, "The red badge of courage is ours at last!" The red breast which God had foretold must be earned was to be forever the identifying mark of Robin Redbreast.

Selma Lagerlöf had another Christ legend that the Swedes like to recount: the tale of the donkey, the beast so closely identified with Christ all through His life. At the beginning of the world, when all things were created, the donkey got his long ears because he could not remember the name that had been given to him. No sooner had he taken a few steps over the meadows of Eden than he forgot, and three times he had to return to inquire what his name was. At last God grew somewhat impatient and taking him by his two ears, said, "Thy name is ass, ass, ass!" And, while He thus spoke, He pulled both of the ass's ears that he might hear better and remember what was said to him.

Gilbert Keith Chesterton, who charmed the reading public of the English speaking world with his verse during the first third of the twentieth century, has given us the rest of the story in his poem "The Donkey":

> *When fishes flew and forest walked*
> *And figs grew upon thorn,*
> *Some moment when the moon was blood*
> *Then surely I was born.*
>
> *With monstrous head and sickening cry*
> *And ears like errant wings,*
> *The devil's walking parody*
> *On all four-footed things.*
>
> *The tattered outlaw of the earth,*
> *Of ancient crooked will;*
> *Starve, scourge, deride me: I am dumb,*
> *I keep my secret still.*
>
> *Fools! For I also had my hour,*
> *One far fierce hour and sweet:*
> *There was a shout about my ears,*
> *And palms before my feet.*

An old Scandinavian legend states that the swallow flew near the Cross on the day Christ was crucified and, being grief-stricken, yet not knowing what to do, called out, *"Svale! Svale!"* which means "Cheer up! Cheer up!" Since then the swallow has been called the "bird of consolation" and its evening twitterings are soothing sounds. The Scandinavians also believed that, since the swallow was not seen in the wintertime, having hibernated in the mud, his emergence in the spring was like a new birth or resurrection. In religious paintings, swallows on the roof serve as an emblem of the Resurrection.

Llewellyn Lloyd, a Londoner, the son of an English banker, went to Sweden to hunt bear more than a century ago. He stayed on, fascinated by the customs of the Swedish people, and, in a sense, may have paved the way for Selma Lagerlöf by writing *Peasant Life in Sweden,* which was published in 1870. In more recent years, Sweden's Uppsala University has become widely known for its work in ethnology.

Swedish housewives, as do all Scandinavian women, give their homes a serious spring cleaning before Eastertide. They bring flowers indoors and use yellow blooms whenever they can, for yellow is to Easter what red is to Christmas.

On Shrove Tuesday—Fat Tuesday in Sweden—a *Semla,* or Fat Tuesday bun, is eaten. This large, wheat-flour bun, filled with almond paste and whipped cream, is served floating in a bowl of hot milk. In Iceland they call it the "cream bun"; in both countries many of them are consumed. For the Icelanders it is Bursting Day, an occasion for eating to excess.

During Lent, while trees are still leafless, it is customary to cut birch branches and decorate them with chicken or rooster feathers which have been dyed red, yellow, purple, orange, or green. As the weeks advance, the twigs gradually produce shoots. At Easter time, the feathers are removed; small cotton chickens, clay birds or flowers made of broken eggshells are added to the branches.

Belief in witchcraft is deeply rooted in Swedish folklore. It was believed that its influence was ever present and fear of witches reached its height on the Thursday of Easter week. In the dark of the night that separated Wednesday from Holy Thursday, it was held that the hags set off through the air for the witches' sabbath at Blåkulla, or Blue Hill. There, meeting with the devil, they engaged in orgiastic rites. The witches were always served by the devil a most delectable dish—frogs and snakes!—after which they danced weird, ritualistic dances to the music of magpies. Since magpies were always missing in Sweden on Holy Thursday, they were linked with the devil, no matter what the day.

Those persons who were brave and curious and yearned for adventure could use a cow, a goat, a rake, a broomstick, or any other mode of transportation and, standing beside their own fireplace, make a wish to join the witches' party. All that was necessary to go ariding was to mutter softly, "In Satan's name straight up and away, past every corner to the end of the world." Legend has it that a servant girl, overhearing her mistress repeat the "code" and seeing her disappear up the chimney, thought she would try it for herself. She straddled a broomstick as she stood by the hearth, but forgetting the magic words, she said, "In Satan's name straight up and down." Poor thing, throughout the night she was violently hurled up and down the chimney and never saw the witches' rendezvous.

It was believed to be necessary to take great precautions while the witches were away at their meeting, which lasted until Easter night. One was not to forget to shut the damper of the stove early in the evening to guard against the possibility that an old hag might tumble down the chimney and land on the hearth. Also, one was not to light a fire after the sun had set or before it had risen, because as far as the smoke curled outward and polluted the air, that far the witches had power to play tricks during their nightly raids. In fact, everything in the house had to be protected against "witch-need." Oven rakes, dung forks, and particularly broomsticks had to be hidden, for they were "witch-steads." In order to insure that cattle would not be commandeered, a cross was drawn on their noses with a tar stick. Likewise, a cross painted on the door of a farmer's house or barn was a good precaution—the more effective if the one who did it wore a red skirt. A sandwich was never handed to a tramp, for if a witch grabbed it and smeared butter from it on her hands, she held complete power over all dairy products. Naturally, children were curious about witch habits and had to be protected carefully lest their curiosity lead them into witches' harm.

Besides witches' "notions," many other unusual superstitions were once prevalent. Those connected with Holy Thursday prohibited a woman from spinning on that day; otherwise, she would experience difficulty in childbirth. If water was taken from the spring early on this Thursday morning, about an hour before birdsong, one was assured of protection from sunburn that year.

Another witch tale was told about a farmhand who shot a magpie on Easter morning. When he went to pick it up, he discovered he had shot a witch. Upon closer examination, he realized that the hag was none other than his master's wife.

The "Easter witch" comes alive today when, on Easter Eve, small girls with red on their cheeks and soot on their noses and eyebrows parade around dressed up in long skirts, gay blouses and scarves. Each always carries both a broomstick and a copper coffeepot, for witches love hot, black coffee.

Selma Lagerlöf, in her autobiography, *Memories of My Childhood,* has recorded her experiences with witches. Growing up at "Mårbacka," she soon realized that in the middle of the afternoon of Easter Eve the maids always stole out of the kitchen, carrying bundles of clothing under their arms, and headed for the cow barn. In the barn, they made a "witch" out of the clothing by stuffing straw into blouse, skirt, sleeves, and gloves. For the head, a coarse gray kitchen towel was tied together at the four corners and stuffed with straw. Eyes, nose, mouth and two or three wisps of hair were sketched with charcoal, and the head was topped with an old screen bonnet which the housekeeper used in the summer when she went to capture a swarm of bees. Then the witch was placed outside the entrance, and the children were called to see her. The children all remembered being "awfully frightened," Miss Lagerlöf recalls.

It was much more fun and more creative to write Easter letters. Miss Lagerlöf stated that they were never written with pen and ink; rather, they were painted. In the middle of the page of every letter stood a gay-colored Easter man or woman holding a broom, a rake, a horn and other Paschal implements. It was important to the youngsters to receive as many letters as possible and the only way to be sure was to make as many as possible to give away.

In Sweden, Good Friday is solemnly observed—even newspapers suspend publication. In olden times, families practiced the Good Friday custom of "birching" or switching one another with birch branches in remembrance of the lashings Jesus suffered before the Crucifixion. Fried salt herring, green peas, and beer soup are the traditional Good Friday food.

Easter Sunday was a good time to find out who really was a witch. Hags went to church the same as ordinary people, but if one listened carefully one would discover that a witch said her prayer backward!

Painting Easter eggs is a contradiction in Swedish upbringing. Children are taught not to play with their food, but Easter eggs are different. Egg eating at Easter time is a real ritual, for it used to be forbidden to eat eggs during Lent. Thus, eggs were saved for a feast on the great day. Coloring the eggs is enjoyed by all. The eggs are cooked, with hay, flowers, coffee grounds, onion skins or birch leaves being used for coloring. To achieve a lovely pattern, the eggs are wrapped with a variety of leaves, flowers or threads before boiling. Egg rolling has been a popular Easter sport for the last 500 years.

Easter fires are still common in western Sweden and are usually located near the center of the village. This practice is accompanied by much shouting, dancing, and merrymaking and may last until dawn.

The Monday after Easter is set aside to commemorate Jesus' walk to Emmaus with the two disciples whose "eyes were opened" as He sat with them at meat, blessed bread, and broke it. In Sweden, friends and relatives spend the day visiting and sipping tall glasses of *äggtoddy* (egg toddy), a delicious beverage made of egg yolk, sugar, sherry, and boiling water—as traditional to Easter as *glögg* is to the Yuletide festivities.

TRADITIONAL AND REGIONAL RECIPES

Fat Tuesday Bun (Semla)
(served after a main course of pork and brown beans!)

1 package active dry yeast	1 egg beaten
¼ cup warm water	⅓ cup sugar
½ cup butter	3 cups sifted all-purpose
⅔ cup milk	flour

Filling

8 oz. almond paste	powdered sugar
½ cup whipping cream	

Dissolve yeast in warm water. Melt butter and add milk. Pour the tepid mixture over yeast. Add half of the beaten egg, sugar, and 1 cup flour. Beat well and add more flour, a little at a time until dough is smooth but not too firm. Let rise in bowl for 30 minutes. Turn dough onto floured baking board and knead until smooth and elastic. Shape into a dozen round buns. Place on buttered cookie sheet, cover with towel and let rise in warm place until double in bulk.

Brush tops of buns with remainder of beaten egg. Bake at 400°F. about 12 minutes or until golden brown. Let cool on rack. Cut tops off buns and scoop out a little from the inside. Insert a slice of almond paste into each bun. Garnish generously with whipped cream. Put the lid on top and sprinkle with powdered sugar. Serve in soup bowl with hot or cold milk.

On Sheer Thursday (Holy Thursday), a green soup is served by the Swedes, not so much because of its nutritional value, but because the green leaves are suggestive of the approaching spring.

Green Soup (Grönsoppa)

1 lb. kale, spinach, or very young nettles	1 tbsp. butter
	2 tbsp. flour
2 cups water	2 cups beef bouillon
1 tsp. salt	White pepper

2 tbsp. chopped chives

Wash the leaves and look them over. Cook in water with salt for 10 minutes. Strain, saving the liquid. Chop leaves finely. Melt butter and stir in flour. Add bouillon and cooking liquid; simmer for a few minutes. Stir in the greens and season with pepper and chives. Add more salt if needed. One-half cup light cream may be added to the soup for a milder flavor. Serve with poached eggs or wedges of hard-boiled eggs floating in the soup. Makes 4 servings.

Good Friday Beer Soup With Bread (Ölsupa Med Bröd)

4 slices rye bread	½ tbsp. grated lemon rind
2 cups beef bouillon	½ tsp. cinnamon
2 cups light beer	Pinch of nutmeg
2 tbs. sugar	⅔ cup sour cream

Soften the bread in the bouillon and break by beating. Add beer and spices. Bring to boil. Taste for seasoning and serve hot with a dab of sour cream on each serving. Makes about 5 servings.

Switzerland

*A*T four o'clock in the morning on Shrove Tuesday, the lights go out all over the market square in the city of Basel and into the darkness come the sounds of fifers, drummers, and groups of young people wearing masks and weird costumes. In each group there are four men, the "standard-bearers," who carry immense transparent lanterns which satirize mercilessly the local politicians and their views. The sentiments expressed are easily discernible in the dark because many of the marchers carry colorful lanterns on long poles which further illuminate the transparencies. These are created in secret by skilled artists who aim for a prize in any of several categories. At five o'clock the lights are turned on again, signifying that the carnival is over. All the spectators, as well as the drummers, fifers, and marchers hurry into the taverns and inns to warm themselves with a bowlful of thick brown flour soup that is part of the celebration in Basel. The soup takes its color from flour browned in shortening. Milk, salt, water, and eggs are added to produce a stabilizer, or antidote, for too much merriment.

Carnival has always been a happy time for all in Switzerland, except for eligible girls who were unmarried and were approaching spinsterhood. In many towns the custom was to single out these girls, drench them with wine, and force them out of the Carnival dances in which their younger companions were taking part.

Each town has its own way of celebrating Carnival. In Schwyz, at Einsiedeln, Carnival runners move through the streets tirelessly, from Sunday until the start of Ash Wednesday, carrying heavy bells. These runners, burdened down by the weight of the heavy metal, have to bend their backs to support the bells, which emit a resounding, incessant clang with every step the runners take along the highways and byways. In addition, these runners wear grotesque false faces. This ancient custom is patterned upon the primitive practice of the "driving out of winter" with fearsome, deafening noise and horrible faces, and ringing in the welcome spring. Wooden masks, handed down from father to son for generations, are worn by the folk of Flums in a similar celebration.

The sound of bells is an integral part of life in Switzerland. That unforgettable reverberating ring, spanning hill and vale, produced by the crescendo of cowbells, the tinkle of sheep bells, and the resonance of church bells, culminates in a fugue of tonal warmth to welcome Easter. Equally soul-stirring is the magnificent church music, and everyone attends services on Easter Sunday. Then the rest of the day is spent in family merrymaking and festivity. In Lutheran churches, all newly confirmed children attend services in a body for the reception of Holy Communion. Boys are confirmed on Palm Sunday and girls on Good Friday.

Preparing Easter eggs in Switzerland involves more than ordinary skill. Minute flowers and leaves are bound onto an egg before it is boiled with onion peel, to produce a white pattern on the tinted background. A weed called scarleteen, not unlike parsley in appearance, is one of the plants used. Sometimes a design, a message, or the name of the recipient is traced on the already dyed egg with a white wax pencil; or the color is carefully scratched off with a sharp knife leaving white lines and letters behind. Scratch-carved eggs were popular in Switzerland as early as the 1880's. Parents hide the eggs on Easter morning under trees and shrubs and elsewhere in the garden. Besides the hens' eggs which have been dyed, there are sugar eggs in great variety, and the famous Swiss chocolate eggs, decorated with colored sugar fluting. These wondrous eggs have been left by "the Easter Hare"; to prove it, the children are given little chocolate and marzipan rabbits!

There are egg games that the boys play; in some places there is a lively egg competition in which one group throws a given number of eggs into a flat basket while another covers a specified distance on foot or on horseback. The matching of eggs is a popular Easter pastime at home, in restaurants and wherever people gather, for the person who smashes the most eggs gets the largest reward.

An *äggtoddy* is drunk in Switzerland on Easter Eve. It is a foamy drink made of spirits, boiling water, sugar, and egg yolk. A similar egg toddy is traditional in Sweden on the same Holy Saturday.

Easter Monday is a holiday in Switzerland, and the school year begins the following day, which is also the starting day for young apprentices in the various trades. A special cheese pie is served on Easter Monday and some of the natives refer to the day as "cheese pie" Monday.

Swiss chocolates play an important part in the Easter delicacies and sweets that are served, as does Osterfladen, the Swiss Easter cake, which is made according to several recipes. Here is a recipe from Zurich, furnished by Anne Mason:

For Pastry

8 tbsp. flour	2 tbsp. very fine granulated sugar
Dash of salt	1 egg
4 tbsp. butter	

For Filling

1 pint milk	Grated rind ½ lemon
pinch salt	3½ tbsp. ground almonds
3½ tbsp. groats (barley, oats or wheat)	¼ teaspoon cinnamon
2 tbsp. butter	3 tbsp. sultanas (variety of raisin from Smyrna)
2 tbsp. sugar	¾ cup sour cream
4 eggs, separated	

Make the pastry by sieving flour and salt into a basin, then rub butter in lightly with tips of fingers until mixture resembles fine bread crumbs. Add sugar, and beat egg with water, adding just enough to mix to a firm dough. Turn onto a floured board and pat out into a rectangle to fit into a deep baking tin.

For the filling, boil the milk, then stir in groats and salt, and simmer until thick, stirring occasionally. Cream butter and sugar, and beat in egg yolks, add lemon rind, almonds, cinnamon, sultanas, and sour cream and mix with cooked groats. Beat egg whites until stiff and fold into filling. Spread this mixture over pastry and cook in a moderate oven (350° F. or No. 5) until pastry is golden and filling cooked.

The Ukraine

I   N the Near East, all through Lent, many priests keep a total fast for two days out of every three. Among the Ukrainians, the Russians, and other Slavic peoples, it is common practice for the faithful to fast until three in the afternoon. Children fast voluntarily until noon. Since neither meat nor dairy products are used by those who keep a strict fast, Lenten meals consist of vegetables, fruit, honey and a special bread. In the Ukrainian Church, Wednesday of the fourth week in Lent is called "Middle Cross Day," on which little cakes baked in the shape of a cross are eaten.

On Palm Sunday, the Ukrainians and Poles strike each other gently with the pussy willows which they use as "palms"; this custom they call God's Wounds (Boze Rany) and they sing:

It is not I that strikes, it is the palm
Six nights hence—the great night!
A week hence—the great day!

Holy Thursday is called the "Thursday of the Passion" by the Ukrainians. On this day, the Volhynian Ukrainians used to bathe in a nearby river, for it was believed that the water held special curative power. At night special dishes were served commemorating the Last Supper. The service celebrated on Good Friday is known as the "Royal Hours," so-called because originally the East Roman Emperors used to attend.

On Easter, the "Great Day" (*Velikden*), the Ukrainians greet each other by saying, "Christ is risen"; the response is, "He is truly risen." Church bells are rung at short intervals all day long on Easter Sunday to remind the faithful that it is the greatest feast of the entire year.

Both the Ukrainians and the Poles decorate eggs with plain colors or simple designs; these eggs are called *krasanki*. However, the *pysanki* are those most sought after, for they are exceptionally beautiful in design, made in a most distinctive manner with unusual ornamentation. Each is a masterpiece of native skill, exquisite workmanship and, above all, patient labor, inspired by ancient Byzantine art. Melted beeswax is applied with a stylus to the fresh white eggs, which have been blown of their contents. They are then dipped in successive baths of dye. After each dipping, wax is painted over the area where the preceding color is to remain. Gradually, the whole complex pattern of lines, colors, and geometric splendor emerges. No two *pysanki* are alike. Although the same symbols may be reused, each egg is designed with originality. The sun, for good fortune; the hen or rooster, for fulfillment of wishes; the stag or deer, for good health; flowers, for love and charity—these are some of the symbols used. Intersecting ribbons, dots, checkerboards, and rhombic designs are employed by the egg artists.

The *pysanki,* as well as all eggs used at Easter, are blessed by the priest before they are given to the recipients, and many are kept from year to year as heirlooms. Six or seven hours to decorate a single egg, using intricate designs, is not unusual, but time is of little moment where love is concerned. When a girl dropped an Easter egg in a stream, she hoped it would be retrieved by her suitor, for her name was inscribed on it and he would be the man she would marry. It was customary with the younger girls to rub the red-dyed eggs against their cheeks to make them glow so that they would have a cheerful, healthy appearance at the Easter family feast.

In the villages of the Ukraine, the joyful Easter celebration lasted several days so that farm workers seldom resumed work until the Thursday after Easter. The time was spent visiting, playing cards, singing, and dancing the traditional *hahilki*. In fact, during the weeks following, until Ascension Day, many kinds of festivity were enjoyed. Despite political strife, the Ukrainians have clung tenaciously to their beloved customs down through the years. Even in America, where, in many communities, they have their own churches, they have adapted their traditions to present-day living. Shortly after Easter they hold a special church dinner at which food, blessed by the priest on Easter Sunday, is served. This includes sausage, borsch (a rich soup made of beef, vegetables including beets and cabbage, herbs, and sour cream), *pirozhki* (a kind of cheese pastry filled with a mixture of beef, onion, and dill), ham, *babka* (a kind of coffee cake), *paska* (their Easter bread), cheesecake and a variety of pastries. The blessed food was considered symbolic of the hospitality of the home as well as good health and good fortune. Pussy willows, greens, and decorated eggs are used to decorate the table.

Wales

To a great extent Wales shares many of the Easter customs of England. However, Easter is not nearly so important as Christmas to the Welshman, who, nonetheless, is a devoted follower of tradition, as signified by his pride in his strange-sounding language. The language of Wales, essentially that of the Britons in ancient times, has been kept alive largely through the Sunday Schools. As one poet expressed it, the Welsh are:

Ancient folk speaking an ancient speech
And cherishing in their bosoms all their past.

The feast of St. David on March 1 usually falls in the Lenten season and the observance of this day is associated with wearing a leek or a daffodil. The custom can be traced back to the Battle of Hatfield Manor A.D. 653, when the Britons defeated Edwin of Northumbria and wore leeks in memory of St. David, the patron of Wales, who is reputed to have survived for several years on such meager sustenance as bread and wild leeks. The reference was well documented in Shakespeare's time, the passage being found in his play *King Henry V*. Fluellen tells the king: "The Welshmen did goot service in a garden where leeks did grow, wearing leeks in their monmouth caps; which, your Majesty knows, to this hour is an honorable pledge of the service; and I do believe your Majesty takes no scorn to wear the leek upon Saint Tavy's day."

Alexander Howard in *British Cavalcade* reminds us that the Welsh students at Jesus College, Oxford, always wear this green emblem on March 1, as do the officers and men of the Welsh Guards and Welsh Regiment. "At the officers' mess of the Welsh Guards the drum major, accompanied by the regiment's all-important mascot goat, bedecked with rosettes and red and blue ribbons, marches round the table after dinner carrying a tray of leeks. Every officer and his guest who admits to never having eaten a leek is required, as a token of being a true Welshman, to do so there and then by standing on his chair with one foot and on the table with the other. All the while, the drummer, standing behind the chair, beats a roll."

Another belief has it that the Welshmen "beautify their hats with verdant leek" from the custom by which every farmer, in bygone times, contributed his leek to the common repast when he went to the Cymortha, or association, to help another with the spring plowing. The daffodil, or Lent lily, is associated with St. David's Day in Wales, for it was believed it would always be in flower for this feast.

Sul/y/Blodav, or Palm Sunday, is popularly known as Flowering Sunday, when Welsh families visit their cemeteries to place bouquets of fresh flowers on the graves of their beloved dead.

Sunrise services are part of the observance of the Chapel Holiday, as Easter Sunday is called. Special music and responses mark the day. Wearing new finery, however, is reserved for Whitsunday. Decorating eggs and all the attendant festivities are the delight of the children. A thirteen-year-old girl living in Goytre wrote: "On Easter morning we, my brother, my sister, and myself, eagerly hunt the garden for Easter eggs which Daddy and Mummy have hidden among the flowers, bushes, grass and leaves. When we find them we set them in the middle of the table in a dish while we eat our breakfast. Afterwards we cut one of them into five portions and eat them before we drink our tea. This is just a little tradition. Daddy says he used to do it when he was small, and I enjoy doing it now."

In Anglesey it is customary for children to go the rounds of farms begging for eggs. Known as "Clapio wyau," the youngsters "clap two pieces of slate, held between their thumbs and first two fingers, to give a castanet effect, and make out that they are in want singing:

> *Clap, clap, gofyn wy,*
> *Bechgyn bach ar ben y plwy.*

> (Clap, clap, ask for an egg,
> Small boys on the parish.)

188

The Lore of the Egg

O F all the folk symbols associated with Easter, none is more conspicuous than the egg, the symbol of fertility and new life. To most of us, it is an even more familiar example of the beginning of life than the seed of a plant. Actually, the significance of the egg in Christian tradition and folklore is only part of a fabulous story. The egg as a cosmogenetic symbol, indicating the origin of all things, is an integral part of the mythology of all races.

From the lore of ancient Egypt and India we learn that the egg was a symbol of the creation of the world. These beginnings were associated with Geb, whose body was the earth, and Nut, the queen, who was the sky. The son of this union was Osiris, lord of the underworld. These two also produced an egg from which the universe developed. From this egg came the extraordinary Bennu bird or Phoenix, symbol of the sun. The early Christians adopted this bird as a representation or symbol of Christ, the Savior. The phoenix was chosen for the belief that it died and came to life again. This feat was accomplished by the bird, which set fire to its nest and burned itself to ashes. In the ashes was an egg, which hatched to produce the destroyed bird. This strange event, it was believed, took place every 500 years. In religious art, the phoenix resembles the peacock, another symbol of Christ's Resurrection.

Also of Egyptian origin is the story of Ptah, chief of the gods, who fashioned a golden egg at a potter's wheel while seated on his throne. He is described as "Father of beginnings, and creator of the egg of Sun and Moon."

From ancient Hindu culture we learn of the World-Egg (often referred to as the Mundane Egg), which was formed in the "waters of chaos" before time began. This was also a golden egg, from which Prajapati, the father of all creatures, came forth. Another version of similar origin credits this god as the creator of the World-Egg, formed from his own perspiration. This egg also contained both heaven and earth. In his book *Easter, Its Story and Meaning,* Alan W. Watts quotes a Hindu scripture: "In the beginning of this world was

189

merely non-being. It was existent. It developed. It turned into an egg. It lay for a period of a year. It was split asunder. One of the two eggshell parts became silver, one became gold. That which was of silver is the earth. That which was of gold is the sky. What was the outer membrane is the mountains. What was the inner membrane is cloud and mist. What were the veins are the rivers. What was the fluid within is the ocean. Now, what was born therefrom is yonder sun."

Old Phoenician culture has given us a similar story of the origin of the egg from water. The Chinese believed that the first man had sprung from an egg, dropped from heaven to float upon the primordial waters.

Investigations made in prehistoric tombs in Russia and Sweden revealed the presence of clay eggs believed to be emblems of immortality. An ancient belief held that an egg placed in the walls of a new building would protect it against evil and witchcraft. The Romans described a disaster by saying, *Ovum ruptum est* (The egg is smashed). Charles Godfrey Leland, author of *Gypsy Sorcery and Fortune Telling,* has gathered a large basket of egg proverbs among which are the following:

> His eggs are all omelette (French).
> Eggs in the pan give pancakes but nevermore chicks (Low German).
> Never a chicken comes from broken eggs (Low German).
> Bad eggs, bad chickens. Hence in America "a bad egg" for a man who is radically bad, and "a good egg" for the contrary.
> Eggs not yet laid are uncertain chickens; i.e., Do not count your chickens before they are hatched.
> Tread carefully among eggs (German).
> The egg pretends to be cleverer than the hen.
> He waits for the egg and lets the hen go.
> He who wants eggs must endure the clucking of the hen (Westphalia).
> He thinks his eggs are of more account than other people's hens.
> One rotten egg spoils all the pudding.
> Rotten eggs and bad butter always stand by one another.
> Old eggs, old lovers, and an old horse
>   Are either rotten or for the worse.
> "All eggs are of the same size." he said, and grabbed the biggest.
> As like as eggs (Old Roman).
> As sure as eggs.
> His eggs all have two yolks.
> If you have many eggs you can have many cakes.
> He who has many eggs scatters many shells.
> To borrow trouble for eggs not yet hatched.
> Half an egg is worth more than all the shell.

In November, 1969, United Press International flashed on the wires from Helsinki, Finland, a bit of contemporary egglore which was widely published: "John Groenvall has been repairing broken eggs for forty years. The British

Easter-egg heads. (*Photo: H. Armstrong Roberts*)

Museum and many others have sought his services. Only two other persons in Europe can fix a smashed egg and one of them was Groenvall-trained. Because the eggs he repairs are used mostly for scientific purposes, they must weigh almost the same after they are mended as before they were broken. Repairing an egg requires infinite skill and patience from fitting the fragile parts together, to gluing, to coating with thin enamel to fill the cracks, and simulating missing pieces. It may take him as long as ten hours to mend an egg.

"He has been paid as much as $720.00 for repairing a single egg, but usually he collects $2.98 an hour for his work, or more, depending on the rarity of the egg and the damage involved. Until two years ago, he spent two months a year classifying and labeling eggs with lettering which measured one millimeter high (one twenty-fifth of an inch)."

These wondrous accounts seem remote, in a way, from the brightly colored egg trees of German origin, the delightful customs of Christian Europe and parts of Asia, the egg-rolling contests in Washington, D.C., and the delectable candy eggs and similar confections of our own day. And yet, the egg as a symbol of death and life has been apparent to practically every race down through the ages. The shell may well be compared to a tomb which encases a germ of life. When the shell is broken or disintegrated, a new life is born.

Thomas Aquinas, the great theologian of the thirteenth century, taking his inspiration from an earlier Greek philosopher, posed the riddle, "Which came first, egg or hen?" The preponderance of the argument indicated that the hen came first. The great religionist wrote that "every imperfect thing must needs be preceded by some perfect thing: for seed is from some animal or plant." The ancient myths of Egypt and India were based on the same reasoning. Geb was referred to as "the Great Cackler" or Gander. Hamsa the divine swan, a symbol of Brahma, was often portrayed in Hindu art floating on the waters of chaos with the World-Egg beneath him. In *Easter, Its Story and Meaning,* Alan Watts states, "In the Finnish epic known as the 'Kalevala,' by Elias Lönnrot, the earth, sky, sun, moon and clouds are said to have been formed from the broken eggs of a teal sent by Ukko, the highest god, to nest upon the knee of the Water-Mother."

The Hawaiians believe that the large island of Hawaii was produced by the bursting of an egg that had been laid on the water by a bird of great size, and that there was no other land. Did not the instinct of our own forefathers, too, give utterance to this oracle: "Everything springs from the egg; it is the world's cradle"?

In Hutchinson's *History of Northumberland* we read that the Jewish people adopted the Egyptian concept of the egg "to suit the circumstances of their history, as a type of their departure from the land of Egypt; and it was used in the feast of the Passover. . . . The eggs were boiled until hard and served as symbols of a bird called Ziz, a storied creature in Hebrew tradition."

In medieval days, the curious symbol of the World-Egg appears in the work of the alchemists. Strange performers and dabblers, these men were seeking to do many things that smacked of superstition and occult practices. One of their

The Easter egg as an art form has been an integral part of Russian culture for centuries, reaching its most magnificent portrayal in the work of Peter Carl Fabergé (1846–1920). A jeweler and craftsman par excellence, Fabergé created dazzling jeweled Easter eggs for the imperial family of Russia and the aristocracy of Europe as well.

A jewel box made from a goose egg; inspired by Fabergé and designed by Helen Buzby. (*Photo: Richard Merrill*)

Inspired by the masterpieces of Fabergé, twentieth-century housewives have delved into bureau drawers for trinkets and odds and ends of costume jewelry to fashion their own interpretations of these fabulous collectors' items. Women versed in the cakemaking arts have drawn on Fabergé's designs. The results are delectable and artistic creations on a larger scale in spun sugar—eggs in the form of baskets with delicate latticework, simulated Wedgwood covered dishes, and vases filled with exquisitely formed sugar flowers: roses, pansies, lilies of the valley, all in natural color. See the color section for examples. Like Fabergé, talented craftswomen have perfected the art of transforming simple substances into magnificent creations.

A selection of Easter oddments found in English shops. The egg-shaped cardboard candy boxes with colorful lithographs and gold braid, popular since Victorian days, were made in Germany. (*Photo: Photographic Illustrators Corp.*)

Popular since the turn of the century, the "look-inside" Easter egg has delighted generations of confection lovers, since every part of the egg is edible. Tradition has it that the first look-inside egg was fashioned in Latvia. Beatrice Knaoppik, with a flair for cake decorating, created this one. (*Photo: Richard Merrill*)

Left, a Spanish egg; right, German marzipan. (*Photo: Photographic Illustrators Corp.*)

A candy-egg necklace and a baby chick emerging from a chocolate egg are typical Easter trinkets offered in Spanish confectionery shops. (*Photo: Photographic Illustrators Corp.*)

A so-called "thousand-year-old" egg from China—a hen's egg wrapped in clay. The Chinese preserved eggs in this manner and presented them as gifts. The older the egg, the more meaningful was the gift. (*Photo: Richard Merrill*)

A decorated wooden egg from Russia made in the twentieth century (*Photo: Richard Merrill*)

A papier-mâché egg box, probably made in Russia, found in an English antique shop. (*Photo: Richard Merrill*)

A group of decorated eggs from Spain. The large egg in the center featuring a caricature of a farm woman bartering for the sale of a duck is a goose egg. The egg at the extreme right, done in an etched floral motif, is known as a "mother-in-law" egg. (*From the collection of Priscilla Sawyer Lord; photo: Photographic Illustrators Corp.*)

aims was to transform lead into gold. Curiously enough, the vessel used was called the aludel and was shaped like an egg. This was placed in a furnace which served as a kind of incubator to hatch the philosopher's stone that would change lead to gold by merely touching the earthly metal. Drawings of the period indicate the presence of a bird which appeared to be a composite of a phoenix, a gander, and a pelican.

Again, we have a link with Thomas Aquinas, since the pelican was associated with Christ in the folk mind, for it was believed that this bird fed its young with its own blood. A prayer of this Italian theologian describes the belief: "Pelican of mercy, Jesu, Lord and God, cleanse me, wretched sinner, in thy precious Blood; Blood, whereof one drop for humankind outpoured, Might from all transgression have the world restored."

If the resurrection of the body had been a tenet of the ancient Egyptians, undoubtedly they would have thought an egg to be a highly important symbol. The emergence of a living creature by incubation after a long period of dormancy is a process so truly marvelous that, if it would be disbelieved, it would be thought by some a thing as incredible as that the author of life would be able to reanimate the dead.

The links between these ancient myths and the use of eggs in Christian tradition are not easily traced. Early missionaries, or the knights of the Crusades, may have been the bearers of the egg tradition, which assumed significance at an early date in the Christian era. Surely no more fitting symbol could be used to teach the story of the Resurrection than an egg.

"We beseech thee, O Lord, to bestow thy benign blessings upon these eggs, to make them a wholesome food for thy faithful, who gratefully partake of them in honor of the Resurrection of our Lord Jesus Christ." This is the prayer offered by Roman Catholic priests in various countries of Europe when eggs to be given as gifts are brought to the church. In *The Easter Book*, Francis X. Weiser reminds us that the egg was a symbol of the "rock tomb out of which Christ emerged to the new life of His Resurrection."

After the yolk and white were removed, Helen Buzby skillfully attached a small metal hinge with glue to make an egg box. (*Photo: Richard Merrill*)

Bermuda

MORE than one hundred years ago, a vessel in distress was forced to anchor in the old Bermuda town of St. George's. Among the passengers was a missionary returning from Japan who happened to be a friend of the Reverend Mr. Roberts, Episcopal rector of Hamilton parish. The missionary was also a botanist and had brought home a collection of seeds, plants, and bulbs. Among the bulbs were those of a white lily found native in the Ryukyu Islands south of Japan. It was known to the natives as the blunderbuss or gun lily. He presented some of them to Mr. Roberts and to the local postmaster. In no time, the bulbs multiplied under the ideal growing conditions of Bermuda, and were soon widely planted in various parts of the island.

In the 1880s, Mrs. Thomas P. Sargent, an enthusiastic amateur gardener of Philadelphia, made a trip to Bermuda, where she saw gardens filled with white trumpet lilies, known locally as Bermuda lilies. She was so greatly impressed with the fragrance and the beauty of this white lily that she arranged to bring bulbs back to Philadelphia. They soon came to the attention of William K. Harris, a local nurseryman who introduced them to the florist trade under the name of *Lilium Harrisi*. Shortly thereafter, they were featured at spring flower shows in various parts of the country. Ten years later, sizable shipments of bulbs were being made to the United States and England from Bermuda, and a lively trade developed. The exporting of Easter lily bulbs was once one of the nearest things to an industry in Bermuda. It was not long before the famous Bermuda lily became known as the Easter lily all over America. The new lily had great appeal for indoor decoration and for use in churches as well, because it could be forced easily for the Easter season.

Visitors to Bermuda never fail to marvel at the extensive plantings which are seen there from early spring to midseason. Twenty million lilies form broad white carpets in the fields, matching in splendor the multicolored tulip carpets of Holland. Easter lilies have become a kind of symbol of Bermuda.

When a blight attacked them in their adopted home, efforts were made to grow them in the United States. As a result, the Croft lily, named for Sidney Croft of Bandon, Oregon, was introduced in 1931. Several growers in the Pacific Northwest and in California now produce the majority of bulbs, forced by the millions each year for Easter.

Bermuda is a mecca for hundreds of tourists and young people on holiday for the Easter vacation. They find that not only do the lilies transform the island into one enormous garden, but also the snapdragons, delphiniums, gerberas, petunias and a host of other flowers which flourish there.

On Good Friday every child who is able goes out to fly his kite and there are contests for the biggest, most beautiful, longest flown, running the gamut of prize categories. The basis for kite flying on this particular day is traced to a Bermudian who had difficulty in explaining Christ's Ascension to Heaven to his Sunday School class. Accordingly, the teacher and his class climbed a high hill on Good Friday where he launched a kite bearing a likeness of Jesus Christ. Once it had caught the air current and was borne aloft, reaching the end of its string, he cut it loose and the kite soared out of sight in the sky. To this day, the children of Bermuda fly their kites on Good Friday to show how well their predecessors remembered the lesson demonstration.

True to the tradition of the island, British breakfast fare on Good Friday morning is the hot cross bun. The breakfast for Easter morning is known as the "Codfish and Banana Breakfast." Two pounds of boneless, skinless salt cod are soaked over Saturday night in a pot of water. Sunday morning the water is poured off and the fish is covered with fresh water in a saucepan. Small, peeled whole potatoes are added and cooked with the fish for about fifteen minutes, or boiled until the potatoes are tender. When the fish is served, either olive oil is poured over it, or a dollop of mayonnaise tops it. A dish of bananas, sliced, makes this the typical Bermuda Easter Breakfast. (In the Canary Islands the fruits are cut lengthwise, for when cut across they show the symbol of the Crucifixion.) In the evening most homes serve a "little Christmas" dinner, with ham but no turkey. The bread usually served is the Portuguese sweet bread, known as folar. (A recipe appears in the section on Portugal.)

Everywhere in Bermuda, sunrise services are conducted to greet the dawn of Easter Sunday. The churches are decorated by the women of the various congregations who use masses of Easter lilies in addition to a profusion of spring flowers. It has become a tradition to spend the afternoon going from church to church to see the floral arrangements. One of the most spectacular events of the Bermuda calendar year is the Floral Pageant—the Easter Parade. Everyone who is not in the parade throngs the parade route in Hamilton to view the floats, which are decorated with fresh flowers, featuring the Easter lily. Some floats may boast as many as 10,000 lilies each.

Betsy Ross of Bermuda provides this recipe:

Hot Cross Buns

2 cups scalded milk	¾ cup sugar
2 tbsp. sugar	3 eggs
1 cake fresh yeast	½ cup raisins or currants
3 cups sifted flour	1 tsp. salt
½ cup butter	

Dissolve the sugar in the scalded milk. Cool to lukewarm, then add the yeast. Sift in the flour and beat the batter until smooth. Cover and let rise until it is light and full of bubbles.

Cream the butter and the ¾ cup sugar and add to the batter with the well-beaten eggs, raisins and salt. Add sifted flour to make a dough just stiff enough so that it can be handled without sticking. Turn onto a floured pastry cloth or broad and knead thoroughly. Place in a greased bowl and cover.

Set in a warm place, free from drafts, until the dough has doubled in bulk. Pinch off small pieces of the dough and form into smooth round buns and place these in a shallow, well-greased pan. Let rise again until light—about 1 hour.

With the back of a silver knife, mark a deep cross on the top of each one and brush the tops with an egg, beaten with 1 tablespoon of cold water. Bake at 375° F. for about 20 minutes. Remove from the oven and while still hot, glaze with a sugar icing.

Sugar Glaze Icing

1 cup icing sugar	Warm water
½ tsp. vanilla	

Sift the sugar and add just enough warm water to make a fairly thick paste. Add the flavoring and spread over the buns while they are hot. The icing will melt and form a glaze.

The Islands of the Caribbean

*T*HE many islands that dot the Caribbean all have their share of Lenten and Easter customs, but a much larger volume would be needed to record them all. Each has its own concept of Carnival and each has its own dance in which the performers interpret the infectious music. If the island is French-dominated, it is called the beguine; Trinidad has its calypso; Barbados has its "jump up." In South America, Brazil has its samba; Argentina, its tango.

In Haiti, although the pre-Lenten fete, Carnival, is held officially on the three days preceding Ash Wednesday, the natives get into the spirit the Sunday after Epiphany and roam from place to place in *bandes,* dancing to the rhythm of their drums. Costumes, masks, colored streamers, rum, candy and even a Maypole are part of the show that is as noisy as it is colorful. Official Carnival involves a wide array of masks, costumes, musical instruments, and noise-makers. Everyone who can move about takes part. Even the traffic policemen enter into the spirit by wearing masks. Floats built for the celebration are designed with great imagination, featuring plumage of tropical birds, palm fronds, seashells, flowers, dyed flour sacks and tops of pop bottles as well as the usual ribbons, baubles, and streamers. Nothing is sacred when it comes to making fun, even at the expense of politicians, public figures and established institutions.

At Port-au-Prince in Haiti, visitors during Holy Week go to see the murals in the Episcopal Cathedral of the Holy Trinity. These have been painted by Castera Bacile, Wilson Bigand and Rigaud Benoit. Both black and white faces are curiously intermingled in these paintings. In the "Crucifixion" painted by Obin, all of the figures are swarthy, or truly black, except Mary, the mother of Jesus, who is white. In another painting, Adam and Eve are raven black; in the portrayal of the "Last Supper," the disciples are mulattoes or blacks, but Judas is white!

In Puerto Rico, the Holy Week pageants and processions are unique for the attention which the natives give to large floral monuments, truly works of art. The Passion Play is presented at San Juan during the week and on Holy Thursday the cityfolk make special visits to each of the city's seven churches, of cathedral size.

Among the natives of the Virgin Islands, the fashion of placing decorated eggshells on the spring stems of yucca plants is a practice of long standing. On St. Kitts everyone flies a kite on Good Friday while, on Barbados, a children's parade is held on Easter Day, with kite flying as the order of the day on Easter Monday.

The classic sports event of the year takes place on Guadeloupe on Easter Sunday—the annual soccer game between Martinique and Guadeloupe. Carnival time begins immediately after Christmas on Guadeloupe and continues until Ash Wednesday. Every Sunday a masquerade is held, but the real Mardi Gras comes just before Lent. Marching bands lead the frenzied crowds of costumed revelers who sing as they strut. The high point of Carnival is the burial of the god Vaval with lengthy ceremony. Conspicuous among the characters in the parade is *moco-zombie,* a man in woman's attire wearing a metal face mask who stalks in and out of the parade on high stilts. Private homes and public ballrooms resound with merriment as tireless dancers with seemingly boundless energy do the beguine until the dawn of Ash Wednesday. Other dances, less popular, are called the quadrille, the tom-tom, the *lerose,* and the *gragé,* an ancient dance inspired by the pounding of cassava into flour with emphasis on intricate footwork.

Carnival, which begins in the middle of January and continues to Ash Wednesday in Martinique, is made up of equal parts of costumes, parades, music, and rum. It is a wild jamboree and spirits run high. Most of the festivities take place in a broad park (Fort-de-France's Savane) which stretches back from the waterfront where Josephine, Napoleon's empress, stands in swirling robes on her pedestal, proud of her homeland and the prestige she brought it. At the end of Carnival and the dancing, a great bonfire is lighted and King Bois Bois, the devil in effigy, is burned in the leaping flames.

Trinidad is a fascinating amalgam of cultures, tongues, and races. Some 800 years before the birth of Christ, the Ciboney Indians occupied Trinidad. The Arawaks, a gentle race, came later; Columbus, too, saw this island. The Spaniards came and so did the French, all leaving some mark of their own, but it was the French who really gave Carnival its verve. Each Trinidadian saves for a whole year to acquire his Carnival costume, and not only a great deal of designing, but also a vast amount of research, is required plus the money to pay for it. Correct to the last detail, some are historical; others are imaginative dragons, devils, demons, animals, birds or butterflies; still others feature grotesque heads made of papier-mâché. At Port of Spain, the calypso bands begin rehearsing in January, knowing the greatest honor to be bestowed on a local composer is to have his composition chosen as the "road march" for Carnival.

The Saturday before Carnival, the king and queen of the Carnival are chosen, as well as the queen of the bands. On the dawn of Monday, Carnival opens with "Joo-Vay"—"Jou Ouvert." The whole place starts "jumping up," literally leaping straight into the air to the compelling rhythms of the steel bands, which try to outdo one another in an effort to win public approval and to "be better than last year." As the vibrant throbbing of the bands crescendoes, the pace of the dancers accelerates, and, unconsciously, the entire watching crowd, regardless of profession, position, or disposition, catches the spirit and everybody dances. Such gaiety is not only infectious, it is irresistible! Monday's performance flows into Tuesday and everyone continues to dance until midnight. Only the arrival of Ash Wednesday's gloom dispels the revelry.

When Easter arrives, Trinidad is a gorgeous paradise. The yellow *poui* are abloom along the hillsides; the purple Petrea, poinsettia, *alamanda,* hibiscus, bougainvillea, jacaranda, cassia, frangipani, ixora, anthurium, and the island's national flower, *chiconia,* in all its brilliant red beauty—all burst into a profusion of bloom to welcome Easter.

Latin America

Argentina

*I*N Argentina, Carnival is celebrated with warm enthusiasm in the small northern villages even though interest has waned to a considerable degree in most of the larger cities. Each year village life is stimulated anew by the shrill sounds of the Indian flute, the jangling of the ukulele-like *charango*, and the beat of small drums. Dressed in their native blankets, both the men and women with their young strapped to their backs gather in a circle before their little whitewashed village church to perform the *carnavalito*, a modern version of an old round dance. Some of the dancers wave corncobs or sprigs of sweet basil, a carry-over from ancient harvest traditions. The dancing, enjoyed by the hour each day, often continues for a whole month.

Carnival preparations begin when the algarroba beans are ripe. After the harvest, the women mix the starch which is used for smearing the faces of the revelers. Two favorite drinks—*aloja,* made from the beans, and *chicha,* a fermented corn liquor—are produced in great quantities. The aromatic herb, basil, which is gathered to ward off evil, serves to decorate the hats and ponchos of the revelers. Everything is cleaned and buildings are whitewashed in preparation for the celebration.

The *tincunaco* ceremony is celebrated on the Thursday before Ash Wednesday. Two groups of women, mothers on one side and godmothers on the other, form lines on each side of an arch of willow branches decorated with flowers, fruit, cheese, sweets, and tiny lanterns. The two groups meet under the arch and pass a symbolic child, usually made of candy, from one to another as they touch each other's foreheads. This sacred ceremony unites the women in a tie that only death can part. Afterward, rockets are shot off, starch is thrown and the feasting and dancing begin.

On Sunday, Carnival reaches its climax. The women, wearing wide ruffled skirts, colorful ponchos, and white hats, transform their faces with starch and water. After lunch, everyone washes and returns with a fresh supply of starch and confetti. Singing folksongs, the people ride on horseback to the house where they are to dance in honor of Pukllay, the spirit of Carnival. Dancing is interspersed with horseplay as Carnival finally ends. Pukllay, a rag doll dressed in native costume, is buried while the woman playing the part of his widow sobs and others beat drums and sing Carnival songs. Each participant throws a shovelful of dirt into the freshly dug grave as all sing:

>!Ya se ha muerto el carnaval!
>Ya lo llevan a enterrar;
>Échenle poquita tierra
>Que se vuelve a levantar.
>
>(Carnival is dead now!
>They are burying him;
>Throw just a little dirt in
>So he can rise again.)

Bolivia

CARNIVAL in this Andean country is filled with excitement, but caution soon becomes the watchword of every spectator because water pistols are discharged and firecrackers called "bangers" hurled about with abandon, and anyone present may become the target. In La Paz, although the celebration opens officially at eleven o'clock on Sunday morning with a children's procession, small masked revelers arrive earlier and fill the city, all the while attacking one another with "slappers and bangers." Even the police are likely to become good-natured targets for these missiles. Everywhere there are children in all sorts of costumes, who dance up and down the streets to the music of a band while the procession is passing.

The adults hold their own parade in the afternoon. The first segment is typical of Carnival parades in other countries, but the Indians in their native costumes create an unforgettable spectacle. The men wear peg-top trousers and short jackets embroidered in gay colors. With brilliant scarves wound around their waists, wool or cotton bags slung over one shoulder, and the traditional knitted caps with ear flaps, they become the dandies of the day. The women put on their best skirts made of brocade, velvet, or plush with bright shawls over their shoulders topped by black, gray, or brown derby hats, for which these women are famous. A woman of the Altiplano must acquire a new skirt for each Carnival if she is to retain her standing; and each year she wears them all to prove how many Carnivals she has attended. Naturally, the older she gets the bulkier she becomes. Women from other regions seem to prefer white embroidered petticoats to the brightly hued skirts. To add to the native flavor of the occasion, each group of Indians brings its own band of panpipes as well as other primitive instruments and the players cavort and dance.

In *Fiesta Time in Latin America,* Jean Milne describes the masked clowns called *pepinos,* who are a feature of the La Paz festivities: "They wear striped costumes and are armed with a cardboard baton known as *mata-suegra* (literally, 'Kill-your-mother-in-law'). Talking in falsetto voices to avoid recognition, they roam through the crowds hitting people and getting hit in retaliation. It is necessary to get a police license to wear the costume and to pin the license number in a conspicuous place so that anyone causing bodily harm or property damage can be easily identified." This entire festival is a rough-and-tumble affair.

Carnival ceremonies used to be held in every small town in Bolivia, but recently people have tended to gather in the larger cities. Hordes of Indians flock to La Paz, Sucre, Cochabamba, and Oruro, staying with relatives or camping outside the city. Many sell a variety of homemade items to help defray expenses. After the initial activities of Carnival have concluded, they linger to dance and drink and celebrate in open fields nearby for as long as a week. In mining towns, Carnival takes on a special significance. A bull is sacrificed in front of the mine and the warm blood is sprinkled over the entrance. This ceremony is carried out partly to thank *Pacha-Mama* (Mother Earth) for the abundance of ore she has bestowed on them, but primarily to prevent any fatal accidents during the coming year.

An eighteenth-century romance with mystical overtones is part of Carnival tradition here. A notorious bandit called Niña-Niña lived in Oruro. His reputation was familiar to the civil authorities, but his identity was unknown. Later it was learned that he worked in a local tavern and was madly in love with his employer's daughter. Despite his wicked habits, Niña-Niña made his way each day to the altar at the entrance to the Cock's Foot Silver Mine to light a candle before a picture of the Virgin which was painted on a rock. After some time he summoned courage to ask the tavern keeper for his daughter's hand, but naturally was refused. When the couple attempted to elope, the girl's father discovered them, and Niña-Niña was found lying in the street, his throat neatly cut and streaming with blood.

That very evening a lady of good breeding knocked at the door of St. John's Hospital and brought in a badly wounded man. After assisting to make him comfortable and requesting that he be properly cared for, she disappeared and was never seen or heard of again. A priest was called, and hardly had the confession been heard and the last sacraments been administered than the victim died. Later the priest told the story of Niña-Niña based on the bandit's confession and his account of how he had arrived at the hospital.

Niña-Niña related that he lost consciousness following the attack, but when he regained his senses, he was being attended by an unknown lady who escorted him to the hospital. As she was leaving, he recognized her as the Virgin of the mine. When the startled townspeople went to the miserable quarters in which Niña-Niña had been living, they were astonished to find that the Virgin's image appeared on the wall. Touched by their patron's benevolence toward one so unworthy as Niña-Niña, they changed the mine's name from Cock's Foot to The Mine of the Virgin (El Socovón de la Virgen).

At that time they promised to commemorate the occasion as a feast in honor of the Virgin each year on the Saturday of Carnival, since that was the day on which the tragedy occurred.

On Carnival Saturday people of all ages flock to the main street to watch a unique procession. No less than sixty mules and oxen are used to haul a king's ransom of gold and silver objects and other precious items, piled high on the saddle of each animal. To large pieces of cloth, spread over the animals' flanks, are attached rows of spoons, knives, and forks, as well as earrings, brooches, bracelets, and other pieces of jewelry, which gleam and sparkle in the sunlight. Even the mules wear great collars embellished with silver; both the bridles and the reins are ornamented with hundreds of silver coins. Thus, each family displays its wealth in lavish fashion. A further touch of luxury is afforded by some of the wealthy residents who ride in silver-hung cars or trucks. Following them come the masqueraders in *comparsas,* each group doing its own special step.

Despite the lavish display of jewels and precious metals, it is the troupes of devils, the Diablada, who are the central attraction. Dressed in gaudy colors, they are truly spectacular dancers. Two luxuriously costumed dancers, representing Satan, head the group, which also includes St. Michael and the China Supay (she-devil), the only female figure in the group. Behind them, stretching out for blocks, come hundreds of dancers dressed as ferocious demons. Each performer wears an enormous mask similar to those seen in Tibet, with huge horns, popping eyes, and ugly jagged teeth, all painted in vivid shades of red and green, black, white and gold. To add to his grotesque appearance, each demon carries an evil-looking toad between his horns, or it may be a lizard, or a serpent. Blond horsehair wigs fall over their pointed ears, which vibrate with each movement that the devils make. Since to the natives of Bolivia, fair hair is characteristic of foreigners, the blond wigs are most appropriate.

Typical costumes consist of pink tights, a silk or velvet cape embroidered with dragons and serpents, a jeweled and fringed breastplate, a short four-flapped native skirt embroidered with gold and silver thread, embellished with precious stones. Heavy boots with spurs that drag create some of the noise to be heard. Even "devils" display pride and a feeling for inheritance since some of the costumes fashioned completely of silver coins, resembling coats of mail, are antiques. Many of these have been inherited, and each new owner adds whatever he can afford to create an elegant effect.

The presence of demons is very real to these miners since both spend much of their lives in the bowels of the earth. The miners identify the devil with Supay, one of their black pagan gods, and erect altars to him within the mines. Furthermore, they refer to the devil as "uncle," El Tío, since he is known to be sensitive and prefers not to be called by his real name. They believe that he is quick to avenge the slightest offense; yet he will do a good turn if so inclined. Originally the Indian mine workers impersonated the devils in this parade, but in the late twenties the slaughterhouse workers adopted the custom.

Later those of higher social position joined the ranks. Several groups of *Diabladas* now exist in Oruro, but all seem to be similar in their performance.

While some of the spectators remain along the street to watch the parade and the dancing of the *comparsas,* others move on to see the procession arrive at the church of the Virgen del Socovón. The dazzling costumed figures make their way up the slope to the church and each group enters separately to perform its ritual dance, accompanied by a high-powered band. Using a bell for a signal, the leader then halts the dance and offers a prayer in Quechua. The rite then follows as the performers proceed to the high altar where the Virgin stands surrounded by banks of flowers. As one group dances its way out, another enters until all have paid honor to their protector. The group remaining outside the church continue their gyrating movements with a strange, restless frenzy.

A curious dramatic note is introduced when members of the *Diablada* pause to perform an allegorical play which symbolizes the rebellion of the devils in the constant earthly struggle between good and evil. It begins with a heated discussion involving Michael, who represents harmony, and Lucifer, the symbol of discontent, evil, and bitterness. The seven cardinal sins are represented by seven demons who line themselves up with Lucifer while seven angels representing the seven virtues rush to the aid of Michael. First the devils emerge victorious, but when the play ends, the forces for good have achieved victory.

On Carnival Sunday, the area around the church looks like fairyland with what seem to be monstrous gold and silver blossoms appearing everywhere, gleaming and shimmering in the sunlight. Actually, what at a quick glance looks like flowers is actually the vessels and jewels carried by the mules and the oxen in the parade of the previous day. Several guards sit over their precious hoard resplendent in the fiery reds and intense greens and blues of their Spanish shawls, while they and their treasures are viewed at close range by the natives and the tourists.

The *comparsas* who perform throughout Carnival present plays which date back to the sixteenth-century Spanish moralities. However, the Inca *comparsa* offers the most appealing historical interest, since it describes in vivid detail the entrancing story of the Conquest, in which the Incas speak Quechua and the Spaniards Castilian.

Brazil

ORDS are inadequate to describe what John Gunther defines as "collective dementia" in the word picture he paints of Carnival time in Rio de Janeiro. Others, less vocative, exhaust themselves with superlatives in attempting to describe the endless hours of mad

Carnival in Brazil is said to be one of the greatest folk spectacles on earth. For four days preceding Ash Wednesday, revelry runs riot as numerous balls and parades are held. All ordinary workday activities are put aside and everyone joins in the fun. The air is filled with music, confetti, and perfume. (*Photo: Brazilian Government Trade Bureau*)

Samba "schools" or clubs meet throughout the year in Rio to prepare songs and dances for Carnival. A new theme is selected annually, and time, money, and energy are devoted to producing original folk music. Many of the tunes become "hits" and are heard for the rest of the year. Clubs consist of 200 or more members and perform before thousands of spectators. (*Photo: Brazilian Government Trade Bureau*)

During Carnival, Brazilians shed their customary reserve and throw themselves wholeheartedly into the festivities. Everyone dresses in costume ranging from silly hats to elaborate creations varying in style from medieval elegance to ultramod. (*Photo: Brazilian Government Trade Bureau*)

Wearing traditional Indian garb, a *caboclinho* dances to the birdlike music of native instruments. Spinning and leaping with mathematical precision, he portrays the Indian's bitter struggle to avoid domination by the white man. (*Photo: Brazilian Government Trade Bureau*)

Centuries of tradition are reflected in the fanciful headdress and facial makeup of a "Knight" dressed for masquerade in Maceio, Brazil. Time and talent make Carnival a memorable occasion each year. (*Photo: Brazilian Government Trade Bureau*)

Religion plays an important part in the Carnival celebration in Alagoas, Brazil. Here, natives of this northern state prepare for a pageant in which battles of the Crusades are reenacted. (*Photo: Brazilian Government Trade Bureau*)

Carnival in Recife is noted for its folkloric representations. The *maracatús* perform dances of Negro origin dating back to colonial times. They parade through the streets, stopping to dance before the door of each church they pass. In the foreground is the Queen, accompanied by her retinue. (*Photo: Brazilian Government Trade Bureau*)

music and dancing. What began in a modest way a little over a century ago with settlers from the Azores has become not only a festival of floats, masks and the fanciest of costumes but also a constant barrage of confetti, streamers, and scent squirters. The leading samba schools, those of Portela, Mangueira, and Salgueiro, bring in blocs of dancers with their music to produce a spectacle that for sheer skill, inventiveness, and stamina seems at times to overwhelm both the spectators and the performers.

Preparations for Carnival, which lasts from the preceding Saturday until Shrove Tuesday evening, actually begin months in advance. When the appointed time arrives, what has been described as "the greatest folk spectacle in the world" takes precedence over all ordinary activities. Stores, businesses, and government offices close, and all known thieves and shady characters are locked up. Brazilians, rich and poor, shed their customary reserve and inhibitions and throw themselves wholeheartedly into the festivities. For the big event, everyone dresses in costume ranging from silly hats to elaborate creations. Some years thematic costumes are in order; men often masquerade as women. As temperatures soar at this time of year, attire is apt to be scanty.

In colonial days, Carnival was opened by Zé Pereira, a big bass drummer who led people through the streets like the Pied Piper. In recent times, the central figure has been King Momus, whose arrival by means of modern transportation is greeted noisily by his loyal subjects.

Attired in bathing suits of crepe paper, with faces, arms and legs gaudily painted, the natives rush to the beaches on Sunday morning and astound tourists as they dash into the water, their costumes disintegrating. (The average tourist does not realize that regular bathing suits are worn underneath.)

On Monday night *the* social event of Carnival takes place. A gala ball is held at the Municipal Theater with prizes given for the best costumes and songs. The spontaneous activities of the masses continue outside. On Tuesday evening a parade of elaborate floats is held along the Avenida Rio Branco. Floats designed by leading Brazilian artists and sculptors compete for prizes and popular acclaim. There are two general types: true artistic representations of historic and cultural subjects, and caricatures of current events or local politics. Carnival is officially over with the end of this parade, and people head wearily home.

The final parade takes place the next day when the "bull pens" are opened; celebrants who got out of hand and had to be taken into custody are freed and must pass curious crowds that have gathered. Actually, considering the size and scope of the activities, there are few disturbances of the peace or incidents of drunkenness during the four days of Carnival.

Other cities in Brazil also have noteworthy celebrations; among them, Recife, Salvador, and São Paulo. The festival at Recife is noted for its folkloric representations. The two most typical Carnival dances, the *maracatú* and the *frêvo,* originated here. The latter is an amazing combination of grace and virtuosity. The former is of Negro origin, dating back to colonial times when plantation owners and their families dressed their favorite slaves in elaborate costumes and even lent them jewelry for an impressive ceremony in which Negro rulers of each district were crowned. The sound of approaching drums signals the arrival of the *maracatús,* who stop to dance before the doors of all the churches they pass. First comes a small cart carrying the figure of an African animal, such as a lion or elephant. The king and queen follow in their royal regalia; behind them come the members of their court. Accompanied by a band of primitive instruments, the court engages in a ritualistic dance.

Another interesting group participating in the Recife Carnival is the *caboclinhos.* Wearing traditional Indian garb and accompanied by native instruments, they perform dances portraying their struggle against the white man.

The village of Fazenda Nova, a small primitive resort town in northeastern Brazil, has become famous in recent years because of its passion play. In 1950, Luiz Mendonça, a native son, returned to the village for a visit. Finding the small town boring after life in the big city, Mendonça, an actor, decided to put on a passion play. Enlisting the help of his family and friends, he set to work. They began to study the Bible and selected significant episodes. Then parts were assigned, costumes designed and rehearsals begun. On Wednesday of Holy Week in 1952, the first performance was held. It was not a polished one but was enjoyed by those who came to see it. Little did the Mendonça family know that their pastime would make the town famous.

Its fame spread by word of mouth and the play became well known for its spontaneity and originality. More money and actors were solicited. The play was no longer merely a pastime. In 1955, due to the increase in attendance, the play was taken out of the theater and was performed on the streets and in the fields of Fazenda Nova. Spectators of all races, creeds, and walks of life came to see it. In 1962, the play was performed before more than 12,000 persons.

Plineo Pacheo, the brother-in-law of Mendonça, left his job in Recife to join the family enterprise. At first working single-handedly, then joined by others, he has been responsible for reproducing many of ancient Jerusalem's buildings and walls. A commission, working without pay, directs the construction of all the buildings, done voluntarily by local residents. The stonecutters are the only paid workers on the project. The seventeen-acre site is surrounded by a stone wall.

Today more than 500 actors participate without pay. The play is performed from 9 to 12 on Maundy Thursday and Good Friday mornings. At least 10,000 attend each performance. All episodes of the story are represented as faithfully as possible, including the hanging of Judas, which is a dramatic point in the performance.

This play has been performed each year since it began. Even the spectators are involved, becoming the "extras" in the various scenes as they follow the actors through the town. In both these respects the play differs from the one at Oberammergau, which is performed on a stage once every ten years.

The script is faithfully written from accounts in the Bible, but the dialogue has been modified slightly. A famous young Brazilian playwright, Ariano Suassuna, revised the script to make it more objective and concise.

As a result of these production activities, Fazenda Nova is completely changed during Holy Week, invaded by tourists in all kinds of vehicles. The play has been subsidized by the Pednambuco Legislative Assembly, and Luiz Mendonça and his family and friends continue to work to improve the play.Thus a young man's pastime has brought his town international attention.

Holy Week begins with the blessing of the palms in churches on Palm Sunday. Many of the palm branches carried are woven into intricate forms: banners, crosses, spears, and letters. In Salvador, palm vendors fill the streets, selling sabers, hats and various articles of clothing woven of palm fibers. The following legend portrays the significance of the palm tree to the Brazilian:

Long ago, a South American Indian tribe suffered from a drought. They prayed for relief, but in vain. Finally only three Indians remained: a man, his wife, and their child. They left in search of a new home, traveling during the night. The next day they took refuge from the hot sun under the shade of a palm tree. The parents were so exhausted that they fell asleep.

The little boy, who remained awake, was afraid. He prayed to the god Tupan for help. Suddenly he heard a voice. Looking up, he saw an Indian woman in the top of the palm tree. She introduced herself as Carnauba and said she would help him. She explained that she and her people had perished from drought many years ago. After her death, the moon had changed her into a palm tree so that she could save the stricken. She told the boy to do the following things: cut open her trunk and drink the sap; eat the fruits of her tree; cook the roots and use them as medicine; dry the leaves and beat them to obtain wax for candles; weave useful articles from the straw that remained.

In exchange, she asked the boy to plant the nuts from her tree so that new trees would grow. Then she told him to use the lumber from the trunk to build a hut. The boy did all these things.

Some years later, palm trees grew where the desert once had been. The young Indian, now a man, said good-bye to his parents and set forth to carry the coconuts of "the good tree of Providence," as the natives of Brazil call it today, to Indians everywhere.

One of the most striking forms of cactus carries the common name of Easter lily cactus. This native of Brazil is found abundantly in the U. S. western desert and when the spring rains come, it bursts forth in all its glory, like a gorgeous Easter lily.

Colombia

POPAYÁN, Colombia, is famed for the beauty of its Holy Week celebrations. Noted for its splendid colonial architecture and rich history, this city provides an atmosphere of rare dignity for the Holy Week processions. Actually, preparations begin many weeks before Palm Sunday. Houses are freshly calcimined in pastel colors, gardens are spruced up and trimmed and church interiors are redecorated. Beautiful objects of silver and gold from colonial times are put on display.

A group of men known as *cargueros*, or bearers, gather the day before Palm Sunday at the Chapel of Bethlehem overlooking the city to prepare the religious images which they carry in the processions. Since their position is one of great honor, the *cargueros* are men of the highest social standing in the city, and the honor is usually handed down from father to son.

The blessing of the palms takes place on Palm Sunday morning, and in the afternoon the images are carried in a great procession from the Bethlehem chapel amid waving palms.

The Feast of the Prisoners, a unique ceremony, takes place on Tuesday afternoon. There is a procession of litters covered with an abundance of food, accompanied by the archbishop, government officials, schoolgirls and the army band, to the prison. The prisoners are brought into the courtyard, where they listen to speeches and are served a feast. In a ceremony symbolic of the choos-

Thousands of pilgrims and tourists from all over Colombia and the continent throng to the ancient city of Popayán, Colombia, for the candlelit Holy Week processions. Beautiful religious images are carried out of the churches and into the streets on large decorated litters. (*Photo: Colombian Government Tourist Office*)

A wealth of jeweled ornaments and objects, dating from colonial times, are displayed in ancient churches in Popayán during Holy Week. Shown above is "La Encarnación." Religious images such as this Virgin are carried in the Holy Week processions. (*Photo: Colombian Government Tourist Office*)

Carnival in Barranquilla is an exotic, colorful affair. Dressed in elaborate costumes and masks, the celebrants crowd the streets. Parades featuring floats and folklore dances, a battle of flowers and an aquatic festival are included among the many activities. (*Photo: Colombian Government Tourist Office*)

Each year during the week prior to Lent, Barranquilla becomes *una ciudad loca,* a "crazy city." Music and dancing combine Spanish, Indian, and Negro cultures, and many colorful folkloric costumes are seen. (*Photo: Colombian Government Tourist Office*)

A unique spectacle is located in the ancient city of Zipaquirá, thirty miles north of Bogotá, Colombia. The famous underground Cathedral of Salt, formed by a vast excavation in the salt mine which dominates the city, has four great naves and can accommodate 15,000 people. Impressive Easter services are held here (*Photo: Colombian Government Tourist Office*)

ing of Barabbas, one of the prisoners is selected, given donations of food and money, and set free at the end of the day.

On Tuesday night, the first of several beautiful candlelight processions takes place. Large decorated litters, bearing saints or scenes from the life of Christ, are carried through the city. Many years ago, one of these processions was credited with saving the town from invasion. Mountain tribes planning to attack the city were startled by strange music and the sight of a fiery serpent winding its way toward them; they fled, leaving their weapons behind.

Early records show that Easter ceremonies were held at Popayán as early as 1558, and they have continued uninterrupted since that time. Even during wars and uprisings, truces were called so that Easter might be observed in all its pomp and splendor. One incident in Popayán history demonstrates the respect for tradition and justice of which Colombia can be proud. General José María Obando, famed for his good looks and conduct, had declared himself an enemy of the government and was being hunted by city officials. Despite this fact, he decided, to carry out his obligation as one of the bearers of the statue of Our Lady of Sorrows in the Good Friday procession. Although the procession began on that day with his place vacant, suddenly he appeared in his hooded cloak and took his place. Surprise and admiration ran through the crowd as they realized the danger in which he had placed himself. Even his enemies respected the significance of the tradition in which he was involved and allowed him to participate in the parade and return to his hideout afterward.

Each year, in the week before Lent, Barranquilla becomes what its inhabitants call *una ciudad loca*—a "crazy city." Crowds fill the streets day and night dressed in exotic costumes and masks. The Negro dances performed at this time are especially colorful because of their fast, frenzied pace, which presents a marked contrast to the slow, quiet dances of the Indians. The *Danza de los Pájaros* (Bird Dance) is performed by men dressed as birds. Wearing bright plumage and masks with beaks, they imitate birds in flight. The *Coyongos* dance-drama depicts birds known for their fishing skill. These "birds" pursue a "fish" and try to eat him in a colorful dance interspersed with dialogue. In the comic *Maestranza* (household) dance, the men dress as women, carrying brooms, pots, pans and various other household utensils. The "mother" supervises the work while the "daughters" go about their various household tasks with grotesque movements.

There are parades of floats and folklore dances and music, a battle of flowers, a beauty contest, an aquatic festival and finally the night before Ash Wednesday, the burial of "Joselito Carnaval," the spirit of the celebration, for another year.

Costa Rica

$\mathcal{I}$N Costa Rica, real-life "angels" lend a touch of drama to the Good Friday processions. This custom had its origin in Spain and Portugal. Although the small children who participate often look a bit awkward as they march along, especially if their "wings" are a bit too big or are not securely attached to the rest of their costume, the presence of a "tired little angel" along the line of march lends a warmly human feeling to an otherwise solemn affair. The entire performance is filled with dramatic incidents from beginning to end. At the outset, the dramatic image of the cross-burdened figure of Christ on its litter makes the onlookers aware of the day they commemorate. At the first stop, a beautiful girl, representing the Samaritan woman at Jacob's well, steps forth from the crowd, offering a jug of water to the image with its haggard, painted face. A little later, Mary Magdalene appears in a similar manner to anoint the Savior's feet with oil from a small crystal flask. Another Bible story is recounted as a lovely Veronica wipes His brow with a sparkling white cloth. Finally, a litter bearing an image or picture of Mary, mother of Jesus, joins the procession.

Typical of the accumulated folklore of the common people that has evolved over the centuries, when the image of Christ is removed from the cross, it is not wrapped in a shroud, but is placed in an elaborate casket and carried through the streets. The little "angels," girls two to seven years of age, some holding banners bearing the last words of Christ, are conveyed on platforms along the line of march. Other litters follow with the Samaritan woman, Veronica, and Mary Magdalene.

Cuba

$\mathcal{I}$N Cuba, African folklore is evident in the pre-Carnival celebration which begins with the Day of the Kings on January 6, in observance of the day of freedom granted each year to the slaves in former times. The participants wear masks with their bizarre costumes and dance in the streets, all the while collecting money as tribute from those who look on. Organized into societies called *cabildos,* they complete with one another, and many of the Negro performances seen in later-day Carnivals originated in early folklore.

Carnival in its present form took place during the early years of the republic. Groups of Negro dancers, the *comparsas,* performed in the parades in which community leaders and prominent local citizens joined, riding in carriages or on horseback. The first floats, introduced from the New Orleans custom at the turn of the century, depicted such fantasies as *Gulliver's Travels* or scenes of historic episodes relating to the Middle Ages. In the years that followed, Havana developed a parade of floats which rivaled those of New Orleans and Rio.

Carnival traditionally began on the Saturday before Ash Wednesday, but continued with sporadic performances on Saturday and Sunday nights for most of Lent. Over the years, the dancing has far outshone that of all the other great Carnival festivals, due to the extraordinary talent of the *comparsas,* of which there are about eighteen. The groups, which drew their talent from all parts of the island, were not professional dancers; rather they were men and women of all ages, sizes, and degrees of color, a cross section of the native population, who danced for the sheer joy of it. Born actors, they made each performance a production worthy of Broadway and were known as The Scorpions, The Snakes, The Marquesas, The Sultans, The Gypsies, The Gardeners, and The Cane Cutters. Some of these groups have been in existence for nearly 100 years, and naturally rivalry among them has always been intense. On Carnival Saturdays, the groups assembled at sundown on the avenue called Malecón and began to dance their way beneath the laurel trees of the Prado. It was well past midnight before the last *comparsa* passed the reviewing stand at the national capitol. Near the end of Lent, prizes were awarded.

Jean Milne gave her impressions in *Fiesta Time in Latin America* when she wrote: "The approach of the *comparsas* is heralded by the dull throb of the drums, and soon the *farolas* come into sight. The latter are huge multicolored lanterns of silk or paper perched on top of tall poles and carried by the leader of each group. Sometimes a bearer will twirl the lantern skillfully as he advances; occasionally one will show off his ability by balancing the long pole in its pouch and dancing down the street without touching it with his hands. Following the lantern-bearers come long files of featured dancers and chorus members, from fifty to one hundred people all gliding along in the well-known conga step. This step is said to have evolved from the shuffling walk of the chained slaves who could take but three steps in any direction and had to drag their shackles on the fourth."

Each *comparsa* furnishes its own native band and stops several times along the route to give its choreographic spectacle. Oriental themes always have had strong appeal because of the brilliant costuming required. Richly colored silks, turbans with plumes, and yards of gauze in floating clouds made the dark-skinned performers all the more striking. They found particular delight in portraying the tragic existence of their forebears as slaves. Little that was ever worn in the way of period costume was unknown to them. Elegance and grandeur provided that feeling of well-being so essential to the success of this type of moving pageantry enlivened by choreography. The parade of decorated floats and the confetti battles took place on Sunday, but all of this has changed since the rise of Castro in Cuba.

Guatemala

*I*n Indian countries like Guatemala, spring, Lenten and Easter customs are often so intermingled with pagan rites that it is difficult to distinguish between them. Nor is it important since the lore of these folk is deeply rooted and meaningful. Coming as it does in March or April, Holy Week coincides with the fertility rites held in ancient times to bring rain and good crops. All during the week, in the picturesque little church of Santo Tomás in Chichicastenango, the Quiché Indians may be seen kneeling in prayer over parti-colored ears of seed corn. Their belief rests on the notion that the first men created were molded from corn paste into which the "Heart of Heaven" breathed life. Corn is their staple food; it nourishes their poultry and their livestock and provides the thatched roofs of the houses in which they live. They raise two crops each year with the first crop seeded in March. On the Sunday before planting, they bring their seed to church to be blessed. They use lighted candles, incense, and the petals from flowers, placing them on the floor as they kneel in a circle to pray. Mosaics laid out on the floors of their houses in beautiful designs of red, white, and yellow corn kernels, with candles as a feature, are a part of this ancient rite. The night before the seed is sown, the women pray indoors while the men go into the fields to burn incense and sprinkle the soil with aquardiente, a kind of brandy. When the seed has been covered with soil, the women go into the fields carrying food for a feast to celebrate the event.

In some Guatemalan towns ceremonial burlesque goes hand in hand with solemn religious observances. In Chiantla, it was the custom for the apostles to escape from the Good Friday procession and hide in ravines. Men and boys dressed in purple robes and peaked headdresses took off in pursuit, and eventually all the apostles were dragged back to the procession.

Antigua is noted for Holy Week processions of extraordinary beauty. The entire populace, including members of various religious orders, Indian and non-Indian, turn out for the events. Statues pertaining to the life of the Savior, placed on great, elaborately decorated litters, are borne by *cucuruchos,* who wear purple during the first part of the week and change to black after 3 P.M. on Good Friday. These impressive processions begin on Palm Sunday and continue throughout Easter week. There are more than eighty monasteries, churches, and public buildings along the line of march. Perhaps the most outstanding of all the religious tributes is the *Procesión del Nazareno,* observed on Maundy Thursday, which is distinctive for the magnificent carpets of flowers, sand, pine needles, and dyed sawdust made by the natives. Sawdust is sprinkled over a cutout pattern which serves as a stencil for the design underneath. Contests are held between the various parishes in the city to select the most beautiful carpet. The great procession begins early in the morning and lasts until late afternoon. Because the burden is a heavy one and many wish to participate, the *cucuruchos,* who carry the litters, change places every block. The marchers sidestep the carpets as they move along. Only the litter bearing Christ and the cross is allowed to pass over the carpets, thus destroying them.

Mexico

*T*HE land that gave so many "p's" to the celebration of Christmas—posadas, piñatas, *puestos* and poinsettias—continues to add "p's" to the Easter celebration: papier-mâché fireworks, the passionflower, and pinole, a specially prepared Easter food.

The passionflower (*Passiflora caerulea*), which is native to Brazil, grows abundantly in Mexico and it is to this country that the legend marking it as *the* special flower of Easter belongs. Dr. Harold N. Moldenke, author of *Plants of the Bible,* delineates the story for us:

"In 1610 a Mexican Augustinian friar, Emanuel de Villegas, brought a drawing of a passion-flower (Passiflora) to Jacomo Bosio, who was then preparing a work on the cross of Calvary. Here was born the legend of this flower's connection with Jesus. Its bud was taken to be symbolic of the Eucharist; the half-opened flower suggested the Star of the East that guided the Wise Men. The normally ten sepals and petals were regarded as representing the ten apostles present at the Crucifixion (Peter and Judas being absent). The corona,

which is usually present as an outgrowth of the receptacle inwardly from the corolla, was symbolic of the crown of thorns placed on Jesus' head. The usually five stamens suggest the five wounds inflicted in Jesus' body on the cross. The three central styles, with their capitate stigmas, represent the nails used to fasten Him to the cross. In species with only three stamens, these are regarded as representing the hammers used to drive in the nails. The long, axillary, coiling tendrils are symbolic of the cord-like strands of the scourges used to beat Him. The often digitately lobed leaves represent the hands of His persecutors.

"In some species the corona is tinged with red, representing to some the bloody thorns of the crown, to others the bloody scourges. In some species there are five red spots, suggesting blood from the five wounds; in other species there are said to be 72 filamentous divisions of the corona, suggesting the 72 thorns said by tradition to have pierced Jesus' brow. In some species the leaves are shaped like the head of a lance or pike, symbolic of the spear used to pierce His side; other species have the lower leaf-surface marked with round silver spots, suggesting the 30 pieces of silver for which He was betrayed."

Above all else the Mexican loves fireworks and they are an integral part of every Mexican ritual. They are costly in terms of labor and especially pesos, but all villages in Mexico, even the poorest, have their own elaborate fireworks for display at festival time. Perhaps the most beautiful of all are those representing castles, often of enormous height, and others made in sections to represent saints, crowns, flowers and countless other forms. These marvelous fireworks are so designed that each section goes off separately until, as with the castle, the entire structure bursts in a dazzling splendor of flame, shedding light everywhere.

One of the popular customs is that of the burning of papier-mâché Judases on the Saturday before Easter. Figures are hung on the dummies before the burning and shot off so that the local boys may scramble for these mementos as they fall. Another kind of handcraft symbolic in this country is the tinware which the natives make. At Eastertide quantities of roosters made of tin abound in the markets. They are used in great numbers for decoration in the homes and adobes of the natives.

Frances Toor, well-known folklorist, has recounted the plethora of fiestas, dramas, and games which are the Mexican tribute to spring and Holy Week. The Mexicans delight in fiestas; furthermore, their keen interest in games, pageants, and dramas makes them eager participants in the drama that surrounds Passion Week. Descendants of the Toltecs, Aztecs, Mayas and Spaniards, the Mexicans had a well-advanced civilization when the Spaniards, led by Hernan Cortes, destroyed the Aztec empire in 1519 and brought Roman Catholicism to the country. Even today a mixture of pagan "cult" and Christian "myth" is discernible in all the fiestas.

The common passionflower (*Passiflora caerulea*), introduced to garden and greenhouse cultivation from Brazil in 1699, is one of several related species which tell the wondrous story of Christ's Passion in the bloom structure. (*Modeled in glass by Rudolph Blaschka for the Ware Collection of Glass Models of Plants, Botanical Museum, Harvard University, Cambridge, Mass.*)

Although the Spaniards introduced the idea of Carnival as the last fling before Lent, the following verse expresses the Catholic command to abstain:

Miércoles de Ceniza
Se desiden los amantes
Y hasta el Sabádo de Gloria
Vuelven alo que eranantes.

(*On Ash Wednesday*
Lovers take leave of love
Until Saturday of Glory
When they love again.)

Hilarious and unrestrained merrymaking mark the season of Carnival in Mexican cities. It is the joyous tumult that one remembers rather than any infectious music. The outstanding carnivals take place in Mazatlán, Vera Cruz, and Mérida, but they lack the brilliance of yesteryear. On the other hand, the celebrations in the small Mexican villages have preserved their vigor and color down to modern times. The natives participate in Carnival games, which often have serious religious and dramatic elements coupled with real burlesque and humor.

In Huejotzingo, Puebla, the most elaborate of the village carnivals dramatizes the capture and death of Agustín Lorenzo, a famous bandit. He used to rob convoys between Mexico City and Vera Cruz, and then hide with the loot in the nearby mountains. According to the plot, he ran off with the beautiful young daughter of a rich hacendado, took her to one of his hideouts and was in the midst of the wedding celebration when federal soldiers fell upon them. About one thousand men make up the various battalions of the carnival "army." Each group has its own colorful costume, some of which are very expensive, costing a hundred pesos or more. Also, a great deal of money is spent on gunpowder, fireworks, and music. Although the merchants of the village contribute toward the expense since the carnival attracts many outsiders, the greater part of the financial burden falls upon the actors, who are essentially poor. Besides being impoverished, the actors grow tired, for they must spend months in advance on rehearsal.

The most dramatic features of this carnival are the actual enactment of the kidnapping, the pursuit of the kidnapper by the soldiers, the wedding ceremony, and the final capture and execution of the bandit. The actors, mounted on horseback, wear costumes that are as elaborate as they are dramatic. No one seems to have any reliable data about the origin of this drama, nor does anyone care! All that matters is that the *juegos* (games) be good, and, according to the natives, they are never better than when a few soldiers are actually killed in battle!

In two other villages the carnivals take place in the form of a battle. In Huixquilucán, a long-existing feud between two barrios culminates on the Tuesday before Lent in clashes so spirited that the village police must be on hand to prevent serious injury. The feud revolves around the loyalty of one barrio to the Virgin and the other to its Saint Martin. The people of the barrio of Saint Martin have perpetuated a little love affair between their saint and the Virgin, claiming it is common gossip that the saint rides over to visit the Virgin every night. Inevitably, those loyal to the Virgin indignantly deny that she would receive a man at night, or at any other time—even a saint! During the ensuing "battle" both sides use as missiles various kinds of fire-crackers, bad eggs, eggshells filled with paint and, when this supply has been depleted, they resort to sticks and stones. Dolls, dressed to represent the saint and the Virgin, are displayed by each side, then blown to pieces with fireworks. The battle rages for two hours and is halted only when authorities force both sides to retire. Never knowing which side wins, both claim victory. The result —some are wounded; sometimes, corpses are produced to prove that the fight has been a good one.

In Zaachila, a village near Oaxaca City, the battle is between devils and priests, terminating in victory for the devils. The costumes and masks of the devils present a kaleidoscope of bright solid colors which shine brightly in contrast to the black cassocks of the priests, their white masks and black, pointed hoods. Canes which have geometric hooks at the ends are used by the devils, while the priests have whips and sticks for weapons. The fight con-tinues until after dark, affording a beautiful spectacle of bright colors dancing in the dim torchlight and the night shadows.

The Huichol carnival at Tuxpan, Jalisco, revolves around the singing of the Christian "myths," the bull dance and the burlesque of the Mexican treasure hunters. Lasting nine days, it takes place in the Casa Real, the temple reserved for Catholic ritual. For this fiesta a special food is prepared, called the pinole; it is made of cornmeal, mixed with honey and formed into tasty "beads."

On the first night of the fiesta, pagan myths are sung and the altar of the Casa Real is adorned with bulls' horns and lighted candles. From then on, Christian myths are sung and devotions held nightly, followed by processions to the officials' houses.

For the second part of the carnival, the bull dance is performed by a boy who, for one month before carnival time, must deny himself meat, salt, and sex. The bull, according to legend, is a descendant of the deer-snake of Nakawé; therefore, he is at once both pagan and Christian. The bull-boy performs bull-like antics, charging, roaring, digging his horns into the dirt, rolling on the ground while a group of dancers surrounding him throw dirt on him as they yell and leap into the air. Finally forming a corral around him, they move in on him until he succeeds in making his way out by jumping over them; then the dance starts all over again.

The third part of this carnival concerns the mockery of the Mexican treasure hunters. Using sticks for steeds and carved wood for pistols and sabers, soldiers arrive at the homes of the Huichol officials, arresting them and threat-ening them with hanging if they do not reveal the hiding place of the treasure.

The officials feign ignorance until they note that the soldiers, using reed tubes as field glasses, are about to hit upon the hiding place anyway.

An interesting and rather gory aspect of the Huichol carnival is the sacrificing of a bull during one of the processions. The bull-boy and the soldiers smear themselves and their sabers with blood from the slain bull, immediately engaging in a good-humored sham battle, feigning great ferocity. After the battle, the bull dance is once again performed. The fun of the entire Carnival is provided by the bull-boys. Sometimes they capture and pretend to make prisoners of the officials' wives and infants. Later, with the boys chasing the captives by pushing them with their horns, all scurry indoors. Then one of the officials and his wife are expected to bring forth a bottle of liquor, tossing it up into the air; it becomes the prize of whoever jumps the highest to get it.

On the last day, "Carnival Tuesday" (the day before Lent), a thanksgiving ceremony takes place. All gather at the Casa Real, and the "fiscal," the Christian official, sits in state while the civilian officials pass by and take his hand as if to kiss it, as they have seen the Catholics do to their priests. On Ash Wednesday, the officials put ashes on one another's foreheads. The ashes come from burned candlewicks, which must be removed carefully by children with scissors as commanded by the Christians. Lent is observed by fasting until noon on Wednesdays and Fridays.

Although Lent is observed so far as fasting and abstinence are concerned, many fiestas take place during this period. The good weather is conducive to these events, and the people are free from their agricultural tasks at this time of year. On Ash Wednesday a fiesta, this time really a pilgrimage to the Señor del Sacromonte (the Lord of the Holy Mount) is observed near the old Aztec town of Amecameca. Pilgrims make their way on their knees up the steps to the chapel on the mount, where a life-sized figure of the Señor lies in a glass coffin. Near the chapel stands one of the ancient ahuehuete trees, a sacred tree of petitions, on which are also hung offerings symbolical of new prayers or favors granted. These may include an old hat, a piece of clothing or a lock of hair. The townspeople believe that the Señor del Sacromonte is a miracle worker and that the town of Amecameca cannot be destroyed while he is there. Whenever the town has been attacked, some disaster has befallen the enemy; when it was threatened by a great forest fire, heavy rains—sent by the Señor!—saved the town from destruction.

A large fiesta takes place on the fourth Friday of Lent in Tepalcingo, Morelos. This attracts vendors of folk arts from the neighboring states of Mexico, Guerrero, and Puebla. Lacquer objects from Olinala, Guerrero, and painted fiber bags from villages in Mexico are offered for sale. Craftsmen will paint any design requested while one waits. Vendors also sell herbs and love charms; the red-crested woodpecker is a favorite.

Besides the traditional blessing of the palms on Palm Sunday, which is universally practiced, a unique custom is observed in Cheran, Michoacán, where a young, unmarried couple from each barrio carry an adorned cross to church on Palm Sunday. The girl decorates the arms of the cross with pinole balls made from white corn, mixed with brown sugar and wrapped in painted corn husks; in addition, she attaches attractive fiber bags and green leaves to it. While the boy carries the cross, the girl carries a pole so heavily laden with fruit that it is a struggle to bear it. However, the girl who has the best decorated pinole balls, the greatest number of bags, and the heaviest burden of fruit wins the most praise for her barrio.

The Passion is always dramatized. Before the Reform Laws of 1857 forbidding religious manifestations, the Holy Week processions were held out in the streets. Now they are held in the city churches, whereas in the villages the atrium or courtyard is used.

One of the most beautiful folk dramas presented in Mexico is The Passion as Tzintzuntan, a poor village situated on the edge of Lake Pátzcuaro. Here a reenactment of the entire last week of Christ's life is portrayed seriously and beautifully by the townspeople. Those who do not take part in the drama itself carry candles and sorrowfully sing *alabanzas* during the descent and burial procession.

Here Holy Week is also a time when persons pay their *mandas* or promises for favors received from Heaven. Men, women and even children can be seen crawling on their knees over rough ground, wearing crowns of thorns. The worst, self-inflicted torture, however, is that of the *penitentes*. They hobble their ankles with grills which cut and mangle the flesh as they hop around. Another form of self-punishment is to carry huge bundles of cacti fastened together with rope; the bundle is laid across the nape of the neck and, to support the burden, the wearer must keep his arms extended at shoulder level. Some even hold a lighted candle in each hand as added penance.

The role of Judas is unique in this region. From Wednesday until Saturday of Holy Week, "Judas" and others around the lake are given the powers of policemen. They arrest and fine mischievous boys or men who pretend they are committing misdemeanors, knowing that the fines incurred will go to the church. On Saturday at the hour of the Mass of Glory, the "Pharisees" and soldiers drive Judas away from the church. A merry chase takes place at the end of which the mob pretends to hang Judas from a tree and then carry him away "dead." In other regions the Judases are huge papier-mâché figures, strung with fireworks. These are shot down after the Mass of Glory, but not until the fireworks have been touched off.

A widespread practice, carried out after the Mass of Glory, is to lift children by the ears to make them grow. In some places they pull their ears and beat them on the buttocks with branches so that they will obey not only the Lord but their parents as well. When children misbehave, their parents often threaten, "Just you wait; you'll get your Glory for this." Adults pull one another's ears in fun and say, "Here's your Glory, Judas." Fruit trees also are beaten to make them yield well.

A most important event of Holy Week among the Mayas of X-Cacal is the lighting of new fires. At midnight on Friday all the fires in the homes are extinguished and at four in the morning the married couples gather in the church. The new fire is started by the friction of rubbing two pieces of wood together; from the fire thus started, a candle is lighted and taken to the altar, where a Low Mass is said. The men in the congregation then light their own firewood and return home to rekindle the fires on their hearths, which will be kept burning until the following year. Some of the Mayas believe that the first flames are the spirit of Jesus Christ returning to life; others, that the fire-kindling ceremony commemorates Jesus' ascent to Heaven over a long cold road, along which He had to stop occasionally to light a fire for warmth.

An interesting custom is observed by the Yaquis during their Holy Week processions. Those who represent the Pharisees wear painted masks of goatskin, with big ears, long noses and sometimes beards. These masks are a symbol of their power; they can do nothing without them. When putting on or taking off a mask, they must lie down on the ground and make the sign of the cross. Each has a medallion of the rosary in his mouth to keep him from spitting or talking while wearing the mask. When it is necessary to communicate with one another, they do so by hitting their machetes against their lances and by making signs. If it is necessary to speak, they must lie down near one another, remove their masks, cross themselves, and whisper. If they do not observe these rites, their souls will be lost after death and they will wander forever.

In remote and still primitive villages, where there are no resident priests, the Passion is much less historical. In one such village, Oxchuc, in Chiapas, the apostles are given a noon meal on Thursday, after which they spend the rest of the day praying. On Good Friday, they sit around a coffin sadly and are not allowed to eat, but a little comforting drink is permitted. No ordinary work may be done on this day because it is believed that all nature is converted into the body of Christ. If one were to plant something, His body would be wounded every time the planting stick made a hole for the seed; if one were to cut wood, every blow of the ax or machete would bruise His flesh. On Saturday morning the "little resurrection" is celebrated by shooting off fire-crackers. The "big resurrection" is observed on Sunday because He is in Heaven and completely recovered.

It is believed here that Tatic Maestro, their savior, was killed by very bad men, called *juros,* who have all died since that time; that He was sent by God to settle all the quarrels among men on earth, so it is strange that He should have been killed. Sútash, a rag doll representing the soul of the Jew who ate the soul of Tatic Maestro is kept in the belfry from Thursday until Saturday morning, when the resurrection takes place. Then it is taken to jail as punishment. On Sunday, Sútash is released from jail and burned in a big bonfire in front of the cabildo amid mockery and laughter for his failure.

Passion Week as observed at Taxco is a truly magnificent pageant. Early on Palm Sunday people from the neighboring village of Tehuilotepec set out for Taxco bearing an image of Christ riding a donkey. The villagers, carrying arches and bouquets of flowers as well as palm fronds, proceed to the church of Santa Prisca, where the residents of Taxco have gathered for the blessing of the palms.

On Monday and Tuesday images borne on litters are carried in evening processions, accompanied by groups of musicians and followers who carry staffs decorated with gourds and paper streamers. The *almas en cadenas* (souls in chains) who appear, dressed in mourning, with chains around their ankles, dramatize the souls in purgatory awaiting deliverance.

Following an afternoon service on Wednesday, symbolizing the dark hours which Christ spent is the Garden of Olives, another evening procession is held in which Adam and Eve appear. On Thursday morning the courtyard of the church is transformed into a kind of paradise with bowers of branches, singing birds in cages, and little girls dressed as angels, complete even to silver wings, to prepare for the long vigil. Later in the day the ceremony of washing of the feet and the Last Supper are reenacted. The Sayones (disbelievers), dressed as Roman soldiers, appear in colorful costumes together with "Judas" and "Pontius Pilate." Meanwhile, processions from neighboring villages arrive, bearing images of the Crucifixion, accompanied by natives carrying flowers, lanterns, and candles together with the penitents, in black, with their burdens of thorny branches.

All the incidents of history and tradition related to Good Friday make the observance truly lifelike after which the crucified Christ is placed in a coffin for conveyance to the tomb, accompanied by a mourning procession. Saturday morning is ushered in with the joyous peal of bells, while the Sayones fall by the wayside in dismay at the news of the risen Savior. Sunday's procession, with all its trappings, is one of triumph. Aside from the stirring religious episodes of Holy Week, in this and other Mexican towns, there are the colorful regional dances and the fireworks.

Panama

THE days extending from pre-Lent through Easter are part of "summer" in Panama, since the weather from January through April is the dry season; the rest of the year is considered "winter," with abundant rains expected at any time. During summer, the thermometer often soars to 110°–115° F. at high noon and the nights are warm. The evening warmth is greatly enhanced by the delightful perfume of the frangipani and star jasmine, among the many, many flowers in bloom. In the evening, too, the stars seem to be more numerous than in other lands and just barely beyond the reach of man. Panama is truly a land of flowers, and a kind of "terrestrial paradise" may be enjoyed by visiting the small mountain village of Boquete, seated on a ridge of the multipeaked Volcán Barú. Fields of Easter lilies, dancing in the dazzling sun, are among the delights.

Nearer Panama City, up in the hills, the agricultural experiment stations, Summit Gardens, are open to visitors, who enjoy the many kinds of orchids.

The hens and chickens on the farm there are literally fed small vanda orchids because they are rich in vitamins. Panama's special orchid is the dove, or Holy Ghost, orchid, *Peristeria elata*. Considered one of the most astonishing examples of symbolism in the orchid family, it is native to Panama, where it is referred to as "el Espirito Santo." The white, waxlike blossoms, which are shaped like a dove with wings spread, as though it were lighting on an altar, measure three inches across. They are delightfully fragrant and as many as thirty to forty or more blossoms open, usually three at a time, up the stalk of the plant, for a period of six to eight weeks. The native Panamanians venerate this beautiful orchid which they believe has mystical qualities because of its close resemblance to the dove. Unfortunately, it has become exceedingly rare in the wild because of the careless exploitation by curiosity seekers who gather the blooms and destroy the plants by improper handling. Even in cultivation it is by no means common.

Margaret Thornington Preston describes this extraordinary orchid in her poem "Flower of the Holy Spirit":

Espirito Santo, flower of the jungle,
  Message of mystical light;
Born in mysterious gloom,
  Breath of an Infinite Might;
Sweet benediction, dove in a blossom,
  Poised in a chalice of white,
Prayerfully bending thy head,
  Spreading thy wings as for flight.

Panama's orchid, sign of the Spirit,
  Flower with a bird in thy heart;
Rarest of tropical bloom,
  Symbol of wonder thou art.
Traceried sunlight sifts through the woven
  Roof of the jungle, to guide
Natives in searching for thee,
  Lighting their way to thy side.

Miracle blossom, clad in thy waxen
  Raiment, surpassing the King's:
Taking no thought, yet behold!
  Flower of the Spirit, with wings.
Radiant Passion flowers, flashing around thee,
  Seem to be flouting thy sign;
Dove of the mystical realm,
  What is thy message divine?"

For centuries the language of symbols, especially those linked with nature, has been an integral part of the everyday lives of those who live close to the soil. It is easy to understand the veneration which the natives of Panama hold

Native Panamanian beauties riding on a gaily decorated float in the Carnival parade are attired in the pollera, the traditional two-piece dress with ruffled blouse and voluminous embroidered skirt. These ornate costumes are usually handed down from generation to generation.

Watching the Carnival festivities is a young Panamanian lady. Her exquisitely embroidered pollera with its lace trim and fat pompon is typical of the costumes worn by tamborito dancers. In her hair she wears balcony combs and *tembliques*. Many *tembliques* are made of rare jewels and are worn only at Carnival time.

Tourists visiting Panama at Carnival time often participate in the gala festivities and many enjoy dressing in native costume. Roberta and Beverley Lord, daughters of the author, posed for this picture when they visited Panama as young girls.

These native Panamanians are ready for Carnival festivities in Porto Bello. Visitors invade this sleepy town twice a year—in spring for Carnival and in October for the Festival of the Black Christ. The wall in the background is the one on which Henry Morgan placed nuns as hostages when he ravaged the isthmus. The wall to the right is that of the oldest church in the western hemisphere.

for the dove orchid. The dove is closely linked with the life of Christ, personifying the Holy Spirit. This white bird, symbolic of His earthly qualities—gentleness, love, purity, and humility—is the emblem of peace. Biblical scholars tell us that during Christ's childhood, doves were sold in the marketplace, and there were dovecotes everywhere in the Holy Land.

The folklore of plants in the Old World is widely known, but we are inclined to overlook the tropical areas of the world, whence came the passion-flower and the Holy Ghost plant. M. A. Purdan, noted orchid enthusiast, painted a vivid picture of Easter in the jungle in an article which he wrote for the *American Orchid Society Bulletin* more than twenty years ago:

"Does the jungle know it is Lent? Every day of the year, the jungle has blooming orchids tucked somewhere among its green frills. Just now the jungle may be likened unto a great cathedral with trees as columns upholding the ceiling which is decorated by the Maker of orchids. In fact the jungle is keeping Lent and making ready for Holy Week by preparing thousands of purple orchid blossoms. Locally these highly perfumed blossoms are called 'Semana Santa,' being in full bloom at this time.

"In remote regions where humble folk know not their city kin, this orchid is now much in evidence. It sings a purple harmony of love and faith by its beautiful presence at every little wooden cross at the roadside. The pretentious shrines have their blossoms in earthen ollas of cool water so the blossoms endure several weeks. Church altars are purple with these orchids. The patron saint of every mountain home is beflowered, purple and sweet.

". . . The entire plant is attractive—a fragrant cluster of bright blossoms on a long, slender stalk, a bunch of fat, green and bronze bulbs ending in long, green leaves. Each precious blossom has six petals, five are long, slender, curving backward then forward and are usually brownish purple. The ornamental sixth petal which always hangs down is large, heart-shaped with edges a bit ruffled. The color may be pale mauve with crimson lines where the white column peeps out, or it may be the deepest, richest purple of the color pots of Persia.

"And the perfume? It is such a mystery. Yesterday the little girl, Libby Lundy, dissected this blossom, making a botanical sketch. Long after the petals had been severed, the child marveled each petal exhaled its innate perfume bringing to mind: 'sweet mystery of life if I could know thee'—

"The scientists of the orchid world speak of this orchid as 'Epidendrum atropurpureum,' but we who know it intimately like to say 'Semana Santa'—it ripples over the tongue like music—it really is a short Gregorian chant without an amen, for it never ceases but blows or scatters on and on over the coastal and interior low lands of Panama."

The Easter bunny in Panama is the *conejo* or "painted" rabbit who brings the Easter eggs. This rabbit has smaller ears than the rabbit of the United States and its brown back sports white spots quite like the markings of a fawn—thus the name "painted" rabbit. Children chant this little rhyme about the Panamanian bunny:

Miss Conejo goes out walking
When the days are nice and sunny;
She looks like a piggy
And a little like a bunny!

The week before Lent, an air of excitement permeates the Isthmus of Panama. In cities and towns, one is likely to see toldos being erected. These are dance platforms, covered with thatched roofs, where the populace enjoys native dances: *curachas, cumbías,* and the tamborito. Invitations to pollera balls, held at many of the social clubs, are sought by the elite, and every eligible young lady hopes she may be elected queen of the carnival which is held for three days prior to Ash Wednesday. Americans stationed in the Canal Zone and other visitors take lessons in the tamborito, for all take part in this, *the* event of the year.

The native Panamanian girls wear the traditional dress, the pollera, an exquisite costume, usually handed down from generation to generation. It includes a blouse with two wide circular ruffles which slip off the shoulders and cover the upper arms; short sleeves; an insertion in the neckline interwoven with colored wool and two fat pompons, one on the breast and the other at the back of the neck. The voluminous skirt, with its elaborately embroidered tiers, is worn over starched petticoats of white linen, trimmed with lace and an insertion which matches the blouse. At the waist are two *gallos* of ribbon, one in front, the other behind. A *cadena chata,* or flat chain, is worn around the neck, its golden length ending in a cross or coin. *Dormilones,* earrings of gold filigree, and a short gold collar with a showy medal provide further adornment.

It is not only the elaborate pollera which makes the Panamanian girl glamorous, but also her alluring hairdo, which is confined in two plaited buns. In these she wears golden combs of balcony design which may be plain or pearl-studded. Add to this an infinity of *tembliques*—fantasies made of beads, semiprecious or precious jewels representing birds, flowers, butterflies and myriad other designs, each fastened to a hairpin and placed around the entire back of the head. She is all dressed for the ball.

After he had attended one of the carnivals, José Santos Chocano, the Peruvian poet, wrote: "The truth is that the pollera has startling powers of transformation. The foot, unstockinged, is shod in colored velvet slippers without heels. Thus during the promenade, the instep and ankle, which are concealed beneath billows of finest lace, reveal themselves at odd moments with utterly devastating effect. The voluminous skirt undulates in insinuating, voluptuous folds."

Spectators from both American continents and also Europe come to Panama to take part in the pollera balls as well as to watch the Carnival or Mardi Gras processions. Naturally, everyone is dressed magnificently for the balls and every woman is resplendent in jewels. In addition, the parades with their attractive floats and the infectious music make the little isthmus a gay place.

231

The greatest fun of all is the dancing of the tamborito, ar at least witnessing this dance, and the most rigid social conventions are cast aside when there is a "tambor." Even people of recent bereavement come out of seclusion to watch the dancing couples. To quote Chocano: "The Tamborito accomplishes in the monotonous beat of the drum, the resurrection of the dead." Certain it is that no one can resist the witchery of this national dance, filled with passion and typifying gallantry. The gestures of lovemaking, the leaps and dips, the cries and the exclamations are highly dramatic.

As the native drums, the *caja,* the *pujador* and the *repicador,* begin their infectious rhythm, the women gather near the drummers in a semicircle which, as their numbers increase, form a horseshoe facing the drums. Then the Cantadora Adelante (soloist) starts a song while the rest of the women sing the refrain, carrying the beat by clapping their hands. When the singers and drummers are in complete harmony, a man steps out from the surrounding group of men, and approaches the chorus. By nodding his head, or by placing his hat on her head, he chooses a partner, directing himself with dancing steps to the center of the circle, followed by the lady. Then they both approach the drums in order to take three broken steps backward, and immediately go into a whirl. The woman barely suggests the three steps, but the man bends his knees deeply as an act of submission to his lady. After the whirl, which has been executed simultaneously, they perform *El Escobilleo,* in which the woman spreads wide her pollera skirt on one side and gathers it up high on the other, displaying the rich lace on her white linen petticoat. With light movements of the arm, she gracefully takes a series of tiny steps from one side of the circle to the other. Her partner leaps, kneels, shouts and turns in circles, sometimes moving off at a distance. Again he approaches with his arms extended and surrounds her neck or waist without touching her, or fans her with his hat if he has not previously placed it on her head at the moment he asked her to be his partner. The men then throw their hats at the feet of the dancing pair in tribute to their skill. The *Escobilleo* ends with the couple facing the drummers, returning backward to the center of the circle, once again using three backward steps.

The tamborito is danced by one couple at a time, and each pair continues to dance for an unspecified time, taking into consideration those who are waiting their turn. To be called a beautiful tamborito dancer is the height of artistic achievement in Panama.

With the arrival of Ash Wednesday, all gaiety and dancing are put aside and Carnival ends with "the burying of the sardine," which is not a sardine at all, but a thin strip of bacon, or any small dead fish, which is buried with mock solemnity to mark the end of Carnival.

Although the Festival of the Black Christ takes place in Porto Bello on October 21, this unusual statue is an object of great interest to tourists who visit Panama at Easter. Because of the miraculous powers attributed to it, many seek to pay homage to it when the opportunity is presented. The history linked with the image holds strange fascination. During the seventeenth century,

Porto Bello was one of the leading ports of the world and was host, year after year, to the World Trade Fair. To this port Columbus sailed more than once and Henry Morgan, in his heyday, viciously ransacked the place as he cut his swath across the isthmus.

According to legend, a Seville galleon which visited the World Trade Fair at Porto Bello in 1658 tried five times to leave the harbor, and each time was beaten back by a sudden storm. On board it carried a life-sized statue of Christ carrying the Cross, which had been carved in Spain of coccolobis wood for shipment to the Colombian port of Cartagena. The sailors blamed the statue for the queer weather. Throwing it overboard into the depths of the harbor proved that they were right, for as soon as they had rid themselves of the statue, they were able to get under way without difficulty. The citizens of Porto Bello, mostly Negro, found the statue washed up on the shore, which was in itself miraculous since coccolobis does not float in water. They placed it in the Church of Jesus the Nazarene, believed to be the oldest church in the western hemisphere. Soon the edifice earned a worldwide reputation as a healing shrine, and its repute was perpetuated when, in 1821, a cholera epidemic swept the isthmus and left Porto Bello untouched. Since the statue had been washed ashore in the month of October, the event was thenceforth celebrated on the anniversary. It used to last for an entire week with a procession and due homage accorded, but now is observed primarily on October 21.

Until recent years, the only approach to Porto Bello was by sea, and that was no small feat. The Panamanian terrain is hard to control because of excessive rainfall, the rapid growth of the lush vegetation, extensive stretches of mountainous terrain, and the presence of dangerous snakes. In addition, a lack of labor to keep one road open resulted in continued isolation until the advent of the bulldozer. Thus, pilgrimages to the shrine of the Black Christ were few. Even today, if the tourist does not arrive during the week including October 21 or Holy Week he is likely to find the church locked and can gain entrance only by offering a fifth of rum to the keeper. (Rum and American cigarettes open many doors!) The beholder will be amazed at the color of the statue, for the naturally dark wood has blackened with age. Porto Bello today is a sleepy little town, not modernized but astute enough to capitalize on its twice-a-year invasion by visitors.

The native Panamanian has two special days of celebrating—Easter and Candlemas; on both of these days he enjoys the native drink of strong chicha and aguardiente, a spiced alcoholic drink of fermented corn and sugarcane.

Peru

 NTIL recent years, Carnival in Peru was truly a wild affair. Unsuspecting tourists found themselves bombarded with mixtures of flour and water, cheap perfume, shoe polish and other messy substances. Peruvians doused one another with everything from squirt guns to fire hoses. People lost their lives during the celebration and many were injured. Finally in 1958, President Manuel Prado prohibited all outdoor Carnival activities. The following year, Carnival was reinstated for one day only, with street battles forbidden. The only surviving custom is that of the *juego de agua* (water game)—tin tubes of colored or scented water are carried by young and old and sprayed on everyone in sight. People stuff confetti down dresses and shirts and toss buckets or balloons full of water from rooftops onto passers-by below. Since all of these antics are done in jest, it is considered impolite to get angry.

Holy Week is devoutly observed in Arequipa, Peru's most religious city. Here thousands of faithful Catholics participate almost every evening in religious processions. Marching silently in single file, each person carries a small candle. By Easter Sunday the streets are actually slippery as a result of all the wax that has dripped.

Most of the occupants of the city dress in their best clothes on the Thursday evening before Easter to make the traditional visit to the elaborately decorated memorials set up in the churches. Following midnight mass on Saturday, the *quema* (burning) *de Judas* ceremony takes place in the public squares of nearby villages. After satirical speeches criticizing village notables, a straw effigy of the traitorous Judas is hanged from a tree and burned, accompanied by gay dancing.

Pagan and religious observances are mingled in the Andean countries during Holy Week. In addition to the traditional processions, the Altiplano Indians dedicate a ceremony to the pagan god Pacha-Mama and burn herbs and genital parts of lambs or goats as offerings.

A solemn procession of the Holy Sepulcher is held on Good Friday in Puno, as well as a fair at which miniature houses, ranches and other objects are sold. On this day it is believed all wishes objectified will come true.

Uruguay

SEMANA CRIOLLA, or Native Week, in Uruguay coincides with Holy Week, and the festivities center around the gaucho show. The largest, most colorful of these shows is held in the Prado in Montevideo. As the seasons are the reverse of the North American, Holy Week comes in the fall in Uruguay. All normal activity ceases and people flock to see the gauchos, or cowboys, tame a bucking bronco or lasso a bull.

Although Carnival is held officially on the two days before Ash Wednesday, many businesses close for the entire week preceding. The city is crowded with visitors, houses and streets are gaily decorated and mummers and masqueraders parade through the streets, singing and dancing. Flower battles are held and hotels and clubs are filled with masked dancers. Immense open-air stages are set up and each neighborhood erects its own *tablado* (tableau). During the three days of parades, Negro *comparsas* and beautifully decorated floats pass through the streets. Government-sponsored fiestas feature the *pericón nacional,* a lovely, stately old dance. Other popular folk dances are the *estilo, cielito, milonga,* and *ranchera.*

Venezuela

During Carnival in Caracas, Venezuela, *templetes,* or platforms, are erected throughout the city, each provided with an orchestra. Citizens participate in games and races as well as street dancing. The winners are awarded cash prizes and are carried through the streets. Piñatas are popular and so are confetti and the serpentine. Parades of floats and *comparsas,* named after animals, attract crowds of viewers. On Ash Wednesday, *El Dios Momo* (Momus) is buried, but festivities resume the following Sunday when the *octavita* of Carnival is celebrated.

In Venezuela, Easter is known as the "Día de la Resurrección" and is a day for rejoicing. In many small villages, an effigy of Judas is burned and firecrackers are set off.

Around Easter time a spectacular annual migration of thousands of turtles takes place. Traveling hundreds of miles upstream, these freshwater turtles deposit their eggs in the sand. This event coincides with the fishermen's harvest time. The turtle shells are used for ornaments and jewelry, the meat is eaten. Cakes made of turtle meat are considered an Easter delicacy.

The Orient

ALTHOUGH Easter has comparatively little significance in much of the Orient, there are many Oriental legends and ancient beliefs relating to the egg, to the hare, and to spring festivals that, like threads in a tapestry, lend color and background to the overall picture of world folklore in its relation to some of our Easter customs.

To the Chinese, the egg is a sign of good luck and happiness, both of which in their culture are synonymous with fertility. The egg's round, smooth shape typifies a state of well-being, and its lack of corners, tranquillity. Red eggs are offered as gifts by parents when children are born. Even the color expresses good fortune and happiness. When couples are married, good wishes are extended and it is considered most felicitous to ask when relatives may expect red eggs. The so-called thousand-year egg which the Chinese prepare by preserving it in mud may be a chicken or a duck egg. A kind of limy clay, used for coating the shells for a period of six to ten weeks, preserves and colors them. The egg is coated without cooking, but the chemicals that soak into the shell and its contents give the yolk and white of the egg a smooth creamy texture. In appearance an egg so treated becomes translucent, displaying rich blue and green tones, with the yolk a vivid green. Its flavor is slightly fishy. Thousand-year eggs are enjoyed greatly in China and are valued as rich food so that a few bites or half an egg, served cold, is considered ample at the beginning of a meal.

In China and Japan the rabbit or, more correctly, the hare is closely linked with the moon. Both the rabbit and the moon are alluded to frequently in the Easter folklore of Europe. Chinese children have a popular expression which refers to the rabbit who lives on the moon and makes noise by pounding rice cakes in a mortar. The old legend more accurately specifies that he is pounding the drugs of immortality at the foot of a cassia tree. A Taoist fable which depicted the "gemmeous hare as the servitor of the genii who employ it in pounding the drugs which compose the elixir of life" probably came from India originally. Another Oriental belief holds that Buddha once transformed himself into a hare to help a hungry fellow creature and was rewarded by transmigration in that form to the moon, where he dwells. Still another account claims that when Indra, the Vedic god who presides over the deities of the air, disguised as a starving pilgrim, was praying for food, the hare, having nothing else to give him, threw himself into the fire that he might be roasted for the god's benefit. In gratitude, Indra sent the hare to the moon.

China

"MEETING the spring" or "beating the spring ox" was an ancient Chinese rite in which the emperor participated. The culture of grain was of such importance to the economy of the land that each year the emperor used to set the example by a ceremonial plowing of a sacred field. Accompanied by five princes and nine high ministers, he walked behind a highly ornamented plow and turned over three furrows. Then a huge clay image of a cow was placed in the field, surrounded by hundreds of miniature cows. After the plowing had been completed, the images were broken, and the peasants gathered the pieces to scatter them as powder on their own fields, thus insuring a good crop. Although the emperor and his staff gave up the practice several generations ago, the ceremony is still carried out in some rural districts. It is held in the period known as Liu Ch'un, which occurs about February 5, when the farmers have a holiday.

A piece of the iron of an old plowshare was worn, like a medal, by Chinese farmers. Sometimes it was encased in silver with a sharp bit of iron projecting from the silver case; or it was wrapped neatly in paper and placed in a red bag to be worn, like an amulet, to keep away evil spirits.

Three festivals of the dead with Buddhist overtones have long been a part of Chinese tradition. The best-known of these is Ch'ing-ming Day, when each family pays honor to its ancestors by visiting their tombs to sweep them out and make them clean and beautiful once more. The name Ch'ing-ming means "clear brightness" and originally had no association with death. There are no public cemeteries in China since each family has its own graveyard. These are conspicuous, particularly in large open areas, because of the trees planted nearby, a requirement for the burial site. In his book entitled *Chinese Festivals,* Wolfram Eberhard tells of this ancestral tribute: "The feast of Ch'ing-ming is the day when the whole family comes together. Members . . . in distant places try to make the journey home, but if this is impossible, they prepare a small sacrifice wherever they are at the time, in the hope that the 'spirit' of the offerings which they burn may reach their ancestors. This 'sacrifice from a distance' as well as the family ceremony must be performed before sun-dawn or early in the morning, because it is necessary that the spirits of the dead, who sleep during the night, be 'at home' in their tombs.

"The offerings at the tombs are various dishes of food: in poorer families, a coarse millet gruel; among the richer, a whole Chinese dinner. Each ancestor gets his share, and a general sacrifice is addressed to all of them together, so that even those who might be overlooked individually will get their share."

The date of the festival occurs on March 21, which corresponds approximately with Easter. Like Easter, it is a spring festival with buds unfolding and the first traces of green appearing on the trees. As in the West, the willow tree, one of the first to show new life, plays a special part in the ceremonies of the day. Women and children cut willow twigs and stick them in their hair or hang them on their doors. They are also placed on the side of the tomb to ward off evil ghosts and disease as well as to attract good spirits to the dead. In China, as in many countries, it is believed that the willow has the power to attract rain, essential to the sprouting growth of crops in April. Thus, it is used when rain prayers are said.

Another ancient observance is the fire festival, preceded a day earlier by the "cold meat feast." All fires are extinguished, and for 24 hours the house is without warmth. Food prepared the previous day is eaten. Until the thirteenth century, the new fire was lighted by rubbing two willow sticks together, an "age-honored and sacred" practice. The ceremony of eating a cold feast dates back to the sixth century B.C. and commemorates a loyal follower of a petty lord in Shansi province, North China, who had to flee for his life into the mountains. When food ran out, his bondsman cut off his leg, thus saving the life of his starving lord. Later the lord achieved power and position, but forgot his faithful servant. One day recalling the episode which had saved his life, he sought out his loyal follower only to learn that he had become a hermit in the mountains. When all efforts to recall him from his abode failed, the lord ordered that the forest be set afire, but the hermit preferred death to giving up his way of life. Thus the lord ordered that no fire should burn on the anniversary of this tragic event. This legend has many parallels in Shansi province and it is believed that the reference to kindling fires in the open was a practice associated with a nomadic way of life forced upon the natives by wars in ancient times. In any event, the significance of the act was deeply rooted in a struggle for existence.

In ancient China, the "outdoor life" festival began not only with "cold food" picnics and fire ceremonies but also with a celebration for the young associated with courtship and marriage. Singing, dancing, and games were part of it; some of the singing was done by the girls and boys as they rode through the air in swings built between the trees growing along a riverbank. In essence, the festival is best described as a fertility feast, similar in spirit to those of other nations.

Japan

*S*ETSUBUN, meaning "change of season," is the occasion for a gala festival in Japan occurring the day before *risshun* (birth of spring) on February 4. While it has no relation to the calendar year, the age-old belief is that a natural year truly begins with spring. Thus, *setsubun* came to have the same significance to the Japanese people as New Year's Eve. *Fuku-wa-uchi oni-wa-soto* (In with good luck, out with the demon) is the warmhearted expression heard in every household on this day. While shouting these words, the head of the household scatters roasted beans around the room to banish all forces of evil and usher in good fortune. It is a day of festival at home or at one of the big temples where a *toshi-otoko* (man of the year) is selected to throw the beans over the heads of the crowd. To catch one is to be assured of good luck. It is considered an honor and an omen of good fortune for the ensuing year to be chosen man of the year for the occasion. Selections are made from prominent public figures, actors, wrestlers and the like. In recent times, prominent women have been so honored.

It is also customary to eat the beans, one for each year of a person's age and an extra for the New Year, to be assured of good health as well as good fortune. A similar number of beans wrapped in paper and placed at a crossroads after dark assures anyone who steps on the package that he will have freedom from all evils that pursued him during the past year.

As might be expected, various rites surround the day. A dried sardine head and a small branch of holly are placed near the entrance to the house in the belief that the odoriferous fish head will drive away any lurking devils, and the prickly holly leaves will prevent any insect from entering. In some districts, branches are burned in the yard in the hope that the crackling noise of the fire will drive away snakes and insects. Similar customs are practiced in Finland, Greece and other countries.

Some seventy-five years ago Lafcadio Hearn declared that *Bimbogami,* the god of poverty, was one devil who could not be banished with beans or dried peas at *setsubun.* In *Glimpses of Unfamiliar Japan,* Hearn described another custom—"the sale of *hitogata* ('people shapes')." These are little figures, made of white paper, representing men, women, and children. They are cut out with a few clever scissors strokes, and the difference of sex is indicated by variations in the shape of the sleeves and the little paper obi. They are sold in the Shinto temples. The purchaser buys one for every member of the family, the priest writing upon each the age and sex of the person for whom it is intended. These *hitogata* are then taken home and distributed; each person rubs his body slightly with the paper, and says a little Shinto prayer. Next day the *hitogata* are returned to the *kannushi,* or priest, who, after having recited certain formulas over them, burns them with holy fire. By this ceremony it is hoped that all physical misfortunes will be averted by the family during the year.

239

How familiar are all these links with similar beliefs long held in the Western world! Although the Japanese had no knowledge of Easter until the advent of Christian missionaries, they have in more recent times produced countless quantities of Easter ornaments, porcelain eggs, toys and other trinkets for the American trade and that of other countries as well. Their children are as much amused by them as are young folk in the rest of the world, and every Japanese child has been told that a lone rabbit lives on the moon, for they have seen his outline when the dark spots were clearly visible.

The world over, eggs are considered significant gifts. In Japan, where eggs are elaborately painted, the more beautifully created the object, the more respect and honor are bestowed on the recipient. (*Collection of Priscilla Sawyer Lord; photo: Richard Merrill*)

Easter Music

*T*HE music of the Easter season is unusually rich in exalted expression which pours straight from the heart. In concise but spirited phrases, the earliest hymns of Greek or Roman origin tell the story of Easter and its meaning in the language of hope, joy, and wonder. Hymns written in the second century are still sung in both Europe and America. Composers of modern times have had a rich storehouse from which to draw as they turned for inspiration to the early writings of the Christian era and to the productions of later centuries, especially the old hymns which have been translated and adapted to present-day use. As the birds' songs greet the spring, so man sings his praises to God on high at Easter time. During the past two hundred years, countless volumes have extolled and delineated these glorious expressions of faith. Each hymn has its own special place in the fugue of Easter as do the oratorios, the carols, the chorales, the liturgical texts and the superb instrumental compositions which intone the glory and confidence of Easter and its triumphant gladness. References to nature in hymns and carols are frequent and appropriate.

(In a book of this sort, which covers so many facets of the world as it greets Easter, it is not possible to present a comprehensive story of Easter music. The hymns and carols included here have been selected as examples of various periods of writing from several countries.)

Melito of Sardes, a priest from Asia Minor in the second century, wrote a joyous Resurrection hymn, "The Exalted," which is sung in Catholic churches as part of the Easter vigil. It dates from the writings of the early saints. "That Easter Day With Joy Was Bright," a favorite in the Protestant Episcopal Church for more than half a century, can be traced to St. Ambrose of the fourth century.

Many of the hymns of the early Greek and Roman traditions might have remained unknown, except to scholars, had it not been for the tireless devotion of a nineteenth-century translator, John Mason Neale. It was he who "united a monk's love for an old missal to a scholar's evaluation of the treasures of antiquity as he unearthed . . . the crown jewels of the church."

Dr. Neale, the prince of translators, a clergyman of the Church of England, failed to gain preferment in his church, and spent twenty years as warden of "Sackville College," East Grimstead, an almshouse sheltering some thirty poor and aged householders. There he received a stipend of twenty-seven pounds per year. He died in 1866 at the age of forty-eight. Neale wrote several books on theology as well as stories for children, but it is for his translations of old Greek and Latin hymns into English that he is best known. John Brownlie, noted writer of church music, said of him: "He approached his work as a discoverer and a scientist. Neale mapped the territory through which he passed, took the height of its mountains, traced its rivers, and sounded its lakes. Dr. Neale stands forth par excellence the interpreter of the praise literature of the early and the medieval church."

In 1854 he published *Carols for Eastertide*. In it appeared "The World Itself," from his own pen. The chaste beauty of every line reflects the jewel-like quality of the ancient hymns he knew so well:

> *The world itself keeps Easter Day,*
> *And Easter larks are singing;*
> *And Easter flowers are blooming gay,*
> *And Easter buds are springing:*
> *Alleluya, Alleluya:*
> *The Lord of all things lives anew,*
> *And all his works are rising too:*
> Hosanna in excelsis.
>
> *There stood three Maries by the tomb,*
> *On Easter morning early;*
> *When day had scarcely chased the gloom,*
> *And dew was white and pearly:*
> *Alleluya, Alleluya:*
> *With loving but with erring mind,*
> *They came the Prince of life to find:*
>
> *But earlier still the angel sped,*
> *His news of comfort giving;*
> *And "Why," he said, "among the dead*
> *Thus seek ye for the Living?"*
> *Alleluya, Alleluya:*
> *"Go, tell them all, and make them blest;*
> *Tell Peter first, and then the rest":*
>
> *But one, and one alone remained*
> *With love that could not vary;*
> *And thus a joy past joy she gained,*
> *That sometime sinner, Mary,*
> *Alleluya, Alleluya:*
> *The first the dear, dear form to see*
> *Of him that hung upon the tree:*

> *"The world itself keeps Easter Day,*
> Saint Joseph's star *is beaming,*
> Saint Alice *has her primrose gay,*
> Saint George's bells *are gleaming:*
> *Alleluya, Alleluya:*
> *The Lord hath risen, as all things tell:*
> *Good Christians, see ye rise as well!*

The hymn "Hail Festive Day," more familiarly known as "Welcome, Happy Morning!", composed by Venantius Fortunatus before the year 600, was adapted from a long poem addressed to the Bishop of Nantes on the subject of the Easter festival. Fortunatus, noted churchman and scholar, described as the last of the Romans and the first of the troubadours, has left us a rich legacy of florid hymnody:

WELCOME, HAPPY MORNING!

Welcome, happy morning! age to age shall say:
Hell today is vanquished, heaven is won today.
Lo! the Dead is living, God for evermore;
Him their true Creator, all his works adore.

Refrain
Welcome, happy morning! age to age shall say.

Earth her joy confesses, clothing her for spring,
All good gifts returned with her returning King:
Bloom in every meadow, leaves on every bough,
Speak his sorrow ended, hail his triumph now.

Months in due succession, days of lengthening light,
Hours and passing moments praise thee in their flight;
Brightness of the morning, sky, and fields, and sea,
Vanquisher of darkness, bring their praise to thee.

Come, the True and Faithful, now fulfil thy word,
'Tis thine own third morning; rise, O buried Lord!
Show thy face in brightness, bid the nations see;
Bring again our daylight; day returns with thee.

In the eighth century, John of Damascus, "the doctor of Christian Art" and greatest poet of the Greek Church, wrote the "Golden Canon," a song of triumph and thanksgiving, from which we have that memorable hymn "The Day of Resurrection." John of Jerusalem, as he is sometimes called, held public office in Damascus, but later retired to the remote monastery of Mar Saba in the grim wilderness of Judea, where he became a priest and devoted himself to the writing of theological works. It is his poetry that has lived for twelve centuries. From within the stark walls of this and other monasteries came some 5000 pages of hymns and religious poems which were deciphered and translated by John M. Neale.

The day of resurrection,
  Earth, tell it out abroad;
The passover of gladness,
  The passover of God.
From death to life eternal,
  From this world to the sky,
Our Christ hath brought us over
  With hymns of victory.

Our hearts be pure from evil,
  That we may see aright
The Lord in rays eternal
  Of resurrection-light;
And, listening to his accents,
  May hear, so calm and plain,
His own, "All hail!" and, hearing,
  May raise the victor-strain.

Now let the heav'ns be joyful,
  Let earth her song begin,
Let the round world keep triumph
  And all that is therein;
Invisible and visible,
  Their notes let all things blend;
For Christ the Lord hath risen,
  Our joy that hath no end.

"All Glory, Laud and Honor," often heard on Palm Sunday, has a fascinating history. It was written by Theodulph of Orleans, bishop and poet, who was summoned to Charlemagne's court at Aachen about the year 821, where he delighted the great assembly of scholars. After Charlemagne's death, Theodulph was imprisoned because of a dispute in which he was wrongly accused. It was in a monastery at Angers that he wrote the hymn that has lived to this day. In 1854, Dr. John Mason Neale published the English translation used today.

A charming legend has grown up about this hymn. On Palm Sunday, the emperor happened to be in Angers, where Theodulph was in prison. As the grand procession, which the emperor had joined, moved through the streets, it halted by chance beneath the tower where Theodulph was kept. Suddenly from above was heard the *Gloria, Laus,* chanted loudly and melodiously. The emperor was deeply impressed and asked the name of the unknown singer. He was told that it was Theodulph, his own prisoner. Then the gentle and merciful monarch was moved with compassion, and from that hour he delivered and pardoned Theodulph, and sent him back to his church. No doubt this legend was invented by the people of Orleans for the glory and justification of their beloved bishop, Theodulph, but at the same time, it is evidence of the popularity of this magnificent hymn. In later centuries, the tradition surrounding this hymn inspired a dramatic setting for its presentation at Tours and Rouen, where in each instance it was sung at the gates of the city. The gates were closed and the choirboys scaled the walls and there sang the hymn, which in its original form has seventy-eight lines. Symbolically, this setting suggested the imprisoned author and also the Christ's triumphal entry into Jerusalem:

All glory, laud and honor
To thee, Redeemer, King,
To whom the lips of children
Made sweet hosannas ring.
The people of the Hebrews
With palms before thee went;
Our praise and prayer and anthems
Before thee we present.

Thou art the King of Israel,
Thou David's royal Son,
Who in the Lord's name cometh
The King and blessed One!
To thee, before thy passion,
They sang their hymns of praise;
To thee, now high exalted,
Our melody we raise.

Thou didst accept their praises;
Accept the prayers we bring,
Who in all good delightest,
Thou good and gracious King.
All glory, laud and honor
To thee, Redeemer, King!
To whom the lips of children
Made sweet hosannas ring!

An old German hymn, "Christ is Risen," sung to a sixteenth-century tune, was translated into English by Dr. Isaac Watts in the eighteenth century, and has been sung frequently ever since:

Christ the Lord is risen!
Now is the hour of darkness past;
Christ hath assumed his reigning power.
Behold the great accuser cast
Down from the skies, to rise no more:
Alleluya, Alleluya.

Christ the Lord is risen!
'Twas by thy blood, immortal Lamb,
Thine armies trod the tempter down;
'Twas by thy word and powerful name
They gained the battle and renown:
Alleluya, Alleluya.

246

Christ the Lord is risen!
Rejoice, ye heavens! let every star
Shine with new glories round the sky!
Saints, while ye sing the heavenly war,
Raise your Redeemer's name on high!
Alleluya, Alleluya.

All over America the Easter sunrise services are opened with Charles Wesley's version of "Christ the Lord is Risen Today." For fifty years this great Easter hymn was forgotten and might have been lost forever had not an 1830 hymnbook editor discovered a copy of this unfamiliar hymn and inserted it in the *Wesleyan Hymn Book*. To make the words fit an old Easter tune, he added the Greek word "Alleluia" to the end of each line.

The two Wesley brothers—Charles, the hymn writer and the younger; and John, the preacher—worked together for over fifty years as the chief exponents of Methodism. John traveled some 250,000 miles and preached 40,000 sermons; at the age of eighty-six he said that two sermons a day began to tire him, so he limited himself to seven a week! As a writer, Charles was prolific. During his eighty years he wrote some 6500 hymns. Even on the last day of his life, in 1788, he dictated a hymn to his wife, and many of his compositions are sung today in various faiths. Strangely enough, John, who admired his brother's unusual ability, collected the best of Charles's work and published it, admonishing any future editor that it was not to be "tinkered" with. However, in editing his brother's work, John deleted "Christ the Lord is Risen Today"—the hymn that the world now uses to greet the Easter dawn. It lay undiscovered until a "tinkering" editor came along.

Christ the Lord is risen today, Alleluia!
Sons of men and angels say: Alleluia!
Raise your joys and triumphs high, Alleluia!
Sing, ye heavens, and earth reply: Alleluia!

Lives again our glorious King, Alleluia!
Where, O Death, is now thy sting? Alleluia!
Dying once, he all doth save, Alleluia!
Where thy victory, O grave? Alleluia!

Love's redeeming work is done, Alleluia!
Fought the fight, the battle won, Alleluia!
Death in vain forbids him rise, Alleluia!
Christ has opened Paradise, Alleluia!

Soar we now where Christ has led, Alleluia!
Following our exalted Head, Alleluia!
Made like him, like him we rise, Alleluia!
Ours the cross, the grave, the skies, Alleluia!

Hail the Lord of earth and heaven! Alleluia!
Praise to thee by both be given, Alleluia!
Thee we greet triumphant now, Alleluia!
Hail, the Resurrection thou! Alleluia!

In 1831, a New York schoolteacher, Ray Palmer, wrote one of our most familiar Easter hymns:

My faith looks up to Thee,
Thou Lamb of Calvary,
  Saviour divine:
Now hear me while I pray,
Take all my guilt away,
O let me from this day
  Be wholly Thine!

"May Thy rich grace impart
Strength to my fainting heart,
  My zeal inspire;
As Thou hast died for me,
O may my love to Thee
Pure, warm, and changeless be,
  A living fire!

While life's dark maze I tread,
And griefs around me spread,
  Be Thou my Guide;
Bid darkness turn to day,
Wipe sorrow's tears away,
Nor let me ever stray
  From Thee aside.

When ends life's transient dream,
When death's cold sullen stream
  Shall o'er me roll,
Blest Saviour, then, in love,
Fear and distrust remove;
O bear me safe above,
  A ransomed soul!

A Latin hymn dating from 1695, as published by the Jesuit fathers in Cologne, inspired Francis Pott in 1861 to translate these familiar lines sung to a tune which he took from Palestrina's *Magnificat Tertil Toni.*

The strife is o'er, the battle done,
The victory of life is won,
The song of triumph has begun:
  Alleluia

Jean-Baptiste Faure, noted nineteenth-century French operatic baritone who won great acclaim in Europe, particularly in Austria, wrote several songs. One, "Les Rameaux" ("The Palms"), proved to be a great favorite when it was first sung at the turn of the century. Faure gave up his singing career to teach in Paris and to compose songs. Of the several he wrote, only "The Palms" has survived. At one time it was one of the best known of musical works for Palm Sunday the Christian world over. In recent years its popularity has waned somewhat although it is still heard in many churches. An older generation could hardly imagine a Palm Sunday without "The Palms":

O'er all the way, green palms and blossoms gay
Are strewn, this day, in festal preparation,
Where Jesus comes, to wipe our tears away
E'en now the throng to welcome Him prepare:

Chorus
Join all and sing, His name declare,
Let ev'ry voice resound with acclamation,
Hosanna! Praised be the Lord!
Bless Him who cometh to bring salvation!

His word goes forth, and peoples by its might
Once more regain freedom from degradation,
Humanity doth give to each his right,
While those in darkness find restored the light!

Sing and rejoice, oh, blest Jerusalem,
Of all thy sons sing the emancipation,
Through boundless love the Christ of Bethlehem
Brings faith and hope to thee for evermore.

Two other vocal pieces which had their place and still are considered among the better-known English compositions are A. R. Gaul's "The Holy City" and Phoebe Knapp's "Open the Gates of the Temple."

Carols are songs with a religious feeling, simple in form and joyous in spirit, which reflect the pulse of the common folk. Because they usually rhyme and are easy to remember, they have wide appeal. The word "carol," which originally meant "to dance in a ring," gives us another clue to the nature of these folk songs—hilarity. Before Lent and during Easter week, they were sung frequently, particularly by children, with the grownups joining in. This old custom is usually associated with Christmas, but there are carols for many of the important feast days of the year as well, although most of them are little known.

In the Tyrol on Easter Eve, bands of musicians travel about singing Easter hymns to the accompaniment of guitars. They serenade the occupants of every house they pass, so that folk will join with them in the choruses as they rejoice together on this glorious anniversary. Dressed in their picturesque costumes with flower-bedecked hats, they are the delight of the children who follow them about. As darkness approaches, torches of pine are carried to light the way. Hospitality is given in return for their efforts, and the children share it also with gifts of Easter eggs.

The carols that follow have been chosen as a sampling of these delightful old songs which add so much to the joyous spirit of Easter and deserve to be better known, so that they can be sung and enjoyed:

THE SECRET FLOWER

German, sixteenth century   Tr. Eleanor Farjeon

This child was born to men of God:
  Love to the world was given;
In him were truth and beauty met,
On him was set
  At birth the seal of heaven.

He came the Word to manifest,
  Earth to the stars he raises:
The teacher's errors are not his,
The Truth he is:
  No man can speak his praises.

He evil fought and overcame,
  He took from death the power;
To all that follow where he goes
At last he shows
  The Kingdom's secret Flower.

The secret Flower shall bloom on earth
  In them that have beholden;
The heavenly Spirit shall be plain
In them again,
  As first it was of olden.

The Spirit like a light shall shine,
  Evil himself dispelling,
The Spirit like a wind shall blow,
And Death shall go
  Unfeared in her own dwelling.

And by the spirit shall be known
  Heroes and Saints and Sages;
Yea, they shall walk in all men's sight,
Amid the light
  God sent to crown the ages.

THE GARDEN OF JESUS

Dutch, 1633   Tr. E. B. G.

Lord Jesus hath a garden, full of flowers gay,
Where you and I can gather nosegays all the day:

> Where angels sing in jubilant ring,
> With dulcimers and lutes,
> And harps, and cymbals, trumpets, pipes,
> And gentle, soothing flutes.

There bloometh white the lily, flower of Purity;
The fragrant violet hides there, sweet Humility:

The rose's name is Patience, pruned to greater might;
The marigold's, Obedience, plentiful and bright:

And Hope and Faith are there; but of these three the best
Is Love, whose crown-imperial spreads o'er all the rest:

And one thing fairest is in all that lovely maze,
The gardener, Jesus Christ, whom all the flowers praise:

O Jesus, all my good and all my bliss! Ah me!
Thy garden make my heart, which ready is for thee!

CAROL OF THE CHILDREN

Our Lord came to Jerusalem
On that first Palm Sunday,
Not clad in royal robe of fur,
Nor festive garment gay.
No steed had he to ride upon,
No kingly palfrey,
But meekly on a lowly beast,
Rode slowly on his way.

And as he drew near to the gates,
The people thronged around,
They cut palm branches from the trees
And spread them on the ground.
The little children flocked to him,
And sweetly they did sing
Hosanna, Hosanna, Hosanna to the King.

The Merchants' Carol

English Traditional   Frank Kendon

As we rode down the steep hillside,
   Twelve merchants with our fairing,
A shout across the hollow land
   Came loud upon our hearing,
A shout, a song, a thousand strong,
   A thousand lusty voices:
"Make haste," said I, I knew not why,
   "Jerusalem rejoices!"

Beneath the olives fast we rode,
   And louder came the shouting:
"So great a noise must mean," said we,
   "A king, beyond all doubting!"
Spurred on, did we, this king to see,
   And left the mules to follow;
And nearer, clearer rang the noise
   Along the Kidron hollow.

Behold, a many-coloured crowd
   About the gate we found there;
But one among them all, we marked,
   One man who made no sound there;
Still louder ever rose the crowd's
   "Hosanna in the highest!"
"O King," thought I, I know not why
   "In all this joy thou sighest."

A Merchant: Then he looked up, he looked at me;
   But whether he spoke I doubted:
How could I hear so calm a speech
   While all the rabble shouted?
And yet these words, it seems, I heard:
   "I shall be crowned to-morrow."
They struck my heart with sudden smart,
   And filled my bones with sorrow.

We followed far, we traded not,
   But long we could not find him.
The very folk that called him king
   Let robbers go and bind him.
We found him then, the sport of men,
   Still calm among their crying;
And well we knew his words were true—
   He was most kingly dying.

EASTER EGGS

Russian   Tr. A. F. D.

Easter eggs! Easter eggs! Give to him that begs!
    For Christ the Lord is arisen.
To the poor, open door, something give from your store!
Those who hoard can't afford—moth and rust their reward!
Those who love freely give—long and well may they live!
Easter tide, like a bride, comes, and won't be denied.

(Words and melody from the traditional Easter song, "Dalalin, Dalalin, po Yaichenku," in Rimsky-Korsakov's *Russian National Songs*, 1877.)

MOTHERING SUNDAY

German, Fourteenth Century   George Hare Leonard

It is the day of all the year,
Of all the year the one day,
When I shall see my Mother dear
And bring her cheer,
A-Mothering on Sunday.

So I'll put on my Sunday coat,
And in my hat a feather,
And get the lines I writ by rote,
With many a note,
That I've a-strung together.
A-Mothering on Sunday.

It is the day of all the year,
Of all the year the one day;
And here come I, my Mother dear,
To bring you cheer.
A-Mothering on Sunday.

" 'He who goes a-mothering finds violets in the land.' In many parts of the country it was the custom for the children of the family who had left the old home to come back to visit their mother on the fourth Sunday in Lent (Mid-Lent Sunday). The eldest son would bring a wheaten cake—in modern times a plum cake with an icing of sugar, or a simnel-cake. Sometimes cinnamon comfits ('Lamb's-tails'), or little white sugar-plums with a carraway seed, or some morsel of spice, within—such as may still be found at country fairs—were brought for an offering. One of the children home for the day would stay in and mind the house, so that the mother should be free for once to attend morning service at the church."—*The Oxford Book of Carols*

253

THE LAMB OF GOD

Traditional

Awake, awake, ye drowsy souls,
* And hear what I shall tell;*
Remember Christ, the Lamb of God,
* Redeemed our souls from hell.*
He's crowned with thorns, spit on with scorn,
His friends have hid themselves:
        So God send you all much joy in the year.

They bound Christ's body to a tree,
* And wounded him full sore;*
From every wound the blood ran down,
* Till Christ could bleed no more;*
His dying wounds, all rent and tore,
Were covered with pearly gore:

And when his foes had murdered Christ
* And shown their cruel spite,*
The sun and moon did hide their heads
* And went in mourning straight;*
The heavens stood amazed, and angels gazed,
And the earth was darkened quite:

And when Christ's soul departed
* And from his body fled,*
The rocks did rend, the graves did ope,
* And then appeared the dead;*
All they that were there did quake for fear—
'Twas the Son of God,' they said:

It was early in one morning
* That Mary did him seek;*
She saw two angels sitting
* At Jesus' head and feet:*
Mary shed tears while Christ appeared,
And he said: 'Why dost thou weep?'

Then Christ he called Thomas,
* And bid him: "Come and see,*
And put thy fingers in the wounds
* That are in my body;*
And be not faithless, but believe,
And happy shalt thou be":

Then Christ called his disciples,
  Divided by his death,
And said: "All powers are given to you
  In heaven and on earth:
Go forth and teach all nations;
Despise them not," he saith:

"Go seek you every wandering sheep
  That doth on earth remain,
Till I myself have paid your debts
  And turned you back again;
Come all ye heavy laden,
I'll ease you of your pain":

God bless the ruler of this house
  And send him long to reign;
Let many a good and happy year
  Go over his head again,
And all his godly family
That serveth the Lord so dear:

God bless the mistress of this house,
  With peace unto her breast,
And, let her body be asleep or awake,
  Lord send her soul to rest,
And all her godly family
That serveth the Lord so dear:

Sans Day Carol

Cornish   Ibid.

Now the holly bears a berry as white as the milk,
And Mary bore Jesus, who was wrapped up in silk:

And Mary bore Jesus Christ our Saviour for to be,
And the first tree in the greenwood, it was the
    holly, holly, holly!
And the first tree in the greenwood, it was the holly.

Now the holly bears a berry as green as the grass,
And Mary bore Jesus, who died on the cross:

Now the holly bears a berry as black as the coal,
And Mary bore Jesus, who died for us all:

Now the holly bears a berry, as blood is it red,
Then trust we our Saviour, who rose from the dead:

255

Angevin tune

Now quit your care
And anxious fear and worry,
For schemes are vain
And fretting brings no gain.
To prayer, to prayer!
Bells call and clash and hurry,
In Lent the bells do cry,
'Come buy, come buy,
Come buy with love the love most high!'

Lent comes in the spring,
And spring is pied with brightness;
The sweetest flowers,
Keen winds, and sun, and showers,
Their health do bring
To make Lent's chastened whiteness;
For life to men brings light
And might, and might,
And might to those who hearts are right.

To bow the head
In sackcloth and in ashes,
Or to afflict the soul,
Such grief is not Lent's goal;
But to be led
To where God's glory flashes,
His beauty to come nigh
To fly, to fly,
To fly where truth and light do lie.

For is not this
The fast that I have chosen?—
The prophet spoke—
To shatter every yoke,
Of wickedness
The grievous bands to loosen
Oppression put to flight,
To fight, to fight,
To fight till every wrong's set right.

For righteousness
And peace will show their faces
To those who feed
The hungry in their need,

256

And wrongs redress,
Who build the old waste places
And in the darkness shine.
Divine, divine,
Divine it is for brothers to combine!

Then shall your light
Break forth as doth the morning:
Your health shall spring,
The friends you make shall bring
God's glory bright,
Your way through life adorning;
And love shall be the prize.
Arise, arise,
Arise! and make a paradise!

Jean Tisserand, a Franciscan, gave us the carol *Alleluia, O Sons and Daughters,* which was published in Paris in 1525. In dramatic vein, Martin Luther in 1546 wrote an Easter church song which has remained a favorite with Lutheran and other Protestant congregations these four centuries. Francis X. Weiser, noted author and scholar, has given us this translation:

It was a strange and wondrous war,
When death and Life did battle.
With royal might did Life prevail,
Made death His knave and chattel.
The sacred Book foretold it all:
How death by death should come to fall.
Now death is laughed to scorn.

Over the centuries, the master composers of the Continent have written enduring music that contributes greatly to the understanding and the fulfillment of Passion Week. The Roman Catholic Church employs the famous Latin poem, *Stabat Mater Dolorosa,* which, according to Francis X. Weiser, originally was written as a prayer for private devotions by an unknown writer. It is now attributed to Jacopone de Todi.

The *Stabat Mater* remains a greatly cherished Lenten hymn translated from the Latin into the vernacular by a number of composers. First published in England in 1748, it rates as a masterpiece in choral music. Giovanni Pierluigi da Palestrina's *Stabat Mater* (1594) with its original Latin text is considered *the* classic. In 1868 Gioacchino Rossini wrote a cantata, somewhat operatic in manner, which he called *Stabat Mater.* Sixteen years later, in 1884, a more substantial composition of the same theme and title was presented in London, written by Antonin Dvořák. Franz Joseph Haydn, Franz Schubert, and Giuseppe Verdi also set this famous hymn to music. The settings of all six composers are still performed during the Lenten season.

For the past four centuries, German composers have been preeminent in music. Greatest of the baroque composers was Johann Sebastian Bach, born in 1685. Taking his text from the Gospel according to St. Matthew, Bach wrote the *St. Matthew Passion,* which today is an integral part of Easter music and is considered among his greatest works. Concerned with the trial and Crucifixion of Jesus, it utilizes in chorus form the mob scenes and the part they played in the Passion of Christ. Besides the striking dramatic effect achieved by the chorus, there are frequent arias depicting exalted states of feeling. The music shouts for the release of Barabbas, for the execution of Jesus, and it sobs with weeping tones at the tomb. There are simple four-part chorales which Bach intended to have the audience sing, but in actual performance this practice has never been followed. Although Bach wrote five passions, only the *St. Matthew* and the *St. John* have survived. After his death in 1750, his music was forgotten. Seventy-nine years later Felix Mendelssohn insisted on reviving the *St. Matthew Passion.* As a result, a concert given in Berlin on March 11, 1829, created a sensation and restored interest in all the music of Johann Sebastian Bach, which is now a foundation for all musical training.

George Frederich Handel, who was born in Halle in 1685, Bach's natal year, spent most of his life in London. It is significant that Handel, whose oratorios were written primarily for the concert hall, was never a church musician. It is even more remarkable that his famed *Messiah* (1742) with its unsurpassed "Hallelujah" chorus is still the keystone of our joyous Easter music and the term most often used to describe it is "inspired." Part II of this gigantic oratorio deals with the Crucifixion, and Part III with the Resurrection and the redemption of mankind.

Franz Joseph Haydn was born in lower Austria in 1732 and moved to Vienna in 1740. In 1809, at the request of the Cathedral Chapter of Cádiz, Spain, he wrote a composition for solo, chorus, and orchestra entitled *The Seven Last Words.* Slow, moving, meaningful but dolorous, it still holds its place in the music of Passion Week.

It was a stroke of genius that made public one of the now familiar classics, the *Miserere* by Gregorio Allegri, which is often sung by a choir at the Tenebrae services. Written in the seventeenth century, for the exclusive use of the Sistine Chapel at the Holy Week Tenebrae services, it required a double chorus of nine parts. By order of the Popes, the composition was not published. It remained so until 1770, when Leopold Mozart brought his fourteen-year-old son, Wolfgang Amadeus Mozart, from Austria to Rome to listen to the music of the Holy Week services in the Sistine Chapel. The lad, who already had shown his musical genius, returned with his father to his lodgings and that same evening wrote the entire nine-part chorus from memory. Carrying the boy's manuscript, Leopold Mozart returned to the chapel with his son the following day to verify what the boy had written from memory. Only a few notes of the music needed correction. Immediately, Pope Clement XIV was informed of this prodigious feat and sent for the Mozarts. Both father and son feared that the Pope would be indignant at the plagiarism implied in the boy's act. Instead, His Holiness praised him extravagantly and promptly ordered the publication of the *Miserere* for the whole world to enjoy. Hearing this masterpiece is one of the truly moving experiences of Holy Week.

Ludwig van Beethoven, born in Bonn, Germany, in 1770, showed talent in the musical world at an early age. He played the organ in his church, joined the court orchestra, and wrote sonatas, rondos, cantatas and even a piano concerto while still a youth. Since his great skill lay in instrument-oriented music for piano and orchestra, he tended to treat the human voice like an instrument. His contribution to Passiontide rests in *Christus am Oelberg (Christ on the Mount of Olives)*, which is highly regarded by connoisseurs of music.

Richard Wagner's last work was his opera *Parsifal*. In the spring of 1867, on Good Friday, he heard "that sigh of profoundest pity which of old resounded from the cross of Golgotha, and which on this occasion escaped from my own breast." Ten years later the words of the opera were completed, but the musical score was not finished until 1882, the year before he died. Because he considered *Parsifal* sacred in character, he stated in his will that it should never be presented anywhere except in the opera house at Bayreuth, which was devoted entirely to the production of his work. However, in 1903, Heinrich Conried, director of the Metropolitan Opera in New York City, staged an elaborate production, despite the protests of Wagner's wife and family. The Wagnerian concept of opera was concerned with the giving of equal emphasis to both dramatic form and music. Furthermore, he used the same motif to express character and mood. This was innovative—hence the occasion for controversy. In addition, Wagner's operas are longer than those of other composers, and performers find them a test of physical endurance. During the Easter season, Wagnerian devotees never fail to attend performances of *Parsifal*. The music of the "Good Friday Magic Spell" taken from it holds special appeal.

Harry Dickson of the Boston Symphony Orchestra writes that the future of all recorded music has a dubious aspect, for it is very possible that in the next century audiences will not go to symphony halls and opera houses—all music will be electronically transmitted to their homes.

Two compositions of the twentieth century have made their mark as Easter music. In 1908 Nicholas A. Rimsky-Korsakov wrote the *Russian Easter Overture*. Based on themes from Obichod, a collection of canticles of the Russian Orthodox Church, this elaborate overture presents a vivid melodic picture of the Russian Easter Day celebration.

Although it was not inspired by the Gospel narratives, Gustav Mahler wrote a *Resurrection Symphony*. It reflects his contemplation of death and resurrection as a prelude to a new and purified life and so has a place in music for this season of the year. It is his best-known work.

American contributions to Easter music of recent origin include an Easter carol for children by Howard Chandler Robbins—*The Sabbath Day,* written in 1929. A generation or more ago, the Rev. Marion F. Ham, a Unitarian minister, and organist T. Tertius Noble collaborated on the carol "O Who Shall Roll Away the Stone?"

Germany, Austria, Italy, France, Spain, Russia, England, and America are the prime sources of our Easter musical heritage, which spans almost the entire Christian era. In contrast to the folksy spirit and tone manifest in a goodly number of Christmas carols, the music of Easter spells out with splendor and glory the belief in the eternity of the soul. This underlying theme of hope elevates the human spirit in a manner that expresses the power and the majesty of Eastertide. For those well versed in the art of music, this is the season of seasons of the entire Christian year, and even the casual listener cannot fail to respond to the spiritual uplift which the music of Eastertide offers.

Easter and the Fine Arts

HE story of Easter in painting, sculpture and the allied arts is so vast as to warrant a separate volume, copiously illustrated. In fact, the almost countless number of great paintings depicting scenes from The Passion of Christ staggers the imagination and challenges the memory of the most ardent amateur in the field. In this brief essay, an attempt has been made to enumerate some of the best known. As music has been called the servant of religion, painting may be termed the handmaiden.

In his splendid book, *The Shape of Content,* Ben Shahn writes that "form in art is as varied as idea itself. It is the visible shape of all man's growth; it is the living picture of his tribe at its most primitive, and of his civilizaton at its most sophisticated state. Form is the many faces of the legend—bardic, epic, sculptural, musical, pictorial, architectural; it is the infinite images of religion; it is the expression and the remnant of self. Form is the very shape of content. . . .

". . . the Trinity was only one small part of the stimulus to form which arose out of the vivid Christian legend: think of the immense and brilliant iconography which remains detailed for us and our delight—the Lion for Mark, the Ox for Luke, the Eagle for John, the Angel for Matthew; Lamb and Serpent and Phoenix and Peacock, each with its special meaning; symbols of keys and daggers and crosses, all challenging the arts and artisans and architects and sculptors to new kinds of invention. Sin and Temptation, Piety, and a thousand virtues and vices all transmitted into the material of art, into form, remaining for us in mosaics, in frescoes, in carvings, forming capitols, cupolas, domes, inner walls and outer façades, tombs and thrones. Wherever something was made, the legend turned it into form."

Since the dawn of civilization, man's imagination has sought release and expression in religious paintings and even today this category of art continues to hold sway over canvases. The one subject best known and most frequently copied or portrayed in an original manner is that of *The Last Supper* or *The*

The Lord's Supper, in life-size wax figures, an interpretation of
Leonardo DaVinci's famous painting, *The Last Supper*, on permanent display at 6209 Sunset Drive, Fort Worth, Texas.

Mystic Feast. It was and still is the chief artistic expression of the Passion. Authorities versed in the knowledge of classical painters and sculptors have been overwhelmed at the stupendous number of unknown artists who have carved altar pieces, painted icons and friezes and murals, and designed stained-glass windows depicting some moment or event in that last week of Christ's earthly journey.

The best-known religious painting in the Western world is Leonardo da Vinci's *Last Supper,* housed in a poorly lighted, small church in Milan, Italy—that of Santa Maria della Gracie. Painted in tempera on the church wall, it is little wonder that it has cracked and faded. When Napoleon and his army were bent on conquering Italy, members of his cavalry stabled their horses in the "stalls" in front of the picture and even cut a door through the painting itself. Leonardo's dramatic placement of the disciples gathered around Christ at the table has given this painting its reputation as a masterpiece of storytelling art. Leonardo da Vinci (1452–1519) rendered his great work in more vivid colors than can be discerned now; recently the original sketch with the true colors was unearthed and there have been discussions relative to restoring the painting to its original brightness. Heinrich Wöllflin said that the classic element in this painting is found in Christ's silence following his words, "One of you will betray me"; in that silence the original impulse and the action are at once momentary, eternal, and complete.

Innumerable reproductions in wood as well as ivory carvings of this painting have been made during the last few centuries. Here in the United States there is a life-size wax-figure tableau of *The Last Supper* at Fort Worth, Texas, viewed by thousands of visitors annually. At Lake Wales, in Florida, a large replica of Leonardo's *Last Supper* has been executed in mosaic by craftsmen from the continent of Europe.

Andrea del Castagno (1423–1457) painted his interpretation as a fresco covering an entire wall of the refectory of the convent of Saint Apollina in Florence, Italy. The *Last Supper* of Jacopo Tintoretto (1518–1594) hangs in San Giorgio Maggiore, Venice.

Those who visit the Holy Land may see treasures of artwork in the churches of many faiths and denominations. Here, too, one of the subjects most often viewed is that of *The Last Supper* or *The Mystical Meal* as it is most frequently referred to in Jerusalem. The table in all these scenes is round, with the disciples seated, some with their backs to the viewer.

Father Pierre Benoit, one of the world's foremost authorities on Biblical archaeology and a New Testament editor of *The Jerusalem Bible;* Konrad Leube, a young German pastor; and Elhanan Hagolani, a professor of sociology, have collaborated on a book entitled *Easter: A Pictorial Pilgrimage.* It is a beautiful book, rich in feeling and in text, with extraordinarily fine pictures, many of which are in color—it is a most useful book with which to travel to the Holy Land.

The greatest artist of them all, for he was master in many skills, mediums, and techniques, Michelangelo Buonarroti (1475–1564) at the age of nineteen

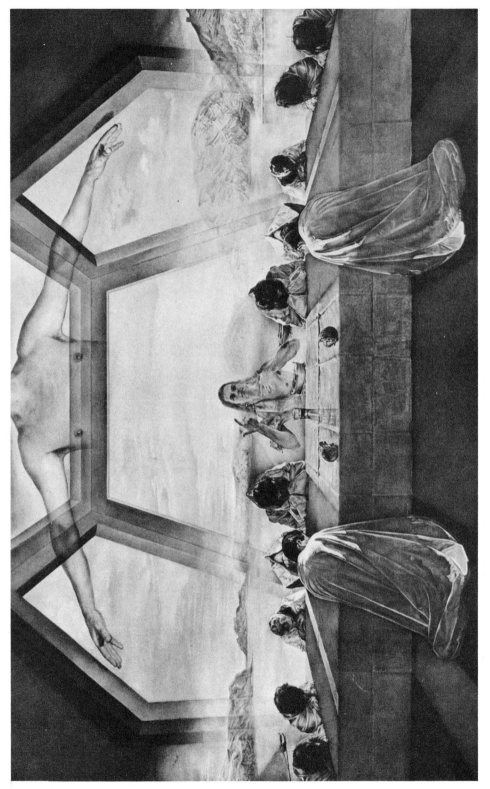

The Sacrament of the Last Supper by Salvador Dali. (Chester Dale Collection. Courtesy, National Gallery of Art)

executed his *Pietà*. Although this famous sculpture rests in St. Peter's Basilica in Rome, it is known the world over and was viewed by thousands of people in the United States when it was on loan for two years during the recent World's Fair in New York City.

The devout Dutch painter of the seventeenth century, Rembrandt van Rijn (1606–1669), painted two different interpretations of the *Supper at Emmaus.* The earlier of the two, painted in 1630, hangs in the Musée Jacquemart-André, Paris; the later one, painted in 1648, is housed in Paris also, at the Louvre.

The United States lays claim to several renowned Passion Week paintings. The *Crucifixion* by Marc Chagall (born in Russia in 1887) hangs in the Pierre Matisse Gallery in New York City. One of the world's leading surrealist painters, a Catalan, Salvador Dali, produced the *Crucifixion* which is displayed at the Metropolitan Museum of Art in New York City. This painting with its clean, cold lines accentuates the aloneness of the event. Dali was also the creator of *The Sacrament of the Last Supper,* which belongs to the Chester Dale collection in the National Gallery of Art, Washington, D.C.

In Boston may be seen the fine work of the Italian artist, Giorgione (1477–1510) at the Isabella Stewart Gardner Museum, Boston, Massachusetts. Mrs. Gardner was so fond of *The Head of Christ* that she always kept a small bowl of violets under the picture; and when violets were not obtainable, violet-shaded browallias were used; her will provided for the continuing of this tribute.

Although born in Crete, El (Domenico Theotocopoulos) Greco (ca. 1547–1614) painted in Italy. In the National Gallery in Washington, D.C., hangs his portrayal of the cleansing of the Temple called *Christ Driving the Traders from the Temple.*

The Museum of Modern Art in New York City displays a painting by the French artist Georges Rouault (1871–1958): *Christ Mocked by Soldiers.* Although this has an almost stained-glass effect and the soldiers look like clowns, it is a picture which communicates emotion to young people.

Michael Munkacsy's *Christ on Calvary* and *Christ Before Pilate* are owned by the John Wanamaker family and are displayed in Philadelphia every year during Holy Week.

Two prints known to Sunday School pupils in the United States are *Christ in Gethsemane,* painted by Warner E. Sallman, and *Christ in Gethsemane,* painted by Hans Hofmann (1880–1966); the original of the latter hangs in a tiny chapel off the vestibule of New York City's Riverside Church. While these paintings do not rate with the great masterpieces, they have served a devotional purpose and have provided inspiration for countless thousands. Jan Styka's *Crucifixion* at the Forest Lawn Chapel in Glendale, California, attracts thousands of viewers every year.

One of the rarest of all these treasures in the United States is the *Chalice of Antioch,* which may be seen at The Cloisters in New York City. An open-work silver goblet cast in an intricate design, with finely executed details, it stands seven and one half inches high. A powerfully drawn historical novel by Thomas B. Costain, entitled *The Silver Chalice,* gives present-day readers a concept of The Holy Grail legend. Mr. Costain writes of Basil of Antioch, a young and skilled artisan who created a decorative chasing for the precious chalice. One may well conjecture that the author must have stood often before the *Chalice of Antioch* displayed at The Cloisters. This fifth-century silver vessel used in the sacrament of the Lord's Supper was discovered near Antioch by a group of Arabs who were digging a well. Engraved on the chalice is a symbolic eagle with outspread wings, perched upon a basket of Eucharistic bread. Christ's throne rises above the bird as though supported by its wings. While He stretches out His arms in blessing, a dove hovers above. The grapevine encircling the chalice represents the Church. Eight other birds are depicted. Its iconography is a bit perplexing, for there seem to be two figures representing Christ, and only ten apostles are depicted.

There are countless other art treasures to be discovered. Unlike Easter music that is airborne throughout the world and familiar to all who are sensitive to the sounds of voices and musical instruments, the products of the visual arts embodied in painting, sculpture, and carving which depict the Easter story are not always readily available to the individual. Down through the ages man has wrought innumerable tributes of rare beauty commemorating this "movable feast." Those treasures are frequently displayed in churches, museums, libraries, schools, and private homes the world over. However, they may be seen and enjoyed only by those who seek them out for renewed inspiration and enjoyment.

One of the greatest treasures of the early Christian era (4th–
6th century A.D.) is the Chalice of Antioch. Discovered in
1910, this famous silver vessel is decorated with the figures of
Christ and the twelve apostles, enclosed by a grapevine. The
outer cup of decorated silver openwork is seven and one
half inches high. No evidence exists that the chalice was the
Holy Grail used at the Last Supper. The seeking of the Holy
Grail is the theme of Wagner's opera, *Parsifal*. (*Courtesy,
The Metropolitan Museum of Art, The Cloisters Collection*)

Christ Bearing the Cross by Giorgione. (*Courtesy Isabella Stewart Gardner Museum*)

Rubens' graphic portrayal of the crucifixion. (*From:*
H. Armstrong Roberts)

Bibliography

ADAMS, CHARLOTTE. *Easter Idea Book*. New York: Barrows, 1954.

ALFORD, VIOLET. *Introduction to English Folklore*. London: Bell, 1952.

ANDERSON, A. W. *The Coming of the Flowers*. New York: Farrar, Straus & Young, 1960.

———. *Plants of the Bible*. New York: Philosophical Library, 1957.

ANON. *The Book of Easter*. New York: Macmillan, 1910.

BAILEY, ALBERT E. *The Gospel in Hymns*. New York: Scribner's, 1950.

BALTRUSAITIS, J. *Lithuanian Folk Art*. Boston Public Library Fine Arts Dept., n.d.

BALY, DENIS. *The Geography of the, Bible: A Study in Historical Geography*. New York: Harper, 1957.

BARBEAU, MARIUS. *The Golden Phoenix and Other French-Canadian Fairy Tales Retold by Michael Hornyansky*. New York: Walck, 1960.

BAZIN, GERMAIN. *A Gallery of Flowers*. London: Thames-Hudson, 1960.

BEECHING, H. K. *Essays and Studies by Members of the English Association*. Oxford: Clarendon Press, 1911.

BELKNAP, E. McCAMLY. *Milk Glass*. New York: Crown, 1949.

BENET, SULA. *Song, Dance and Customs of Peasant Poland*. Great Britain: Roy Publications.

BENOIT, PIERRE; LEUBE, PASTOR CONRAD; and HAGOLANI, ELHANAN (Eds.). *Easter: A Pictorial Pilgrimage*. Abingdon Press, 1969.

BRAND, JOHN. *Observations on Popular Antiquities*. London: Chatto & Windus, 1913.

Brewer's Dictionary of Phrase and Fable. Revised and Enlarged. New York: Harper, 1953.

BROOKE, JOSELYN. *The Flower in Spain: A Calendar of Wild Flowers*. London: The Bodley Head.

BROWNE, LEWIS. *This Believing World*. New York: Macmillan, 1926.

CAMP, WENDELL; BOSWELL, VICTOR R.; and MAGNESS, JOHN R. *The World in Your Garden*. Washington, D.C.: National Geographic Society, 1957.

CARHEDEN, KRISTINA. *Food and Festivals, Swedish Style.* Minneapolis: Dillon Press, 1968.

CARTER, MORRIS. *Isabel Stewart Gardner and Fenway Court.* Boston: Houghton Mifflin, 1925.

CHAMBERLAIN, SAMUEL. *Tour of Italy.* (Recipes translated and adapted by Narcissa Chamberlain.) Gourmet, 1958.

CHAMBERS, R. (Ed.). *The Book of Days.* Philadelphia: Lippincott, 1863–64.

CLAUDE-SALVY. *Quai aux Fleurs.* Paris: Marchot, Librairie Grund, 1952.

COATS, ALICE M. *Flowers and Their Histories.* New York: Pitman, 1956.

COLLINS, ARTHUR H. *Symbolism of Animals and Birds.* London: Pitman, 1913.

COOLIDGE, OLIVIA. *Greek Myths.* Boston: Houghton Mifflin, 1949.

CORCORAN GALLERY OF ART. *Easter Eggs and Other Precious Objects by Carl Fabergé.* Washington, D.C.: The Corcoran Gallery of Art, 1961.

COULTON, G. G. *Medieval Panorama: The English Scene from Conquest to Reformation.* New York: Macmillan, 1947.

DALY, LLOYD W. *Aesop without Morals.* New York: Yoseloff, 1961.

DEARMER, PERCY; WILLIAMS, R. VAUGHAN; and SHAW, MARTIN. *The Oxford Book of Carols.* London: Oxford University Press, 1961.

DOS PASSOS, JOHN. *The Portugal Story.* New York: Doubleday & Co., Inc., 1969.

DREWERY, MARY. *Hamid and the Palm Sunday Donkey.* Hastings House, 1968.

DYER, T. F. T. *The Folklore of Plants.* New York: Appleton, 1889.

EARLY, ELEANOR. *Ports of the Sun.* Boston: Houghton Mifflin, 1937.

Easter Ideals: An Annual. Milwaukee: Ideals Pub. Co., 1950–1961.

Easter Picture Book. Now at the Victoria and Albert Museum. Her Majesty's Stationery Office, 1952.

Easter Stories for Children. Milwaukee: Ideals Pub. Co., 1960.

EBERHARD, WOLFRAM. *Chinese Festivals.* New York: Henry Schuman, 1952.

EMERY-WATERHOUSE, FRANCES. *Banana Paradise.* New York: Stephen-Paul, 1947.

EMRICH, MARION VALLAT, and KORSON, GEORGE (Eds.). *The Child's Book of Folklore.* The Dial Press, 1947.

EVANS, SEBASTIAN. *The High History of the Holy Grail.* New York: Dutton, 1910.

EWING, JULIANA H. *The Peace Egg and a Christmas Mumming Play.* New York: E. & J. B. Young, 1887.

FAISON, S. L., JR. *A Guide to the Art Museums of New England.* New York: Harcourt, Brace, 1958.

FENNER, PHYLLIS R. *Feasts and Frolics: Special Stories for Special Days.* New York: Knopf, 1949.

FERGUSON, GEORGE. *Signs and Symbols in Christian Art.* New York: Oxford, 1954.

Festival Poems: A Collection for Christmas—The New Year—Easter. Boston: Roberts, 1884.

Fodor's Guide to the Caribbean. Fodor, 1969–70.

FOLEY, DANIEL J. *Little Saints of Christmas*. Boston: Dresser, Chapman & Grimes, 1959.

———. *The Christmas Tree*. Philadelphia: Chilton Co., 1960.

FRASER, JAMES G., and GASTER, THEODOR H. *The New Golden Bough*. New York: Criterion, 1959.

FRYATT, NORMA R. *A Horn Book Sampler*. Boston: The Horn Book, 1959.

FUSSELL, G. E., and K. R. *The English Countrywoman*. London: Andrew Melrose, 1953.

GARDNER, HELEN. *Art Through the Ages*. Revised under the editorship of Sumner McK. Crosby. New York: Harcourt, Brace, 1959.

GASTER, THEODOR H. *Passover: Its History and Traditions*. New York: Schuman, 1949.

GENDERS, ROY. *Perfume in the Garden*. London: Museum Press, 1952.

GEUNEP, VAN. *Manuel du Folklore Français Contemporain*. Paris: Picard, 1937–1963.

GOLDIN, HYMAN E. *A Treasury of Jewish Holidays: History, Legends, Traditions*. New York: Twayne, 1952.

GOMBRICH, E. H. *The Story of Art*. New York: Phaidon, 1958.

GOODALL, NAN. *Donkey's Glory*. Philadelphia: McKay, 1959.

GOUDGE, ELIZABETH. *God So Loved the World*. New York: Coward-McCann, 1951.

———. *My God and My All*. New York: Coward-McCann, 1959.

GRABOWSKI, JÓSEF. *Wycinanka Ludowa*. Warsaw: Polska Sztuka, 1955.

GRIGSON, GEOFFREY. *The Englishman's Flora*. London: Phoenix House, 1955.

GUERBER, H. A. *Legends of the Virgin and Christ*. New York: Dodd, Mead, 1896.

HALE, EDWARD EVERETT. *Easter: A Collection for a Hundred Friends*. Boston: J. Smith, 1886.

HALE, WILLIAM HARLAN. *The Horizon Cookbook*, 2 vols. American Heritage Pub. Co., New York, 1968.

HAMILTON, EDITH. *The Greek Way to Western Civilization*. New York: Mentor Books, 1930.

———. *Mythology*. New York: Mentor Books, 1930.

———. *The Roman Way*. New York: Mentor Books, 1932.

HAMILTON, LORD FREDERIC. *The Vanished Pomps of Yesterday*. New York: Doran, 1921.

HARPER, THE REV. HOWARD V., D.D. *Days and Customs of All Faiths*. New York: Fleet, 1957.

HARPER, WILHELMINA (Ed.). *Easter Chimes: Stories for Easter and the Spring Season*. New York: Dutton, 1942.

HARRINGTON, MILDRED P., and THOMAS, JOSEPHINE H. *Our Holidays in Poetry*. New York: Wilson, 1929.

HARTING, JAMES E. *The Rabbit*. New York: Longmans, Green, 1898.

HASTINGS, JAMES D. D. (Ed.). *A Dictionary of Christ and the Gospels*. New York: Scribner's, 1912.

HAZELTINE, ALICE ISABEL, and SMITH, ELVA SOPHRONIA (Eds.). *The Easter Book of Legends and Stories*. New York: Lothrop, Lee & Shepard, 1947.

HEARN, LAFCADIO. *Glimpses of Unfamiliar Japan,* 2 vols. Boston: Houghton Mifflin & Co., 1894.

The Herbalist. Hammond, Indiana: Hammond Book Co., 1934.

HEYERDAHL, THOR. *Aku-Aku: The Secret of Easter Island.* Chicago: Rand McNally, 1958.

HOLE, CHRISTINA. *Easter and Its Customs.* New York: Barron, 1961.

HOTTES, ALFRED CARL. *Garden Facts and Fancies.* New York: Dodd, Mead, 1937.

HOWELLS, VICTOR. *A Naturalist in Palestine.* London: Andrew Melrose, 1956.

HUNT, FERN B. *Floral Decorations for Your Church.* Philadelphia: Chilton, 1960.

HUNTINGTON, VIRGINIA. *In Green Autumn.* Philadelphia: Dorrance, 1941.

HUTCHINSON, RUTH, and ADAMS, RUTH. *Every Day's a Holiday.* New York: Harper, 1951.

INMAN, THOMAS, M.D. *Ancient Pagan and Modern Christian Symbolism.* New York: J. W. Bouton, 1884.

JAMES, M. R. *Abbeys.* London: Great Western Railway, 1926.

JENKIN, A. K. H. *Cornish Homes and Customs.* New York: Dutton, 1934.

JONES, ALEXANDER (Gen. Ed.) *The Jerusalem Bible.* New York: Doubleday & Co., 1966.

JONES, WILLIAM. *Credulities Past and Present.* London: Chatto & Windus, 1880.

JOYA, MOCK. *Things Japanese.* Tokyo News Service Ltd., 1958.

KANE, HARNETT, T. *Queen New Orleans: City by the River.* New York: Morrow, 1949.

KELLER, WERNER. *The Bible as History: A Confirmation of the Book of Books.* Translated by William Neil. New York: Morrow, 1956.

KEYES, FRANCES PARKINSON. *All This Is Louisiana.* New York: Harper, 1950.

KONSTANDT, OSCAR (Tr.). *The Most Beautiful Alpine Flowers.* Innsbruck: Penguin-Verlag, 1957.

KRYTHE, MAYMIE R. *All About American Holidays.* New York: Harper, 1962.

KUBLY, HERBERT. *Easter in Sicily.* New York: Simon & Schuster, 1956.

LAGERKVIST, PÄR. *Barabbas.* New York: Random House, 1951.

LAGERLÖF, SELMA, *Memories of My Childhood: Further Years at Mårbacka.* New York: Doubleday, Doran, 1934.

———. *The Miracles of Antichrist.* Translated from the Swedish by Paulini Bancroft Flach. London: Gay & Bird, 1899.

LAKE, ALEXANDER. *The Past and the Future of the Croft Easter Lily.* Lompoc, California: Flower World Press, 1947.

LAMKIN, NINA B. *Easter and the Spring.* New York: Samuel French, 1935.

La Rousse Encyclopedia of Mythology. New York: Prometheus Press, 1959.

LAVERTY, MAURA. *Feasting Galore: Recipes and Food Lore from Ireland.* New York: Holt, Rinehart & Winston, 1961.

LEHNER, ERNST and JOHANNA. *Folklore and Symbolism of Flowers, Plants and Trees.* New York: Tudor, 1960.

LELAND, GODFREY L. *Gypsy Sorcery and Fortune Telling.* New York: University Books, 1964.

LIPKIND, WILLIAM. *Days to Remember: An Almanac*. New York: Obolensky, 1961.

LORD, PRISCILLA SAWYER, and FOLEY, DANIEL J. *Easter Garland*. Philadelphia: Chilton Co., 1963.

McCLINTOCK, INEZ and JOHN. *Toys in America*. Washington, D.C.: Public Affairs Press, 1961.

McKNIGHT, FELIX R. *The Easter Story*. New York: Holt, 1953.

McSPADDEN, J. WALTER. *The Book of Holidays*. New York: Crowell, 1958.

MARIE, GRAND DUCHESS OF RUSSIA. *Education of a Princess: A Memoir*. New York: Viking, 1931.

MARSHALL, CATHERINE (Ed.). *Peter Marshall's "The First Easter."* New York: McGraw-Hill, 1959.

MARSHALL, M. E. *The Delectable Egg*. New York: Trident Press, 1968.

MEYER, ROBERT E., JR. *Festivals, Europe*. New York: Ives Washburn, 1954.

————. *Festivals, U.S.A*. New York: Ives Washburn, 1950.

MILLER, MARY BRITTON. *A Handful of Flowers*. New York: Pantheon, 1959.

MILLER, SAMUEL H. *The Life of the Soul*. New York: Harper, 1951.

MINTER, JOHN EASTER. *The Chagres: River of Westward Passage*. New York: Rinehart, 1948.

MOLDENKE, HAROLD N. and ALMA L. *Plants of the Bible*. Waltham, Mass.: Chronica Botanica, 1952.

MONKS, JAMES L. *Great Catholic Festivals*. New York: Schuman, 1957.

MUNRO, DANA CARLETON, and SONTAG, RAYMOND JAMES. *The Middle Ages: 395–1500*. New York: Century, 1921.

NASH, ELIZABETH TODD. *One Hundred and One Legends of Flowers*. Boston: Christopher House, 1927.

NEWLAND, MARY REED. *The Year and Our Children*. New York: Kenedy, 1956.

NORTHALL, G. F. *English Folk-Rhymes*. London: Kegan Paul, 1892.

NUTT, ALFRED. *Studies of the Legend of the Holy Grail*. London: David Nutt, 1888.

O'CALLAGHAN, SEAN. *The Easter Lily*. New York: Roy, 1958.

OPIE, IONA and PETE. *The Lore and Language of School Children*. New York: Oxford, 1959.

PARMELEE, ALICE. *All the Birds of the Bible, Their Stories, Identification and Meaning*. New York: Harper, 1959.

PAULI, HERTHA. *The First Easter Rabbit*. New York: Ives Washburn, 1961.

PERL, LILA. *Rice, Spice and Bitter Oranges: Mediterranean Foods and Festivals*. New York: The World Publishing Co., 1967.

————. *Foods and Festivals of the Danube Lands*. New York: The World Publishing Co., 1969.

PRATT, ANNE, and MILLER, THOMAS. *The Language of Flowers, the Association of Flowers, Popular Tales of Flowers*. London: Simpkin, Marshall, Hamilton, Kent, 1892.

PRENTOUT, HENRI. *Les Provinces Françaises.* Paris: 1927.

PRESSE, G. W. SEPTIMUS. *The Art of Perfumery and the Methods of Obtaining the Odors of Plants.* Philadelphia: Lindsay and Blakiston, 1867.

PURDY, SUSAN. *Festivals for You to Celebrate: Facts, Activities and Crafts.* Philadelphia: J. B. Lippincott Co., 1969.

QUINN, VERNON. *Stories and Legends of Garden Flowers.* New York: Stokes, 1939.

RADFORD, EDWIN. *Unusual Words and How They Came About.* New York: Philosophical Library, 1946.

———, and MONA A. *Encyclopaedia of Superstitions.* New York: Philosophical Library, 1949.

ROBB, DAVID M., and GARRISON, J. J. *Art in the Western World.* New York: Harper, 1953.

ROBINSON, HERBERT SPENCER, and WILSON, KNOX. *Myths and Legends of All Nations.* New York: Garden City Books, 1960.

SACKVILLE-WEST, V. *The Easter Party.* London: Michael Joseph, 1951.

SCHAUFFLER, ROBERT HAVEN (Ed.). *Easter: Its History, Celebration, Spirit and Significance as Related in Prose.* Compiled by Susan Trace Rice. New York: Moffat, Yard, 1916.

SCHERMAN, DAVID E., and WILCOX, RICHARD. *Literary England.* New York: Random House, 1944.

SELSAM, MILLICENT E. *Plants that Heal.* New York: Morrow, 1959.

SHACKLETON, ROBERT. *The Book of Washington.* Philadelphia: Penn. Pub. Co., 1922.

SHAHN, BEN. *The Shape of Content.* New York: Vintage Books, 1957.

SHOEMAKER, ALFRED L. *Eastertide in Pennsylvania: A Folk Cultural Study.* Kutztown, Pennsylvania: Pennsylvania Folklife Society, 1960.

SKINNER, CHARLES M. *Myths and Legends Beyond Our Borders.* Philadelphia: Lippincott, 1899.

SMITH, H. A. *Lyric Religion, the Romance of Immortal Hymns.* New York: Revell, 1931.

SMITH, HERMAN. *Kitchens Near and Far.* New York: Barrows, 1946.

———. *Stina: The Story of a Cook.* New York: Barrows, 1946.

SPICER, DOROTHY GLADYS. *Feast-Day Cakes from Many Lands.* New York: Holt, Rinehart & Winston, 1960.

———. *Festivals of Western Europe.* New York: H. W. Wilson Co., 1958.

———. *From an English Oven.* New York: The Women's Press, 1948.

STERMAN, PHYLLIS. *Sweet Sixteen Cook Book.* New York: Sterling, 1952.

STOKER, FRED. *A Book of Lilies.* London: Penguin Books, 1943.

Sunset Books and *Sunset Magazine.* Menlo Park, California: Lane Pub. Co.

SWAYNE, AMELIA W. *The Observance of Easter.* Philadelphia: Religious Education Committee, Friends General Conference.

TAYLOR, GLADYS. *Saints and Their Flowers.* London: Mowbray, 1956.

TEALE, EDWIN WAY. *Green Treasury.* New York: Dodd, Mead, 1952.

———. *North with the Spring.* New York: Dodd, Mead, 1951.

THORNTON, FRANCIS BEAUCHESNE. *The Donkey Who Always Complained: A Parable for Moderns.* New York: Kenedy, 1956.

TODD, CHARLES BURR. *The Story of the City of New York.* New York: G. P. Putnam's Sons, 1888.

TOOR, FRANCES. *Festivals and Folkways of Italy.* New York: Crown, 1953.

———. *A Treasury of Mexican Folkways.* Mexico: Mexico Press, 1947.

A Treasure of Easter Religious Art. Milwaukee: Ideals Pub. Co., 1960.

TUBBY, RUTH P. *A Picture Dictionary of the Bible.* New York: Abingdon-Cokesbury, 1949.

URLIN, ETHEL L. *Festivals, Holy Days and Saints' Days.* London: Simpkin, Marshall, Hamilton, Kent, 1915.

VAN BUREN, MAUD, and BEMIS, KATHARINE ISABEL. *Easter in Modern Story.* New York: Century, 1929.

VAN LOON, HENDRIK. *The Story of Mankind.* New York: Garden City Pub., 1938.

VAN TREECK, CARL, and CROFT, ALOYSIUS. *Symbols in the Church.* Milwaukee: Bruce, 1960.

VANN, GERALD. *The Paradise Tree.* New York: Sheed & Ward, 1959.

WALDO, MYRA. *The Round-the-World Cookbook.* New York: Bantam Books, 1956.

WALKER, WINIFRED. *All the Plants of the Bible.* New York: Harper, 1957.

WALSH, WILLIAM S. *Curiosities of Popular Customs.* Philadelphia: Lippincott, 1897.

Washington, City and Capitol. Washington, D.C.: U.S. Govt. Ptg. Off., 1937.

WATERMAN, PHILIP F. *The Story of Superstition.* New York: Grosset, 1929.

WATTS, ALAN W. *Easter: Its Story and Meaning.* New York: Henry Schuman, 1950.

WEISER, FRANCIS X. *The Easter Book.* New York: Harcourt, Brace, 1954.

———. *Handbook of Christian Feasts and Customs.* New York: Harcourt, Brace, 1952.

———. *The Holy Day Book.* New York: Harcourt, Brace, 1956.

WELLS, H. G. *The Outline of History.* New York: Macmillan, 1921.

WEST, JESSAMYN. *The Friendly Persuasion.* New York: Harcourt, Brace, 1943.

WHITE, T. H. *The Bestiary, A Book of Beasts.* New York: Putnam, 1960.

WILLIAMS, C. A. S. *Encyclopedia of Chinese Symbolism and Art Motives.* New York: The Julian Press, 1960.

WILSON, ADELAIDE. *Flower Arranging for Churches.* New York: Barrows, 1952.

WINKWORTH, CATHERINE. *Christian Singers of Germany.* New York: Macmillan.

WINZEN, DAMASUS. *Symbols of Christ.* New York: Kenedy, 1955.

WOHLRABE, RAYMOND, and KRUSCH, WERNER. *The Land and People of Denmark.* Philadelphia: J. B. Lippincott, 1961.

World Almanac and Book of Facts, The. New York: N. Y. World-Telegram & The Sun, 1961.

WRIGHT, RICHARDSON. *A Book of Days for Christians.* Philadelphia: Lippincott, 1951.

Index

278

288

Trees (*cont.*)
Crataegus oxyacantha, 23
Cypress, 26
Fir, silver, 126
Frangipani, 202, 227
Hawthorn, 23, 178
Holly, 239
Jacaranda, 202
Laurel leaves, 118, 148, 158, 218
Mountain ash, 75, 143
Oak, 66
Olive, 40
Palm(s), 40, 65, 68, 99, 116, 126, 139, 140, 146, 148, 153, 162, 167, 186, 200, 212, 213, 224, 226
Pear, 104
Pine, 26, 141
Rowan, 143
Saw palmetto, 40
Serenoa, repens, 40
Shittah tree, 24
Spruce, 126
Yew, 40
Walnut, 34
Willow, 24, 40, 56, 85, 99, 131, 146, 153, 162, 186, 187, 203, 238
Trimaie, 90
Trinidad, 200, 201
Trinity, the, 261
Trolls, 86, 87, 88
Troyat, Henri, 152, 154
Trombone choir, 42
Trophine, 89
Tsiknopefti, 110
Tunstall, 78
Tupan, 213
Tuxpan, Jalisco, Mexico, 223
Tymintävikko, 85
Tyrol, Austrian, 53, 249
Tyrozoumi, 111
Tzintzuntan, Mexico, 225

Ukko, 192
Ukraine, 157, 186, 187
Ukrainians, 144
Umberto, Bishop of Pisa, 24
United States, 24, 29-51, 105, 156, 167, 197, 198, 230, 263, 265
United States Navy, 40
University College, 125
Unterammergau, 103
Upper Room, the, 43
Uppsala University, 179
Urals, 156, 159
Uruguay, 234, 235

Utah, 44

Valencia, 166, 176
Valladolid, 169
Valley of Kidron, 16
Van Rijn, Rembrandt, 265
Vastenavond, 56
Vatican, The, 130
Vaval, 201
Vaya, 116
Vedic God, 237
Velikden, 186
Venezuela, 235
Venice, 130
Venus, 89
Vera Cruz, Mexico, 222
Verdi, Giuseppe, 257
Vernal equinox, 39
Vezelay, 91
Vienna, Austria, 52, 54, 258
Vienna Easter egg, 107
Vila do Conde, Portugal, 149
Vile Franca de Xira, 149
Virágvasarnap, 123
Virgen del Socovón, 207
Virgin Islands, 38, 201
Virgin Mary, The, 116, 148, 169, 171, 205, 207, 214, 223
Virgin of Good Hope, 169, 171
Virgin of the Mine, 205
Virgin's Lament, The, 117
Virginia, 33
Virposunnuntai, 84
Vizyi, 110
Vlöggelen, 141
Vogatsiko, 111
Volcán Barú, Panama, 227
Volhynian Ukrainians, 186
Von Schmid, Christoph, 107

Wagner, Richard, 259, 267
Wagtails, 119
Wales, 187, 188
Walfeleu, 56
Walloon, 56
Wanamaker, John, 265
Wandering Jew, The, 167
Warwickshire, England, 80
Washing of the feet, 130, 131, 227
Washington, D.C., 23, 35, 157, 192, 265
Washington Monument, 35
Water, Holy, 127, 137, 139
Waterford, 125, 126
Watts, Alan W., 189, 192
Watts, Dr. Isaac, 246
Wax, 77
Wearyall Hill, 23

Wedgewood, simulated, 193
Weiser, Francis X., 53, 104, 176
Welsh Guards, 188
Welsh Regiment, 188
Wesley, Charles, 247
Wesleyan Hymn Book, 247
West Indies, 24
Westmeath, 126
Westminster Abbey, 71
Westminster School, 63, 69
Westmoreland, England, 79
Westphalia, 103
West Virginia, 47
Western Macedonia, 111
White House, 35, 36, 37
Whitsunday, 77, 128, 142, 188
Whitsuntide, 138
Whuppity Scoorie, 161
Wichita Mountains, 43
Wilde, Sir William Robert, 128
Willowswitch Sunday, 84
Wiltshire, England, 66
Wine, 4, 110, 112, 115
Winston-Salem, North Carolina, 42
Witches, 56, 86, 143, 180
Witte Dondeday, 56
Wölffln, Heinrich, 263
Wolsey, Cardinal, 71
World-Egg, The, 189, 192
Worshipful Company of Stationers, 65
Wotan, 143

XB, 155, 156

Yaquis, 226
Yarn Saturday, 85, 86
Yeats, William Butler, 125
Yeoman of the Laundry, 71
Yew, 126
Yggdrasil, 143
Yorkshire, England, 66, 78
Yosemite National Park, 44
Youth festival, 60
Yuletide, 182

Zaachila, Mexico, 223
Zabuski, 155
Zaragoza, 177
Zaterdag voor Pasen, 57
Zebedee, 11
Zeeland, 140
Zé Pereira, 211
Ziz, 192
Zodiac, signs of the, 56
Zubrovka, 155
Zusan Gate of Herod, 17

PRISCILLA SAWYER LORD not only shares the extensive outdoor interests of her family at their seaside home in Marblehead, Massachusetts, but she pursues her own varied enthusiasms in a most perceptive manner. With an extensive background in English and American literature from her student days at Boston University, followed by library training and experience including that of reader's adviser, Mrs. Lord has continued to keep abreast of the latest books published in several of her fields of interest—and her interests are wide and varied.

In the realm of children's literature she is both a collector and narrator, devoting time periodically to story-telling at the Abbot Public Library in her own community.

An avid gardener, she has in recent years directed her attention to the study of herbs and is an active member of The Herb Society of America. In addition, she is vitally interested in Girl Scouts of America, having served the organization in many capacites. She travels and lectures extensively, appears on radio and television, and collects both objects of interest and information relating to Easter, Christmas, and other seasonal festivals. This interest resulted in *Easter Garland,* which she also collaborated on with Daniel J. Foley. She and Mr. Foley are also the authors of the widely-acclaimed and much-honored *The Folk Arts and Crafts of New England,* which is now considered the definitive book on the subject.

During her years of living in Marblehead, she had grown to know and love the streets, the old houses, the harbor, the sense of history that lives there. Her passion for her adopted town caused her to write *Marblehead: The Spirit of '76 Lives Here,* with Virginia Gamage, also to be published in 1971 by Chilton.

Mrs. Lord's husband, Philip Hosmer Lord, is an internationally known yachtsman and she often accompanies him as "crew" on voyages along the New England coast or in the Caribbean.

DANIEL J. FOLEY, landscape architect and horticulturist, has worked with plants since childhood. Often referred to as America's favorite Christmas historian, he has also written *Christmas The World Over, Christmas in the Good Old Days, Toys Through the Ages, The Christmas Tree,* and *Little Saints of Christmas.*

For seven years he was closely associated with Dr. J. Horace McFarland and supervised the planting and development of the famous Breeze Hill Test Gardens at Harrisburg, Pennsylvania. He served as editor of Horticulture Magazine from 1951 through 1957. Widely known as a lecturer, he has appeared before hundreds of audiences, is a frequent contributor to leading gardening magazines and newspapers. He is the author of *Gardening By The Sea, Ground Covers For Easier Gardening, Garden Flowers in Color, Vegetable Gardening in Color, Annuals For Your Garden, The Flowering World of Chinese Wilson, Gardening For Beginners,* and co-author of *Garden Bulbs in Color.*

In addition to his professional interests, Mr. Foley, a native of Salem, Massachusetts, has many absorbing avocations. Pursuit of the history of gardening in America, while a student at the University of Massachusetts, led to research in colonial architecture and furnishings and the every-day life of the early settlers. Later, he became associated as trustee and active participant in the handling of historic landmarks in the field of public relations.